CHRIST & THE MAYA CALENDAR

Other Books by Robert Powell

Christian Hermetic Astrology
The Star of the Magi and the Life of Christ

Chronicle of the Living Christ
The Life and Ministry of Jesus Christ
Foundations of Cosmic Christianity

Elijah Come Again
A Prophet for Our Time
A Scientific Approach to Reincarnation

The Most Holy Trinosophia
The New Revelation of the Divine Feminine

The Mystery, Biography & Destiny of Mary Magdalene
Sister of Lazarus John & Spiritual Sister of Jesus

The Sophia Teachings
The Emergence of the Divine Feminine in Our Time

Other Books by Kevin Dann

Across the Great Border Fault
The Naturalist Myth in America

A Book of Wonders
Marvels, Mysteries, Myth and Magic

Bright Colors Falsely Seen
Synaesthesia and the Search for Transcendental Knowledge

A Short Story of American Destiny
1909–2009

CHRIST
& THE
MAYA CALENDAR

2012 & THE COMING OF
THE ANTICHRIST

ROBERT POWELL
&
KEVIN DANN

LINDISFARNE BOOKS
2009

Lindisfarne Books
An imprint of SteinerBooks / Anthroposophic Press, Inc.
610 Main St., Great Barrington, MA 01230
www.steinerbooks.org

A Note about the Title

The word *Antichrist* is used in the title and throughout this book, and there are
at least two ways in which this word may be understood. The more general use of
the word is found in the Bible and in Christian tradition, in which the Antichrist
is understood to be the human being who bears the incarnated Satan (also called
"Ahriman" in Persian tradition and, in Revelation 13 in the Bible, "The Beast").
This is how the word *Antichrist* is used in this book.

However, this general meaning should be distinguished from another, more
specialized use of the word, as found in the spiritual science of Anthroposophy,
which often uses the word *Antichrist* to designate the Sun Demon, known as
Sorath in the Hebrew tradition, referred to as the "Beast whose number is 666,"
and as "the two-horned Beast" in Revelation 13. In this connection, Rudolf
Steiner refers to "the False Prophet who represents the teachings of The Beast."
The authors of this book discuss the significance of Sorath in chapters 7 and 8.

Cover and design: William Jens Jensen
Cover images: Left: pg. 60, Kingsborough edition of the
Dresden Codex, photograph courtesy of Justin Kerr;
Right: *Fifth Apocalyptic Seal* by Clara Rettich
(based on a design by Rudolf Steiner)

Library of Congress Cataloging-in-Publication Data

Powell, Robert, 1947–
  Christ and the Maya calendar : 2012 and the coming of the Antichrist / Robert
Powell, Kevin Dann.
      p. cm.
  Includes bibliographical references
  ISBN 978-1-58420-071-0 (alk. paper)
  1. Maya calendar—Miscellanea. 2. Antichrist. 3. Steiner, Rudolf, 1861–1925.
I. Dann, Kevin T., 1956– II. Title.
  BF1999.P67 2009
  299.7'8427—dc22
                                                                    2009002509

Contents

About the Cover Images

Page 60 of the *Dresden Codex*, the best-known and most studied of the four Mayan screenfold hieroglyphic books that survived the auto da fés during the Spanish conquest of Mexico. The *Dresden Codex* is a ritual-astronomical text, closely associated with the function of the Mayan calendar. Most of the text is a series of *Tzol'kin* (260-day) almanacs and day counts used for worship and divination. In the upper panel are pictured three gods, the central one—bearing a pair of darts in the right hand, an *atlatl* in the left—is usually referred to as a "Venus god." Early interpretations saw this scene as "the combat of the planets." Beneath the central band of four glyphs indicating Tzol'kin dates is a panel that early interpreters called the "battle of the constellations." On the right a menacing figure stands over a bound captive; facing them, a regent on a rattlesnake carriage/throne is borne by a servant. At their feet lies an open-mouthed rattlesnake head.

The *Fifth Apocalyptic Seal* painted by Clara Rettich. Revelation 12 starts with the great image of the cosmic being Sophia, clothed with the Sun, with the Moon under her feet, and on her head a crown of twelve stars. Rudolf Steiner designated this image as the fifth of the Seven Seals of the Apocalypse and drew a sketch for the painter Clara Rettich to reproduce the image (as well as the other six images) for the Theosophical Congress in Munich, Pentecost 1907. The paintings by Rettich of the seals were on display (in large format) at the Theosophical Congress, where Steiner spoke of their great significance for the spiritual path, as portrayals of realities that are clairvoyantly perceptible as archetypes underlying cosmic and human evolution. The *Fifth Apocalyptic Seal* is particularly relevant to our time, as described in this volume.

PART I

THE MAYA CALENDAR
AND THE APOCALYPSE CODE

BY KEVIN DANN

PREFACE

Katun 11 Ahau is set upon the mat, set upon the throne, when
their ruler is set up.... The heavenly fan, the heavenly wreath
and the heavenly bouquet shall descend. The drum and rattle of
the lord of 11 Ahau shall resound, when flint knives are set into
his mantle.... Ahau 11 is the beginning of the count, because
this was the katun when the foreigners arrived. They came from
the east when they arrived. Then Christianity also began. The
fulfillment of its prophecy is [ascribed] to the east.... This is a
record of the things which they did. After it had all passed, they
told of it in their [own] words, but its meaning is not plain.
                      —*The Book of Chilam Balam of Chumayel*[1]

As we read these words from the *Chilam Balam*—the collection of
Mayan oracular texts—we cannot help but feel grateful for the
honesty of the Maya chronicler who wrote them. Written down in the
nineteenth century, in the Yucatec Maya language, the images and
sentiments stretch back to the time of the Spanish conquest, and there
is much bitterness along with the honesty: "[Katun 11 Ahau:] when
Christianity was introduced by the real Christians. Then with the
true God, the true *Dios*, came the beginning of our misery. It was the
beginning of tribute, the beginning of church debts, the beginning of
the strife with purse-snatching." Thanks to their passionate devotion
to both prophecy and history, the voices of the ancient Maya people
resound into our own time, telling us something about this extraordinary moment through which we are living. Something... "but its
meaning is not plain."

Indeed, despite the explosion of books and videos that claim to
penetrate the mystery of "2012"—the numerical shorthand for the
completion on December 21, 2012 of the thirteenth *B'ak'tun* cycle in

the Long Count of the Maya calendar—consensus about its meaning seems ever more elusive. As metaphysical speculation mounts, professional astronomers and ethnologists dismiss the whole body of modern interpretations of the Maya calendar as New Age gobbledygook. Among the supposed seers themselves—José Arguelles, Carl Johann Calleman, Barbara Hand Clow, Daniel Pinchbeck—doctrinal disputes worthy of academics are now the norm. Scholars have every right to be miffed at the sometimes sloppy thinking and exaggerated claims—which tend toward enthusiastic proclamations of an imminent, universally accelerated psychic evolution—of the seers; the seers have legitimate critiques about the limits of scientific inquiry when it comes to the prophetic traditions of ancient peoples.

For us twenty-first-century moderns, perhaps more than for the anonymous Maya chronicler above, it would be deeply unsettling to think that Christian prophecy could be brought to bear upon the Maya calendar in order to solve the riddle of 2012. That is the premise of this book.

Five centuries ago, the Maya and other native peoples of the Americas saw their lives shattered by the long-prophesied arrival of the strange, cross-bearing peoples from the East. In the case of the Mexica (the name the people called themselves; "Aztec" became widely used in the nineteenth century by English-speaking students of the region), this shattering was facilitated *by* their indigenous prophetic tradition, as the courageous Lord Montezuma, mistaking Hernan Cortés for the Plumed Serpent deity Quetzalcoatl, allowed the conquistadores easy entry into the heart of Tenochtitlan, the capital city of the Mexica empire. Given our historical knowledge of the terrible violence of the human sacrifice practiced there, we could perhaps sympathize with Cortés as he ordered the bloodthirsty idols in the sacrificial temple pyramids to be smashed and replaced by the Cross and the Virgin Mary. Nevertheless, we human beings of today resent the hubris of the act and correspondingly feel incensed by the arrogance of the conquistadores. Today we cringe to think of the destruction by the Spanish of the vast repositories of Mexican and Maya chronicles, which might have helped us unlock the riddles of their calendrical systems, their myths, their prophecies.

Those riddles are vast and persistent and yet demand renewed inquiry. The question of the significance of the Maya Long Count's end date in 2012 has taken on particular relevance, given its imminence, and the variety and vociferousness of some of the claims made about it. In May 2008, in Tulum, Mexico, participants at a week-long field study and lecture series led by Robert Powell and sponsored by the Sophia Foundation of North America were able to take up this question of the mystery of the Maya calendar. Inspired by visits to the Maya ruins at Tulum, Coba, and Chichen Itza and by the discussions among the participants, Powell extended his pioneering research on the Apocalypse Code to help make sense of the "timing" of the Long Count. Building from Rudolf Steiner's important indications about the incarnation of Ahriman, and the activity of Lucifer and Ahriman on the American continent at another crucial moment in human history, he also has brought forth new discoveries about the nature and identity of the spiritual beings whose continued activity have played such an important role in the spiritual history of America and the world. Finally, Robert here presents crucial research about the cosmic dimension to the unfolding events of our own time.

Teaching a course in Modern World History—"modern" in this case meaning from 1500 to the present—I have a wide range of places and times which I can choose to explore with my students. For the past three years I have focused on the encounter in 1519 of Hernan Cortés and the Aztec emperor Montezuma, since it brings so poignantly into focus the confrontation between the magico-mythological worldview of the Mexica and the rational worldview of the Spanish. While the early modern era saw countless encounters all over the globe between European rationalism and pre-modern native *mentalités*, there was for me a special urgency to bring new understanding to the story of the Aztec empire, in light of Rudolf Steiner's stunning revelations about an earlier episode of spiritual battle in the region. Reading Morris Collis's *Cortez & Montezuma* (1954), my students were able to enter into the thought world of the Aztec, deeply enough to suspend their innate skepticism that an entire civilization could mistake Cortés for the god Quetzalcoatl.

Participating in the Tulum field study, and subsequently editing the lecture material, has given me the opportunity to reflect further on both the history of the "Mexican Mysteries," and their relationship to the Apocalyptic events now transpiring. Personally, it has been an extraordinary challenge to walk a path between exoteric and esoteric scholarship; I invite readers to walk that path with me and see what rings true.

Perhaps the year 2012 and what it is bringing also offers an opportunity for a path toward the synthesis of the prophetic traditions of North American native and European newcomer. From the long-misused heart of Christian prophecy—the book of Revelation—and two of its modern interpreters—Rudolf Steiner[2] and Robert Powell[3]—come images that can affirm and extend the deep intuitive wisdom that has rippled down through the ages from the Maya astronomer-priests, scribes, kings, and common folk. Like the images that still adorn the ruins of Maya temples, these Christian apocalyptic images become living only if we take them in deeply and discerningly. The time is truly at hand; let us begin.

1. Calendars Do Not Forget

There is perhaps no single individual who bears as much responsibility for the destruction of Maya "memory" as Diego de Landa, the Franciscan friar who, in 1561, became Bishop of Yucatán. Convinced that all Maya religious practices amounted to demon worship, and that eliminating these practices would help usher in the Second Coming of Christ, Landa never hesitated to destroy suspected idolaters or their sacred texts. The brutal inquisition ordered by Landa culminated in an *auto da fé* on July 12, 1562, in which a vast treasury of Maya codices (from the hundreds to many thousands, with only four surviving) and religious images (as many as 5,000) were burned. It is thus a great irony that Landa's *Relación de las Cosas de Yucatán* (1566) became instrumental in aiding twentieth-century scholars to decipher Maya hieroglyphics, and that it remains the primary contemporary source for Maya history.

Even as he crusaded to destroy Maya cultural memory, Landa was impressed by the feats of memory that he found among the Maya people. Interviewing an elderly Maya man about Maya history, he listened as the man recounted with no hesitation, events from the thirteenth century. "Had I not known of this calculation," declared Landa, "I should not have believed it possible to recall after such a period" (Diego de Landa, *Yucatán Before and After the Conquest,* p. 82). Other speakers told Landa of more recent history, the arrival of the Spanish in 11 Ahau, showing him how they designated this with a cross in that section of the katun wheel.

Actually, the coming of the cross to the Yucatán in 1541 was not just *history* for the Yucatán Maya; it had been *prophecy* long before it became present or past experience. According to Landa,

As the Mexican people had signs and prophesies of the coming of the Spaniards...so also did those of Yucatán. Some years before they were conquered by Admiral Montejo, in the district of Mani in the province of Tutul Xiu, an Indian named Ah-cambal, filling the office of Chilan...told publicly that they would soon shift to fresh calendar bearers, [and] be ruled by a foreign race who would preach a [new] God." (*Yucatán Before and After the Conquest*, p. 19)

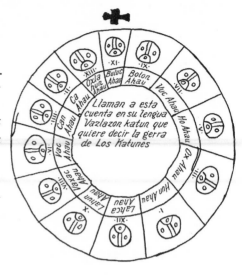

Katun wheel from Landa (1556) from Yucatán Before and after the Conquest

It was no small thing that the *Chilan* (a priest concerned with prophecy and divination) fore-warned of the appearance of the Spanish by anticipating it as the advent of "fresh calendar bearers," since for the Maya people, the calendar was an exquisite tool pertaining to astronomy, history, and destiny. The Spanish might burn their hieroglyphic histories, and the Maya people themselves might grow foggy in their memories of the past, but their calendar could never forget.

The Maya calendar is actually three calendars: the *Tzolk'in*, the *Haab'*, and the "Long Count." Sharing many aspects with the calendars of both earlier Mesoamerican civilizations such as the Zapotec and Olmec and the more contemporary Aztec, it is widely understood that the Maya methods of reckoning time were the most sophisticated. The original name for the sacred calendar is unknown, but it is now called the *Tzolk'in*, meaning simply "count of days." Equivalent to the Aztec *Tonalpohualli*, the *Tzolk'in* combines twenty discrete day names with the thirteen numbers of the *trecena* cycle to give a period of 260 days. There are glyphs for each of the day names, and these glyphs—along with other hieroglyphic texts—adorn nearly every conceivable object left behind by the

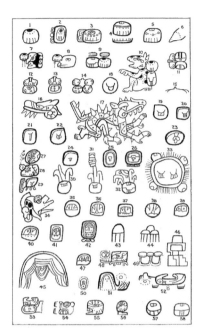

From of the Maya Year: examples of the glyph for the first day sign Imix (Bureau of American Ethnology to the Secretary of the Smithsonian Institution, 1897)

ancient Maya: pottery; bone, shell, jade ornaments, and of course the stelae (incised, or carved, stone commemorative slabs) and murals of their temples and residences, as well as the few screenfold holy books that survived Landa's and other friars' *auto da fés*. One nineteenth-century student of Maya hieroglyphs described them as *"calculiforme"* (pebble-shaped). These day-count glyphs are so common in Maya hieroglyphic expressions that early students of Maya writing claimed that it was almost exclusively devoted to chronology and astronomy. Classic Era (C.E. 250–900) Maya inscriptions are now known to deal largely with dynastic history; each historical statement is immediately followed by a calendrical expression.

The *Haab'* is the Maya solar calendar, comprising eighteen months of twenty days each, plus a period of five days at the end of the year known as *Wayeb'*. Like the *Tzolk'in* days, the *Haab'* months have associated glyphs that vary regionally and over time, but that tend toward images descriptive of the environment—*Sotz* (bat); *Mol* (water); *Pax* (planting time). Neither the *Tzolk'in* nor the *Haab'* system numbered the years, but combining the two calendars of 260 days and 365 days gave a distinct identity for a year, within a fifty-two-year cycle. A particular combination would not occur again for fifty-two *Haab'* years—which was longer that the average Maya life span. The conclusion of a fifty-two-year *Haab'* period, called a "Calendar Round" in modern parlance, was—particularly immediately preceding and after the arrival of the Spanish conquistadores—a time of much anxiety and anticipation among both the Maya and the Aztecs, and was marked by intense ritual activity designed to propitiate the gods.

The calendar with the longest memory is the Long Count, which though often spoken of as measuring the time elapsed since the "creation of the world," actually marks off the time that has passed since the beginning of the most recent Long Count cycle of 5125 years. The Long Count combines glyphs for five different increments of time:

	Long-Count Notation
k'in = one day	0.0.0.0.1
winal = 20-day month	0.0.0.1.0
tun = 360-day Long Count year	0.0.1.0.0
katun = 7200 days (20 tun)	0.1.0.0.0
baktun = 144,000 days (20 katun)	1.0.0.0.0

In Maya inscriptions, these time increments progress from largest to smallest. The stela below, from a site in Guatemala, shows one of the earliest Long Count dates recorded: 7.19.15.7.12, which correlates to the Gregorian calendar date of C.E. 37. The last known Long Count date recorded is C.E. 910—the date taken by archaeologists to mark the end of the Classical period of Maya civilization. Almost all Long Count glyphs record dates in the Classical period, however a few monuments point to much earlier times in a more general way, unconnected to historic events. The glyph for 13.0.0.0.0 in these texts refers to the earlier cycle of thirteen *baktuns*. (Thirteen *baktuns* comprise one cycle of the Long Count calendar.) The present age of thirteen *baktuns* will complete on December 21, 2012. This is of course the date that has generated so much apocalyptic anticipation in our own era.

The present Long Count—and thus the present age—is generally agreed upon to have begun on August 11, 3114 B.C.E. (This correlation emerged among Mayanists at the turn of the twentieth century; a debate continues about whether the precise "zero date" is August 11, 12, or 13). This base or zero date was set in late summer for astronomical reasons. The late scholar of the Maya, Linda Schele, noted that, in mid-August, the Milky Way—called *Wakah chan* ("raised sky," also widely referred to as the "World Tree") in Classical Maya creation myths—rises high in the sky. Realizing that the *Wakah chan* was the principle recurring image of Maya cosmic symbol·ism, Schele discovered that many Maya glyphs depicted the World Tree (Schele et al, *The Code of Kings*, pp. 113–114; 285; 382). In the *Chilam Balam* it is called the *Yax Imix Che*, the "first/green ceiba tree" that is raised in the middle of the cosmos. At Palenque in particular. Schele found a number of depictions of the World Tree. In the image on page 12, a serpent representing the Galactic Equator runs

The World Tree, the Milky Way, and the "2012 Window"
(Linda Schele & Mary Ellen Miller, from The Blood of Kings: Dynasty and Ritual in Maya Art)

through the center, and at the top perches a great bird symboliz-ing the deity *Itzamna*. Below, a water monster's mouth marks the entrance to *Xibalba*, the underworld.

The classical era Maya were of course not the only ancient peoples to recognize the Milky Way as a path toward the Creator. The first-century Roman poet Ovid spoke of the *Via lactea* ("Milky Way") as the "royal road to the throne of Zeus." Asian peoples knew this hazy band of stars as the "Silvery River of Heaven." Though we and all other peoples of the Earth experience the Milky Way as a tree, band, path, or river running above our heads, it is really a great circle, which is inclined at 60° to the plane of the ecliptic. The ecliptic is the appar-ent path that the Sun traces out in the sky over the course of a year; the

Linda Schele's drawing of the central panel of the Temple of the Cross at the Palenque site in Chiapas, Mexico (From Linda Schele and Mary Ellen Miller, The Blood of Kings: Dynasty and Ritual in Maya Art, p. 27)

planets (save Pluto, recently officially reclassified as a dwarf planet) all fall within an 8° band along the ecliptic. The zodiacal constellations constitute a band that is 8° on either side of the ecliptic.

In the movement of the December solstice Sun toward the "Galactic Alignment" (facing page): *A* marks the position where the December solstice Sun was in relation to the Milky Way about 3,000 years ago; *B* is the location 1,500 years ago; and *C* marks the "2012 Window," when the December solstice Sun has converged, as a result of the precession of the equinoxes, with the exact centerline of the Milky Way, or Galactic Equator.

The Earth's rotation is not fixed in space, but wobbles like a rotating toy top, so that the axis falls backward through the fixed stars, 1° every seventy-two years. This movement is called "precession." Since

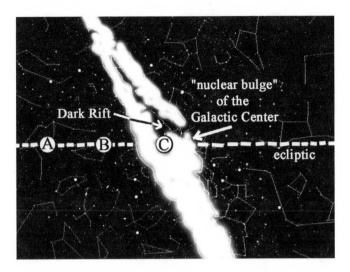

Movement of the December solstice Sun
toward the "Galactic Alignment"
(illustration by John Major Jenkins)

the Sun is ½° wide, the winter solstice Sun takes thirty-six years to precess through the region of the Galactic Equator. Actually, Belgian astronomer Jean Meeus (*Mathematical Astronomy Morsels*, 1997) determined that the precise alignment of the winter solstice point with the Galactic Equator occurred already in 1998. Why then do so many people speak of the alignment of the winter solstice with the Galactic Equator as taking place on December 21, 2012, the end date of the Maya calendar? Since it takes thirty-six years for the Sun to precess through the Galactic Equator, 1998 can be seen as the midpoint for a period that extends from 1980 until 2016. Instead of speaking of "2012" we should speak of the "2012 Window," in the sense that the precise end date of the Maya calendar, on December 21, 2012, falls within this thirty-six-year period centered on the year 1998.

Though we may find ourselves initially disappointed that the date that we formerly believed to be so precise in its identification by the ancient Maya is actually a thirty-six-year time span, consider the enormous span of time between alignments: The alignment of a solstice or equinox point with the Galactic Equator occurs only each quarter precessional cycle, that is, every 6,480 years. The next solstice alignment will take place in 12,960 years. That the Maya calendar, dating back perhaps further in time than our own Christian calendar, could pinpoint this rare, unique, astronomical event with such precision is stunning. Might there be other calendars with similar foresight?

2. The Gospel in the Stars

And I beheld another beast coming up out of the Earth; and he had two horns like a lamb, and he spake as a dragon. And he exerciseth all the power of the first beast before him, and causeth the Earth and them which dwell therein to worship the first beast, whose deadly wound was healed. And he doeth great wonders, so that he maketh fire come down from heaven on the Earth in the sight of men, And deceiveth them that dwell on the Earth by the means of those miracles which he had power to do in the sight of The Beast; saying to them that dwell on the Earth, that they should make an image to The Beast, which had the wound by a sword, and did live. And he had power to give life unto the image of The Beast, that the image of The Beast should both speak, and cause that as many as would not worship the image of The Beast should be killed. (Revelation 13: 11–15)

The Apocalypse Code

Though rarely considered such, John's Revelation—like the Maya Long Count—is both a calendar and an instrument of prophecy, and like the Long Count, its chronological clairvoyance derives from its intimacy with the stars. In Revelation, we find a description of the future in terms of the opening of the seven letters of the seven communities. This relates to our present seven civilizations—our present one being the fifth. Then follow the seven seals, relating to the seven civilizations that will follow on from the end of our seven eras. Seven trumpets follow: these signify a sequence of seven still more distant future civilizations. At the very end of Earth evolution there will then follow seven vials of wrath, taking humanity through seven stages of purging to arrive at the next stage of evolution, called the "Heavenly Jerusalem" in Revelation. The "clock" that measures out these cycles of seven in John's Revelation is the same one that plays into the Maya calendar—the precession of the equinoxes, caused by the wobble of the Earth upon its axis, against the background of the starry heavens.

As mentioned in chapter 1, the Earth's axis falls back through the fixed stars, 1° every seventy-two years; with 30° in each zodiacal sign, it takes 2,160 years (30 x 72) for the Sun's position at the vernal equinox to pass through each zodiacal constellation. A "zodiacal year," also known as a Great Year, or Platonic Year (Plato was among the first to mention it) thus lasts 25,920, or 12 x 2,160, years. Our present cultural age (Pisces) began C.E. 1414.[4] The Piscean cultural age will end in the year 3574; the two following cul-

The Great Beast by Albrecht Dürer
(Apocalypse woodcut series, 1498)

tural ages will bring the calendar to the year 7894. This takes humanity to the end of the seven letters of John's Revelation. The period of seven seals (7 x 2,160 = 15,120) brings the date to 23,014; the final period of seven trumpets carries this apocalyptic calendar to 38,134, denoting the end of Earth evolution, when the great purging (seven vials of wrath) will commence. Surrounded as we are by an array of doom-saying prophets who anticipate that 2012 will bring global catastrophe, John's Revelation is a comforting calendar, looking 36,000 years into the future.

Before this end date is reached, however, humanity must pass through many trials; this is the central message of Revelation. The exact meaning, and the exact timing, of these trials, has confounded readers of Revelation for nearly 2,000 years. Expressed in imaginative pictures from a long lost clairvoyant experience, in the same way that the pictures came to the prophets of the *Chilam Balam*, the prophetic pictures of Revelation elude the modern mind. In addition, the many centuries of erroneous and largely ideologically-driven interpretive exercises have severely lessened the sense that we might have as moderns that this extraordinary text could still have any relevance for us. That its main students in our own time tend to be fundamentalists anticipating an imminent Rapture makes Revelation even less appealing as a source for understanding the signs of the times. Yet if we can muster such titanic effort to penetrate the mysteries of the Maya calendar, can we not bring similar effort to the archetypal work of Christian prophecy?

Linda Schele and her fellow Mayanists worked in the late twentieth century to crack the code of Maya hieroglyphics. They needed a "Rosetta Stone" to help them break through to a full understanding of ancient voices. For them it came one afternoon in 1973, when they managed to decipher the first dynastic list of ancient Maya kings of the city of Palenque. By identifying a particular sign (*K'inich*) as an important royal title, Schele and her colleagues were able to identify and "read" the life histories of six kings of Palenque. After this breakthrough, progress proceeded at an exponential pace, leading to an array of new insights into the mysteries of Maya civilization.

John's Revelation demands a similar "Rosetta Stone." The precessional clock is the "hour hand," allowing only the broadest of correlations between the pictures of the Apocalypse and historical events since John first recorded his visions. A "minute hand" is needed before these pictures can serve as guides for the present and future. Since we are deciphering Christian "long count" prophecy, it is not surprising that we can find both the "Rosetta Stone" and the "minute hand" by following the chronology of the life of Christ to understand the present moment in history. The life of Christ (especially from the baptism in the Jordan until his death and Resurrection, or "Mystery of Golgotha") can be thought of as an embryonic period, a seed from which the future course of world history grows and bears fruit. Every deed performed by Christ has *eternal* significance, so that the rhythm of his life—like the Maya Long Count—does not end, but perennially repeats in new cycles of Time.[5]

We can liken the period between the Baptism and the Mystery of Golgotha to the period between conception and birth.[6] The conception took place at the baptism in the Jordan, on September 23, C.E. 29, when Christ incarnated into the physical body of Jesus. From that date through to Easter Sunday on April 5, 33, is a period of 1,290 days. It is also the period mentioned in the last chapter in the book of Daniel. Each of these days was a preparation for unfolding the future history of humanity. The key—the "Apocalypse Code"—to this unfolding of the Christ impulse is that one day in the life of Christ corresponds to twenty-nine and a half years of history.[7] Readers familiar with astronomy will know that this is the period required by Saturn to make one orbit of the zodiac. Applying the Apocalypse Code, the first day following on from the Baptism relates to the first twenty-nine and a half years of history following the Mystery of Golgotha in C.E. 33, the second day to the second twenty-nine and a half years, and so on. Applying the Apocalypse Code, we can thus actually determine when the end of the Earth will take place. That is 1,290 times this Saturn rhythm of twenty-nine and a half years, which takes us up to the year C.E. 38,000.[8] This date is confirmed by the date (38,134) mentioned earlier in relation to the precessional cycle.

How can we apply the Apocalypse Code to answer the question: Where do we stand now, at the present point in time, in relation to the seed embryo of the life of Christ? Can we correlate the pictures of John's Revelation as precisely as the Maya prophetic calendar anticipated the Galactic Alignment on December 21, 2012, during the "2012 Window" from 1980 to 2016?

In applying the Apocalypse Code, each twenty-nine-and-a-half-year period of history since the Mystery of Golgotha in C.E. 33 reflects the corresponding day in the life of Christ between the Baptism and the Resurrection. Thus, at present we are in the period described in the Gospels as the forty days of temptation in the wilderness. Historically, the period of temptation started on the evening of the Sabbath, Friday, October 21, 29. (The exact period of Saturn's orbital revolution is 29.4578 years. It is this exact period of 29.4578 years that is used to apply the Apocalypse Code, even if for the sake of simplicity the period is referred to as 29½ years.) The interval between the Baptism and the start of the period of temptation was twenty-eight and one-third days. Taking this correspondence (1 day = 29½ years, 28 1/3 x 29½ = 836 years), we have to add this to the year 33, which is the starting point, C.E. 33, being the year of the Mystery of Golgotha. In terms of our calendar, therefore, the beginning of the temptation of humanity started in 869 (= 33 + 836). This was the year of the eighth Ecumenical Council in Constantinople, when the split began between the Eastern and the Western Churches. The year 869 marks the point in time to which we can trace the start of the great conflict between the East and the West. In the Eastern Church they say that from this point in time on, the force of materialism, combined with a lack of understanding of the human being's spiritual nature, came into the Western Church. In 869, humanity began the first day of the temptations in the wilderness.

At the same time, Saturn was in sidereal Sagittarius.[9] Every time Saturn returns to sidereal Sagittarius, we have a further day in these forty days of temptation. If we take the forty days and reckon 40 x 29½ = 1,178 years, and add this onto 869, we find that the *end* of the period of temptation is in 2047, in the middle of this century.

We can be even more precise. The last day in the wilderness, the fortieth day, was the day on which Christ had overcome the temptations. In the Gospel of St. Matthew and the Gospel of St. Luke only three temptations are described. The overcoming of the three temptations is at the same time the overcoming of the forces of destruction. Fundamentally the whole of history is the story of humanity's wrestling with the three temptations. The culmination of the period of temptation was on the thirty-ninth day. The temptations lasted throughout almost the whole of the forty days, but the three temptations described in Matthew and Luke took place on the thirty-seventh, thirty-eighth, and thirty-ninth days. The fortieth day was the day on which, as described in the Gospels, "Angels came and ministered unto him." Going back one Saturn revolution from C.E. 2047, we arrive at the start of the last day, the fortieth day, in 2018, when Saturn will next be in Sagittarius in the sidereal zodiac. Now we are already in the period of the thirty-ninth day. The thirty-ninth day commenced with Saturn in Sagittarius in 1988. At the present moment in time, from its present location in the zodiac, Saturn will pass further around the zodiac to be in sidereal Sagittarius again in 2018. Clearly, the Apocalypse Code (thirty-ninth day: 1988–2018) leads to almost exactly the same historical time frame as the end of the Maya Long Count, or, rather, the "2012 Window" from 1980 to 2016.[10]

What do the Gospels say took place on the thirty-ninth day in the wilderness? This was the day of the third temptation, the temptation of turning stones into bread. This is basically the temptation of materialism, when the material world replaces the spiritual reality of existence, expressed in the words, "turning stones into bread."[11] Christ's reply to this temptation was, "Man does not live by bread alone, but by every word from the mouth of God." In other words, Christ directs our attention to the spiritual, to the divine Word which proceeds from the spiritual realm. Thus, our challenge is to honor the spiritual above the material. It is interesting that Christ says, "Man does not live by bread alone." It is clear we do need bread. We need the material, and we have to respect the material world, but it should not be the sole focus of our attention.

Having said that we do need bread, it is interesting to consider the case of the young Judith von Halle, who received the stigmata, the outer sign of the wounds of Christ, on Good Friday in 2004. At that time, she was in her thirty-second year of life.[12] When she received the stigmata, she had the same experience as other stigmatists before her (such as Anne Catherine Emmerich and Therese Neumann): she found that she was unable to eat any food and, simultaneously, she began to live in visions of the life of Christ—this became her "spiritual bread." Judith von Halle is a living example, at this time of the third temptation in the wilderness for humanity as a whole, of someone who has a different form of existence than the rest of humankind, in that she does not need bread or any kind of solid food. (She does occasionally drink water, but nothing else.) Robert Powell met her personally in November 2008, and described that she looked perfectly normal—in fact, quite radiant—and one would never have thought that she had not eaten for four and a half years. She indicates in one of her books that she is able to live by virtue of the grace

bestowed on her through her visions of Christ: "The life force emanating from the Resurrection strengthens me inwardly so much that
I can be outwardly nourished by it."[13] Judith von Halle does not live
by bread at all, but by every word that proceeds from the mouth of
God. She is thus an example of someone who has overcome the third
temptation in its most immediate form.

There is, however, a more subtle level of this third temptation,
which it is important to understand. At the third temptation on the
thirty-ninth day in the wilderness, Satan/Ahriman commanded Christ
to turn stones into bread. For humanity as a whole, this can be interpreted as substituting something lifeless and mechanical for the living, something that our modern civilization, with the help of technology, has perfected. It has reached the point where millions of people
around the world prefer the television or a computer to the real world.
Virtual reality is the modern means of turning stones into bread, by
which the images on the screen appear to be living, though they are
dead and lifeless. This is referred to in Revelation as "worshiping the
image" (Revelation 13:13–15).

THE INCARNATION OF AHRIMAN

By observing current events, it can be seen clearly that this third temptation is now building to a climax. The global financial crisis that
began in September 2008, precipitated as it was by widespread obsession with the material level of existence ("bread"), is the fulfillment
in our time of the words of Christ spoken two thousand years ago.
We, the whole of humanity, are now passing through this trial, which
is presented by the tempter described in Matthew as Satan, and in
the Persian tradition as the being named Ahriman (this is the Middle
Persian equivalent of the earlier Avestan language's *Angra Mainyu*,
or "destructive spirit"). Knowledge of this being was first brought
into the modern world in the early twentieth century by the Austrian
spiritual teacher Rudolf Steiner (1861–1925), who—in his choice
of terminology—referred back to the Zoroastrian religion, which
portrays Ahriman as the being who opposes the Sun Spirit, *Ahura
Mazda*. Echoes of this theme of a cosmic struggle between good and

evil are to be found in other religions—for example, Satan is the dark power in the Jewish tradition, and Seth (Typhon) is the opponent of Osiris in the religion of Ancient Egypt. It is apparent, through comparison of these religions, that Ahriman, Seth, and Satan are one and the same. By the same token, Ahura Mazda, Osiris, and Christ are one and the same, in the sense that Ahura Mazda and Osiris are two pre-incarnatory forms of Christ at different points in time—i.e., Ahura Mazda for the Persians in the Age of Gemini and Osiris for the Egyptians in the Age of Taurus.[14]

As it is Ahriman (Satan in the Bible) who presents this temptation of turning stones into bread on the thirty-ninth day in the wilderness, it follows that we are living in the time of the incarnation of Ahriman (between now and 2018), or, in traditional Christian terms, the coming of Antichrist. This is the challenge humanity now faces. A source for understanding this trial, or temptation, is found in Revelation 13, where Satan, known in the Christian tradition as Antichrist, is described as "The Beast." There it is described how The Beast comes to rule upon the Earth for a period of three and a half years, which exactly mirrors the period of Christ's ministry. It is also described how The Beast (Antichrist) is assisted by another being described as a two-horned beast, the false prophet, who is able to wield magical powers and to call down fire from heaven. This second individual referred to here is a source or vehicle for the inspiration of the Sun demon, called in the Jewish mystery tradition Sorath, made up of the Hebrew letters *Samech*, *Vau*, *Resh*, and *Tau*. Moreover, each letter in the Hebrew alphabet has a numerical value: *Samech* = 60, *Vau* = 6, *Resh* = 200, *Tau* = 400. If we add this together, we have the number 666. In Revelation this is the number of The Beast. The two-horned beast Sorath works in history in the rhythm of 666 years. Around the time of C.E. 666, Sorath worked very powerfully in an attempt to prematurely bring something along the lines of what we now have as modern science. Sorath worked by way of inspiration especially in the Academy of Gondishapur in Persia. But the working of this influence at that time was weakened through the Muslim conquest, which to some extent curtailed the potentially negative influence of the Academy of Gondishapur (see chapter 7).

The second time in history when the influence of Sorath reached a culmination was in the period around 2 x 666 = 1332. This was in the fourteenth century, when again this negative inspiration worked especially powerfully, leading to the destruction of the Order of the Knights Templar. The third time is now, around 3 x 666 = 1998. Here there is a new influence of Sorath working in. Thus Ahriman, or Satan, who is presenting the third temptation, is assisted by Sorath, the two-horned beast, whose negative inspiration is focused upon the human being who is referred to in Revelation as the prophet of The Beast with ten horns and seven heads (Antichrist or Satan incarnate, the incarnation of Ahriman in Rudolf Steiner's terminology). Chapter 7 goes into greater detail concerning the historical interventions of Sorath at intervals of 666 years.

Here we are confronted with a powerful, negative force. We are living in very challenging times that call upon us to understand the working of these trials and temptations, and to seek ways to overcome them. Just consider the impact that the financial crisis has had, and we can recognize the serious nature of the challenge of these trials.

Coupling the prophetic images of Revelation with the timing given by the Apocalypse Code, we can see that the central theme of the present century is that of the coming of the Antichrist, or the incarnation of Ahriman.[15] On October 27, 1919, Rudolf Steiner was in Zurich, Switzerland beginning a lecture series later published in English as *The Influences of Lucifer & Ahriman: Human Responsibility for the Earth.*[16] He had spoken of Ahriman many times since he first mentioned him on January 1, 1909 (linking the catastrophic earthquake a week earlier in Messina, Italy, to Ahriman), this time in 1919 saw his first mention of an *incarnation* of Ahriman:

> Ahriman skillfully prepares his goal beforehand; ever since the Reformation and the Renaissance, the economist has been emerging in modern civilization as the representative governing type. That is an actual historical fact.... Rulers are in fact merely the handymen, the underlings of the economists. One must not imagine that the rulers of modern times are anything but the economists' agents. And all that has been enshrined as law and justice is, if one scrutinizes it carefully,

simply a consequence of a thinking dictated by economics. In the nineteenth century economics was, for the first time, replaced by a thinking based on finance and banking. And in the nineteenth century was created for the first time the whole financial system which swamps every other relationship.... If people do not realize that the legislative state that safeguards human rights, on the one hand, and the organism of the spirit, on the other hand, must balance and redress the economic order established by economists and bankers, then again, through this lack of awareness, Ahriman will find an important instrument for preparing his incarnation. His incarnation is undoubtedly coming, and this lack of insight will smooth the way for his triumphant advance. [17]

In view of the 2008 financial crisis, highlighted by a $700 billion bank bailout, could there be a more explicit indication of the role of the financial system in preparing for Ahriman's incarnation?

There is something absurdly prosaic about the fact that, on a daily basis, we are living through the very events foreseen so long ago in John's Revelation, and that, a century ago, were pinpointed so precisely by Rudolf Steiner. The cryptic images that John received in a cave on the island of Patmos have become the daily newspaper headlines and, for many of us, pressing practical concerns. With the unfolding global financial crisis, the sweeping changes in policy clearly seem to bring even greater concentrations of capital, and with it an unprecedented level of global economic, social, and political power. Never before in human history has there been a moment as open to the possibility of a world government. In the many centuries since John first recorded his visions in Revelation, "The Beast" of chapter 13 has been recognized in the personages of many despotic kings, popes, emperors, or dictators. All of these erroneous identifications of Antichrist (excepting perhaps those applied to Adolf Hitler, who truly was a "prefiguring" of the coming world ruler) came when the world was a much smaller place, and each "empire" represented a relatively small corner of the planet. At present, global integration has progressed to the point where "World Ruler" is more than just a title; it describes an actual possibility. [18]

The chronology given by the Apocalypse Code for the advent of The Beast of Revelation can be supplemented by the teachings of the Persian/Zoroastrian tradition. The founder of Zoroastrianism, Zarathustra, was evidently the first human being to speak of Ahriman's existence. This account, drawn from the sacred Zoroastrian text of the *Bundahisn,* describes the conflict between Ahriman and Ahura Mazda:

> Then Ahura Mazda, with a knowledge of which way the end of the matter would be, went to meet the evil spirit and proposed peace to him, and spoke thus: "Evil spirit! bring assistance unto my creatures, and offer praise! so that, in reward for it, ye (you and your creatures) may become immortal and undecaying, hungerless, and thirstless." And the evil spirit shouted thus: "I will not depart; I will not provide assistance for thy creatures; I will not offer praise among thy creatures; and I am not of the same opinion with thee as to good things. I will destroy thy creatures forever and everlasting; moreover, I will force all thy creatures into disaffection to thee and affection for myself." And the explanation thereof is this: that the evil spirit reflected in this manner, that Ahura Mazda was helpless with regard to him, therefore He proffers peace; and he did not agree, but bore on even into conflict with Him. And Ahura Mazda spoke thus: "You are not omniscient and almighty, O evil spirit! so that it is not possible for thee to destroy me, and it is not possible for thee to force my creatures so that they will not return to my possession." Then Ahura Mazda, through omniscience, knew that: If I do not grant a period of contest, then it will be possible for him to act so that he may be able to cause the seduction of my creatures to himself. As even now there are many of the intermixture of humankind who practice wrong more than right. And Ahura Mazda spoke to the evil spirit thus: "Appoint a period! so that the intermingling of the conflict may be for nine thousand years." For he knew that by appointing this period the evil spirit would be undone. Then the evil spirit, unobservant and through ignorance, was content with that agreement; just like two men quarrelling together, who propose a time thus: Let us appoint such-and-such a day for a fight. Ahura Mazda also

knew this, through omniscience, that within these nine thousand years, for three thousand years everything proceeds by the will of Ahura Mazda, three thousand years there is an intermingling of the wills of Ahura Mazda and Ahriman, and the last three thousand years the evil spirit is disabled, and they keep the adversary away from the creatures. Afterward, Ahura Mazda recited the *Ahunvar* thus: *Yatha ahu vairyo* ["As a heavenly lord is to be chosen"] once and uttered the twenty-one words; He also exhibited to the evil spirit His own triumph in the end, and the impotence of the evil spirit, the annihilation of the demons, and the Resurrection and undisturbed future existence of the creatures for ever and everlasting. And the evil spirit, who perceived his own impotence and the annihilation of the demons, became confounded, and fell back to the gloomy darkness; even so as is declared in revelation, that, when one of its (the *Ahunvar's*) three parts was uttered, the evil spirit contracted his body through fear, and when two parts of it were uttered he fell upon his knees, and when all of it was uttered he became confounded. [19]

There are several points to note about the conflict between Ahura Mazda and Ahriman. The first is the setting of a time period for the conflict. Contemplating the current state of world affairs, all the signs are that the end of this time period is drawing close, and thus the conflict is approaching a climax. Hence the timeliness of considering the incarnation of the Antichrist (Ahriman) as the likely culmination of his attack on all that which is good (the good in this scenario being the creative work of Ahura Mazda/Christ, the creator of the prototypes of all existence). The possibility is raised that the termination of the conflict will coincide with the end of the Maya calendar at the winter solstice of the year 2012. This date is not exactly nine thousand years from the time of Zarathustra at the beginning of the Age of Gemini in 6266 B.C.E., since the precise time interval between -6265 and +2012 is 8,275 years. (The historical date 6266 B.C.E. = -6255 astronomically.) The "nine thousand years" spoken of in the *Bundahisn* could very well mean an approximate time interval of around nine millennia. Since the period of 8,275 years fall into the ninth millennium following the start of the Age of Gemini, which was the age of Zarathustra when he founded the Ancient Persian culture, it seems quite likely that we have in the Zoroastrian myth of the battle between Ahura Mazda and Ahriman a further support for the chronology given by both the Maya Long Count and Revelation.

Let us consider the possibility that the Mayans were inspired to devise a calendar which ends at the winter solstice in the year 2012 because there was a real spiritual inspiration underlying this. In turn, let us consider the possibility that the inspiration underlying the Maya calendar—in particular, underlying the end date—could perhaps have to do with the deadline indicated in the sacred writings attributed to Zarathustra concerning the time limit set for the cosmic battle between Ahura Mazda/Christ and Ahriman/Satan. If the end of the Maya calendar on December 21, 2012, is indeed the deadline for the conflict between Christ and Ahriman, it is conceivable that the three-and-a-half-year period of the Antichrist will begin around the summer solstice in the year 2009 or a little thereafter. The start of this period would be at the summer solstice if the three and a half years were to be reckoned as solar years. However, if they were to be reckoned as lunar years, which was the normal mode of reckoning in ancient Israel, the start of this period would be on July 31, 2009.

In the summer of 2009, July 22, there is a total eclipse of the Sun at 2:36 a.m. Greenwich Mean Time. The path of the eclipse crosses India, Nepal, Bangladesh, Bhutan, China, the southern islands of Japan, and the western Pacific Ocean. The Moon will be at its perigee (its closest position to the Earth), making it appear larger than the Sun, resulting in a wider path and greater duration. (The arc of the partial eclipse path on this date swings as far north as 60° N, right across northern Russia, and as far south as 30° S, touching the North Island of New Zealand) According to Rudolf Steiner, these conditions will allow for the maximum power of evil (The Beast) to arise from the interior of the Earth should human beings remain unaware of the importance of aligning with Christ and maintaining their own consciousness in a state of wakeful awareness in relation to this event.

At the time of the July 22, 2009, eclipse, there is a triple conjunction of Jupiter, Neptune, and Chiron (formerly called an asteroid, it is now classified as a "centaur," suggesting its dual nature as half comet, half asteroid)—all within less than a single degree, and also a heliocentric opposition of Saturn with Uranus. No doomsday events are forecast for that date; eclipses long ago lost their power to frighten humankind. Indeed, dozens of eclipse-watching tours to China and the South Pacific are already sold out. Sirius Travel's 2009, eleven-day China tour schedule takes in the eclipse from Emei Shan, a sacred mountain in central China; advertisements for the *Sky & Telescope* magazine "South Pacific" tour boasted, "With so few cruise ships available for this eclipse, and only 160 staterooms on the elegant *Paul Gauguin*, this eclipse voyage is sure to sell out"; for $3,499, "Ring of Fire" expeditions takes eclipse watchers out to Iwo Jima island for five minutes and twelve seconds of totality.

Eclipse tourism does not change the fact that at the time of a total solar eclipse, something sulphurous is stirred up. At the time of a solar eclipse, according to Rudolf Steiner, "What spreads out as negativity upon the Earth can be borne up in a luciferic way into cosmic space, where it can bring about further damage."[20] Demonic spiritual beings are more agitated than usual at the time of an eclipse, and thus eclipses, according to Steiner, offer special opportunities for the activity of black magicians. Very few people are able to discern this work of evil during solar eclipses. Could it be that the solar eclipse of July 22, 2009 (the longest eclipse of the twenty-first century, lasting six and a half minutes), signifies the start of the three-and-a-half-year period of the rule of the Antichrist? If so, the incarnation of Ahriman may take place at or around the time of this solar eclipse.

KRISHNA AND THE KALI YUGA

The Maya Long Count begins August 11, 3114 B.C.E. It is interesting that the date for the beginning of the latest *yuga* ("age") in the Hindu cyclic calendar is midnight on February 17/18, 3102 B.C.E. This means that there is only a twelve-year difference between the starting points of these two calendars—incredibly close, given their lengthy duration. Twelve years is a Jupiter period; it is the length of a Jupiter orbit around the Sun. The Mayans, therefore, start their calendar one Jupiter period before the Hindu calendar. According to Rudolf Steiner, the *Kali Yuga* lasts for 5,000 years: 3102 B.C.E. (astronomically –3101) to 1899 (see chapter 6). There is just a twelve-year difference in the starting point, and a difference of 113 years in the finishing point, of the two calendars. Added together, this period of 125 years is itself interesting, because it is one-fortieth of the period of the *Kali Yuga*.[21]

Kali Yuga literally means Dark Age. Why do Hindus consider this period an age of darkness? The start of this period on February 17/18, 3102 B.C.E., was the date of the death of Krishna, the true "soul of India." In fact, Krishna did not incarnate into a human being in the normal sense, but rather manifested through a physically incarnated human being. Rudolf Steiner uses the expression "embodiment" in relation to Krishna and indicates that this great being "became physically visible."[22] Above all, the *Bhagavad Gita* brings to expression that Krishna *overlighted* the soul of Arjuna.[23] From this perspective, Krishna's "death" signified his withdrawal from Arjuna, which was experienced by Arjuna as a loss of clairvoyance and thus the beginning of the Dark Age. According to Steiner's spiritual research, Krishna reappeared as Jesus of Nazareth; thus Krishna and Jesus are one and the same being. Steiner taught that the Krishna soul is the pure and archetypal human soul who, until Jesus, had never before incarnated on the Earth but remained in the cosmic realm and thus did not experience the Fall. The *Bhagavad Gita* is essentially the narrative of the manifestation of this Krishna soul, who reveals himself to Arjuna as the Lord of all existence. Steiner discovered that the Krishna soul incarnated just a single time—as Jesus of Nazareth. Jesus of Nazareth, the incarnated Krishna, was the vessel at the Baptism for the incarnation of a great cosmic being, the Christ, who originated from celestial heights and over a period of several millennia incarnated stage by stage, the final stage (incarnation on Earth in Jesus of Nazareth) being in C.E. 29 at the baptism of Jesus in the River Jordan.[24]

Along with marking the "death" of Krishna—his withdrawal from Arjuna—the last representative of the ancient clairvoyant spiritual consciousness in the Indian culture, the *Kali Yuga* marks the loss of this spiritual consciousness *for all humanity*. We can grasp this by way of the following analogy. Thinking of Jesus of Nazareth, the incarnated Krishna, undergoing temptation during the period of the forty days in the wilderness, we can also conceive of this period as an archetype symbolizing the historical period of *Kali Yuga* from 3102 B.C.E. to C.E. 1899, whereby during these forty "days" amounting historically to the five-thousand-year period of *Kali Yuga*, the knowledge of God was in danger of being totally eclipsed. In the Maya calendar, the "forty days in the wilderness" of the *Kali Yuga* is extended by approximately one "day"—a period of transition to the new Yuga, the *Satya Yuga*, the Age of Light—and thus the Maya calendar ends in 2012 rather than in 1899. *This is the real significance of the end of the Maya Long Count.*

In 1899, the year that marks the end of the Hindu *Kali Yuga*, Rudolf Steiner had an intense, life-changing clairvoyant experience of Christ, which he describes in his autobiography. Until then, his relationship to Christianity was far less inwardly profound. Steiner's inner experience involved what he termed the "Mystery of Golgotha"—the events of the Passion, Crucifixion, and Resurrection. This was the turning point in his life. After this, Steiner became the "prophet" of Christ in his Second Coming, as did John the Baptist for Christ's first coming. Steiner often emphasized that his entire teaching of "Anthroposophy" (or spiritual science) was to prepare for the Second Coming (see, for example Rudolf Steiner, *The Reappearance of Christ in the Etheric*).

In these extraordinary chronological "co-incidences," we can see that the principle events of Christ's life were not parochial, but rather *universal* in the sense that *both calendars reflect the rhythm of Christ's life*. The transition from *Kali Yuga* to the beginning of the New Age, or *Satya Yuga*, proclaimed by the ancient Hindus, was revealed, at least in part, through the appearance of the great spiritual teacher Rudolf Steiner, who began his teaching activity in 1900. His 1899 experience of the Mystery of Golgotha heralded the dawn of this age.

"Second coming" is not an expression that appears in the New Testament, and yet by the twentieth century it had long been in common use. The Greek word *parousia* essentially means "appearance and subsequent presence with." In the original text of the New Testament, *parousia* is used for the prophecies that speak of a future presence of Christ in human evolution. Steiner, however, knew from personal experience that the "coming" was already in progress—

that Christ had continued to be a living presence throughout human history, though recognizable to only a few in any period. Steiner's emphasis was always upon *rhythm*, and the leitmotif that ran through all of his Christological teachings was the dynamic nature of Christ's being, and human beings' response to that presence.

Steiner's immense contribution to overcoming modern materialistic conceptions of the New Testament was his exact understanding of another Greek word: *nephele*. In Paul's two epistles to the Thessalonians (considered by most Biblical scholars to be the oldest part of the New Testament), Paul is the first to ever speak of the Etheric Christ: "Then we which are alive and remain shall be caught up together with them in the clouds, to meet the Lord in the air; and so shall we ever be with the Lord." To Paul, *nephele* meant "cloud," but it also meant the hazy, subtle, and wholly real realm that surrounds and permeates all living things. *Nephele* is the etheric realm; physical clouds are but one of the many manifestations of the living, weaving realm of the etheric (see, for example, E. R. Smith, *The Burning Bush,* pp. 20; 465; 511). The many biblical passages that today strike our ears as meaning "clouds" are actually speaking of the etheric realm. That *nephele* now stands behind the term "nebulous" denotes the change in human consciousness over the past two thousand years with regard to the ability to grasp spiritual reality.

In January 1910, Rudolf Steiner began to speak of the return of Christ, not in a physical form, but *in the etheric realm of the Earth.* In Karlsruhe, Germany, on January 25, he spoke of how Christ went almost completely unrecognized during his own lifetime. He then posed a question to his audience: "Could it, then, be possible that something of infinite importance is taking place today, and that human beings are not taking it into their consciousness? Could it be that something tremendously important is taking place in the world, right now, of which our own contemporaries have no idea?" Since the end of the *Kali Yuga,* or Dark Age, in 1899, Steiner said that humanity would increasingly gain the ability to perceive the etheric world, and thus, to have the "Damascus experience" of St. Paul, that is, to *see* Christ in the etheric realm. Like Paul, people would become "eye witnesses" of Christ. Living experiences of Christ would make documentary evidence, such as that presented in the four gospels, superfluous, or at least supplementary.

At the same time, Steiner warned that the materialistic mind would instead conceive of an actual physical return of Christ, and that certain individuals (such as the Theosophical Society and C. W. Leadbeater's proclamation of Krishnamurti as the physical vessel for the World Teacher, or Christ[25]) would be heralded as the reincarnated Christ. Then, in his lecture, "The Reappearance of Christ in the Etheric," Steiner pointed very particularly to the timing of the new etheric clairvoyance:

> The first signs of these new soul faculties will soon begin to appear in a few isolated souls. Those signs will become clearer during the fourth decade, between 1930 and 1940, and especially in 1933, 1935, and 1937. Faculties that are still rare in people will begin to manifest as natural abilities. Along with this, there will be great changes, and biblical prophecies will be fulfilled. Everything will be transformed for those on Earth, as well as for those who are no longer in a physical body. Regardless of where they are, souls are meeting entirely new faculties. Everything is changing, but the most significant event of our time is a deep, decisive transformation in human soul faculties. (*The Reappearance of Christ in the Etheric*, p. 16)

Steiner added, "It would be a great misfortune if materialists were to triumph and humanity were to overlook these events."

Clearly, Rudolf Steiner's task for twentieth-century humanity was analogous to the one performed twenty centuries earlier by John the Baptist—to serve as witness, as forerunner, and even as facilitator of the descent of Christ, called by Steiner the Sun *Spirit*, into the etheric realm—just as for the corresponding event in the physical realm John had stewarded Christ's descent into the body of Jesus of Nazareth at the baptism in the Jordan. The stunning outpouring of wisdom from Steiner, beginning with his emergence as a spiritual teacher in 1900 until his death in 1925, can be seen as a revelation through which Jesus Christ spoke to humankind at the advent of his return within the etheric realm of the Earth. In the cascade of revelations made by Steiner in this single lecture, there was much more that he was *not* saying. His own biography was in exquisite sync with the process of the etheric return of Christ. If one applies the analogy (identified by Steiner in 1923) that one year in the life of an individual is equal to a hundred years in the life of humanity since the birth of Christ, Steiner's birth in 1861 came at the moment of humanity's "Moon Node." The lunar nodes are the two places where the Moon crosses the plane of the ecliptic each month. The axis of these nodes moves backward around the zodiac, taking 18.61 years to complete a circuit. In the life of the individual, the return of the Moon's nodes is a herald of the spiritual awakening that will transpire at age twenty-one, when the self, or "I," is born. At the moment of the return of the Moon's nodes, each person can experience an opening to his or her higher self. Rudolf Steiner's life work was to awaken humanity to the "higher self" of Christianity.

Rudolf Steiner's proclamation that in 1933 Christ would return into the etheric realm of the Earth would seem to have been soundly repudiated by the events of history; in January 1933, Adolf Hitler came to power in Germany and began a twelve-year reign of terror upon the world. Yet, this "triumph of the will," Hitler's mobilization of the German people in an attempt to bring the whole world under the submission of his will, can be understood as the exact counter-image of humanity's true destiny—to follow not a single human will, or ideology, but God's will. In the words of Jesus Christ, "Not my will, but thine, be done" (Luke 22: 40). Steiner had warned already in 1924 that, if humanity did not recognize Christ in his new form, humanity would have to face The Beast arising from the abyss in 1933.[26]

We see that a confrontation is taking place on different levels, the forces opposing Christ and what he represents. Against the background of the Zoroastrian account about how Ahriman challenges Ahura Mazda, and the time limit of 2012, we can see clearly that the whole period beginning in 1899, highlighted by Hitler's attempt for world dominion beginning in 1933, is the period when *Ahriman is trying to take control of the world*. This also explains why in the Maya calendar the *Kali Yuga* is extended by approximately one "day," since the *Satya Yuga* cannot really begin until this conflict is resolved. The key thing to bear in mind is that humanity is part of this conflict;

it happens in and through us. Ahriman's only way of working is through human beings. Part of his vision is to take over all human consciousness on Earth, establishing it as a fortress from which to attack other realms. We saw an example of this with the January 2005 rocket launch, timed to strike the Comet Temple on July 4, 2005. This extraordinary technological achievement, accomplished with the precision of a cruise missile striking its target, gives a perfect picture of what Ahriman wishes to accomplish in his war against the rest of the universe. We must grasp Ahriman's agenda for world dominion. It is through connecting with Christ that we thwart this plan.

As mentioned, we can see from the life of Hitler an initial attempt to gain world dominion. When he came to power in 1933, it was the time of the onset of Christ's return as a regenerating force in the etheric aura of the Earth. Hitler's counter-attack against this supra-sensory event was to apply the method of inversion through black-magic practices in order to oppose Christ's mission for the Earth. His insignia—the Swastika—was the inversion of an ancient sacred symbol. Christ loved children: "Suffer the little children to come unto me.... Taking them up in his arms, putting his hands upon them, and blessing them" (Mark 10:14–16), and admonished his disciples, "Whosoever shall offend one of these little ones that believe in me, it is better for him that a millstone were hanged about his neck, and he were cast into the sea" (Mark 9:42). By contrast, Hitler embarked on a program of indoctrinating the youth and compelling them to serve him (Hitler Youth, etc.). Whereas Christ was imbuing nature with new life force, Hitler set about creating black-magic centers—the con-centration camps—to desecrate the Earth. And whereas Christ began working in the etheric realm to strengthen the human "I" from within, Hitler opposed this by seizing possession of the "I" of his SS officers, who had to "die" in him and serve him in total obedience.[27] The gift of Christ for the human "I" works in the sense of the words of Paul ("Not I, but Christ in me") and restores the evolutionary poten-tial of the human being toward moral integrity in the service of love, goodness, and regeneration. The human "I" lives in the blood, and the sacrifice of Christ's blood on Golgotha was to bring to birth the true "I"—a continual orientation toward the Good, the True, and the

Beautiful—and to bring regeneration to the Earth. Christ's sacrifice was a Blood Mystery.

On the basis of her clairvoyant view of the Crucifixion scene, the stigmatist Judith von Halle gives the following description of this Blood Mystery:

> Cassius—later known as Longinus—...took his spear and rode his horse decisively up the Crucifixion hill. His deed, which he fulfilled upon the body of the Lord, took place in a few seconds; and yet it seemed that time stood still. He pierced the body with his full strength, from a lower right-hand angle through the rib cage, lung, and into the heart. Then he tore the spear out of the side of the corpse again with a mighty pull, and the bright blood of the Redeemer gushed forth powerfully, pouring out at the foot of the Cross into a depression of greenish rock where it foamed and was contained. Jesus's loved ones cried out in horror, pain, and compassion, but when they saw this blood, this living, foaming blood which shone like the Sun, all were transformed in an instant....Cassius fulfilled the divine plan. His seemingly shocking intervention in fact liberated the elixir of humanity....Only through his courageous deed, the spear stroke, did life pour out into the world...the transformed blood of life....The Grail blood that poured forth from the side of the Lord...was always assigned the property of giving eternal life....The spear-wound mystery is one of transformation, of etherization....Thus the mystery of transformation is a new impulse which Christ has implanted in humanity. Christ reverses the descending evolutionary sequence to make it possible for us to attain a divine state. [28]

3. The Mexican Mysteries

On the American continent, far from the hill at Golgotha, the cross-carrying Spanish invaders encountered in the sacrificial cultures of the Maya and Aztec an inversion of the Blood Mystery, an attack on the "I" that lives in the blood:

> Apart from the festivals which they solemnized by the sacrificing of animals, on occasions of great tribulation or need the priests or *chilànes* ordained the sacrifice of human beings.... When the day of the ceremony arrived, they assembled in the court of the temple; if they were to be pierced with arrows their bodies were stripped and anointed with blue, with a miter on the head.... If his heart was to be taken out, they conducted him with great display and concourse of people, painted blue and wearing his miter, and placed him on the rounded sacrificial stone, after the priest and his officers had anointed the stone with blue and purified the temple to drive away the evil spirit. The chacs then seized the poor victim and swiftly laid him on his back across the stone, and the four took hold of his arms and legs, spreading them.... Then the nacon [captain or chief] executioner came, with a flint knife in his hand, and with great skill made an incision between the ribs on the left side, below the nipple; then he plunged in his hand and like a ravenous tiger tore out the living heart, which he laid on a plate and gave to the priest; he then quickly went and, anointed the faces of the idols with that fresh blood.[29]

Bishop Landa's description of Maya sacrifice is echoed clearly in Bernal Diaz's eyewitness account from Tenochtitlan, the capital city of the Aztec empire:

> On each altar were two figures, like giants with very tall bodies and very fat, and the first which stood on the right hand they said was the figure of Huichilobos [Huitzilopochtli] their

god of War; it had a very broad face and monstrous and terrible eyes, and the whole of his body was covered with precious stones.... All the walls of the oratory were so splashed
and encrusted with blood that they were black, the floor was
the same and the whole place stank vilely. Then we saw on the
other side...the other great image...which they call Tezcat...
and this Tezcatepuca [Tezcatlipoca] was the god of Hell and
had charge of the souls of the Mexicans, and his body was girt
with figures like little devils with snakes' tails. The walls were
so clotted with blood and the soil so bathed with it that in the
slaughter houses in Spain there is not such another stench. [30]

Both Bishop Landa's description from the Yucatán and Bernal
Diaz's account from Tenochtitlan testify to the centrality of heart
sacrifice in the religious practices of Mesoamerica. Both are clearly
inversions of the Blood Mystery enacted by Christ for the redemption of humanity. These historical inversions are uniquely instructive for many principles and processes here on this continent that
have presently become inverted or twisted, and suggest how the
ambitious undertakings of the Aztec empire may have some echo
in our time.

When you visit the Maya ruins at Chichen Itza, Coba, Palenque,
or other sites today, the tour guides typically offer some lurid tales
of Maya ritual bloodletting and sacrifice, but then immediately
explain these away as having been practices brought by the Maya's
imperial neighbors to the west, in the Valley of Mexico. Sometimes
the guides even state that the Classic Era Maya were conquered by
the Toltec, the "master craftsmen" whom contemporary scholars are
still trying to puzzle out as to whether they were an actual ethnic or
political group, or an amalgam of Aztec and other Mesoamerican
peoples' myths. The guides are echoing earlier scholarly consensus
about the Maya; it is only in recent decades that archaeological evidence suggests that there has long been a sacrificial tradition within
Maya civilization as well. But while the scholarly jury is still out
as to whether this sacrificial tradition is indigenous or imposed in
Maya civilization, it has deep and disturbing roots in the Mexican
highlands to the west.

THE SACRILEGE OF BLOODLETTING

If you have seen the film *Apocalypto*, you have been given vivid, ter-rifying images of "Maya" sacrificial practice; these scenes are of course only marginally accurate historically and, if anything, are more descriptive of Aztec than of Maya practices. In the eyewitness accounts of Spanish conquistadores like Bernal Diaz, we have reli-able descriptions of the Aztec ritual of heart sacrifice. From Diaz and the Aztec chronicles, we can imagine at least in part the vio-lence that accompanied the dedication of a temple to the Aztec god *Huitzilopochtli* (the "Hummingbird of the South") that took place in c.e. 1487, which was the year of the death of Tlacaellel, the principal dark agent in promoting human sacrifice.[31]

According to the description we read in historical accounts, a vivid scene presents itself: the *ocelomeh* (Jaguar Warriors) have just returned from a battle with fresh captives for the ceremony that will dedicate the new temple. At the base of the pyramid, a line of plebe-ian captives—their hands tied behind their backs, a leather choker around their throats—is coming through the Tenochtitlan gates. They are met by a band of priests who inspect them and waft incense about each one. Led to the bottom of the temple staircase, they are forced to do reverence before Huitzliopochtli's altar; then they are marched to the palace to perform the same for Montezuma and his priest-advisor Tlacaellel.

A line of captive nobles follows, and at Huitzilopochtli's temple they are made to place the richest gifts of treasure from their own lands. Kneeling before the altar, they pierce their tongues, legs, and ears with maguey spines, and then are compelled to make the ulti-mate gesture of surrender; they place their moistened finger in the dirt and then place it in their mouths. The highest of the lords has been coached by a priest, and makes his prayer: "I come to worship Huitzilopochtli, who gathers unto himself all nations; and now, as his creature, I come to serve him, bringing all my vassals and ser-vants that they too may adore him and recognize him as their lord."

At daybreak the following morning, the captives are among the thousands who have been placed in a close single file line down the steps of the great pyramid (it is over a hundred feet tall, comprising five terraces), through the city out over the causeways, as far as the eye could see. At the ends of the lines there are pens full of thousands of captives, waiting for the line to begin moving. Every road in Tenochtitlan is full of people; this day would see the greatest crowd ever gathered in the sacred city.

Stone relief found in 1978 at the base of the Templo Mayor in Mexico City, depicting the dismembered body of Coyolxauhqui, sister of Huitzilopochtli

At the summit of the new pyramid are twin chapels to Huitzilopochtli and the "Rain God" Tlaloc, their upper sections adorned with intricately carved aromatic wood. Four sacrificial slabs have been set up, one at the head of each staircase. Adorned in their finest royal cloaks, Tlacaellel and the three kings of the Aztec Triple Alliance—Tenochtitlan, Texcoco, and Tlacopan— approach Huitzilopochtli's altar, make prayers, and then take their places at the slabs. As the sun breaks over the horizon, great snakeskin drums begin to throb, and almost synchronous with the beat of the drums, the slaughter begins. Each victim is seized by four priests, one on each limb, and then flopped across the sacrificial slab. A fifth priest slips a hook around the victim's neck, to choke off the sound of the screams, and then the officiant raises the great obsidian knife and lets it fall with the full force of his upper torso. The precisely aimed stroke slices the chest in two, so that the priest can easily reach inside the pulsating pool of blood and tear out the still palpitating heart, to raise skyward in offering to Huitzilopochtli. The carcass is pushed off the slab and kicked over the top step, to tumble down to the base of the pyramid, where another group of priests waits to dismember the body.

The careful ceremonial protocol that marked the usual sacrificial occasions is impossible on this day—the scene at the temple is one of barely controlled mayhem. Over the course of the day, the red rivulets turn into rivers of fresh red blood running like lava over drying, darkening clots, which occasionally break off and bob downstream. At the foot of the pyramid, where blood and bodies come to rest, the priests struggle to keep their footing as they butcher the sacrificial victims. Others bail up blood in jars, then run off with them to all of the temples in the city, to smear the blood onto the faces of the idols there.

By afternoon, the stench of death hangs over the central part of the city, and residents flee to stay with friends and family in the outskirts. But the slaughter continued—for four days and nights—and even the guests of honor fled in panic from their flower-draped boxes in the central square. No ledger was kept of the killing spree, but some of the eyewitnesses told later Mexica chroniclers that 80,000 victims were sacrificed over the four days. (Most historians believe this to be an exagerration, but admit that the number might still have reached over 10,000.) Some accounts state that Tlacaellel and the most stalwart of his fellow priests continued the slaughter until month's end, butchering over 100,000 people to honor the Hummingbird.

THE "PRINCE-OF-THE-HOUSE"
AND THE RISE OF HUITZILOPOCHTLI

Huitzilopochtli,
Only a subject,
Only a mortal was.
A magician,
A terror,
A stirrer of strife,
A deceiver,
A maker of war,
An arranger of battles,
A lord of battles;
And of him it was said
That he hurled
His flaming serpent,

His fire stick;
Which means war,
Blood and burning;
And when his festival was celebrated,
Captives were slain,
Washed slaves were slain,
The merchants washed them.
And thus he was arrayed:
With headdress of green feathers,
Holding his serpent torch,
Girded with a belt,
Bracelets upon his arms,
Wearing turquoises,
As a master of messengers.
—*Hymn of Huitzilopochtli* ("Florentine Codex,"
in D. G. Brinton, *Rig Veda Americanus*)

Chimalpahin, one of the most reliable Mexica historians, wrote:

There were many great kings who inspired fear far and wide, but the one who was the most courageous, the most illustrious in the state, was the great captain, the great warrior Tlacaellel.... It was he also who established the worship of the devil Huitzilopochtli, the god of the Mexicans. (*Codex Chimalpahin*, vol. 1, p. 127)

Before 1428 and the victory of the upstart Aztec led by Itzcoatl over the neighboring people of Atzcapoltzalco, there had been no temples to Huitzilopochtli in Tenochtitlan or its environs. It was around 1428 that Tlacaellel had pronounced himself "Prince-of-the-House," and assumed command of the armies of the Triple Alliance. But more important, he created a new state ideology for the Mexica, with the following edict: "Huitzilopochtli is guiding the destiny of the Mexica. Anyone who opposes the Mexica opposes divine destiny."

All three states of the Triple Alliance had archives filled with codices, maps, and genealogical records that told a remarkably detailed history that extended back into the time of the *Tolteca*, the "master craftsmen" claimed by the Mexica as their ancestors. A widely held legend was that all of Anahuac's (the Nahuatl name for the Valley of Mexico) tribes had come to this continent under the guidance of a single omniscient deity, *Tloque Nahuaque*. Landing near what is today Tampico, they wandered the Gulf Coast north and south before heading inland. After long centuries had passed, their god took leave of them, making this farewell through the priests:

> Our Lord goeth bequeathing you this land; it is your merit, your lot. He goeth, he goeth back, but he will come, he will come to do his duty, he will come to acknowledge you. When the world is become oppressed, when it is the end of the world, at the time of its ending, he will come to bring it to an end. But [until then] you shall dwell here; you shall stand guard here. That which lieth here, that which spreadeth germinating, that which resteth in the Earth, is your merit, your gift. He maketh it your birthright. For this you followed him here. (W. Elzey 1991, pp. 114–135)

After Tloque Nahuaque (also called *Ometeotl*; apparently identical to the Maya *Hunab Ku*) had departed, the Tolteca, still living as a single tribe, moved north and settled in Teotihuacan, where they built the pyramid temples of the Sun and Moon, in a kind of foreshadowing of the principal temples at the Aztec capitol of Tenochtitlan.

In the hands of Itzcoatl's royal historian, Cuauhcoatl, these myths were totally twisted to serve the purposes of the new rulers. An official state history was created and then widely disseminated; it replaced Tloque Nahuaque with Huitzilopochtli, saying that he ordered the Mexica to leave their land, and promised to make *them* princes and lords of all the rich lands of the other six tribes. The older histories were ordered destroyed by Tlacaellel, who declared: "It is not necessary for all the common people to know of the writings; government will be defamed, and this will only spread sorcery in the land, for it containeth many falsehoods." This became a key part of state policy; whenever a temple was destroyed—the ultimate symbol of conquest—its archives were put to the torch, so that the new history could begin unhampered by the old.

Perhaps the most important new myth was that of Huitzilopochtli's birth. From bits and pieces of ancient Toltec myths, Tlacaellel, Cuauhcoatl and the *Pipiltin* ("Sons of Lords," i.e., the aristocratic

Mexica class) told this story: Coatlicue, the Earth Goddess, was one day sweeping the floor of her temple at Coatepec[32] ("Snake Mountain") when a ball of feathers floated down from the sky and touched her upon the shoulder. With this, the child Huitzilopochtli quickened within her womb. When Coatlicue's daughter Coyolxauhqui heard of this shameful news, she incited her brothers, the Centzon Huitznahua (the Four Hundred Stars) to destroy Coatlicue, because her pregnancy brought disgrace on the family. While in the womb, Huitzilopochtli swore to defend his mother and at the moment of birth, he sprung forth in full battle armor and war paint. After defeating the Four Hundred Stars, Huitzilopochtli slew his sister and cast her down the Coatepec hill, where her body broke to pieces on striking the bottom (see reproduction of the stone relief depicting this scene, p. 39).

Tlacaellel ordered the creation of a large round stone on whose face was sculpted the dismembered Coyolxauhqui. Placed at the bottom of the steps leading up the pyramid to Huitzilopochtli, sacrificial victims landed upon it after their hearts had been extracted. The priests of the cult of Huiltzilopochtli were presumed to reenact with every ritual murder, the heroic deed of the newly born Sun God Huitzilopochtli. Tlacaellel had also founded the myth that Huitzilopochtli was "The One Who Makes the Day," inferring that Huitzilopchtli must daily be fed with human blood if the day would continue to be made by the Sun's arcing path. With these two myths, Tlacaellel made human sacrifice the organizing principle of Mexica social, economic, and spiritual life (see E. M. Moctezuma, 1985, pp. 797–813).

In this new mythic universe of the imperial Mexica, Huitzilopochtli was brought into association with Quetzalcoatl, the Feathered Serpent, lawgiver, civilizer, creator of the calendar. In Tlacaellel's version of the myth, demons tempted Quetzalcoatl constantly to commit murder and human sacrifice, but his love was too great for him to succumb. To atone for great sins, Quetzalcoatl threw himself on a funeral pyre, where his ashes rose to the heavens as a flock of birds carrying his heart to the star Venus. A mural in the palace at Teotihuacan shows his first entry into the world in the shape of a chrysalis, from which he struggles to emerge as a butterfly, the symbol of perfection. Quetzalcoatl's promise to return in a 1 Acatl (Reed) year became the fateful catalyst for the Spanish conquest, when the Aztec emperor Montezuma recognized Cortés as the returned Quetzalcoatl.

While Quetzalcoatl was clearly a god with a long history in Mesoamerica (in the Maya culture, he is known as *Kukulkan*), Huitzilopochtli was very little known. In some older accounts that survived Tlaclaellel's 1428 *auto da fé*, the two gods are actually inverted in their characteristics—Quetzalcoatl is the bloodthirsty one, and Huitzilopochtli is a much milder, benevolent figure. The inverted Huitzilopochtli was raised by Tlacaellel to the supreme divinity and he instituted a reign of terror in tandem with the new, inverted stories. Immediately after issuing his second edict—that the Mexica's mission was to bring the worship of Huitzilopochtli to all peoples and nations, even if by force of arms—Tlacaellel sent emissaries to the lord of Xochimilcho to demand that he provide labor and materials for a new temple to be dedicated to Huitzilopochtli. When the lord refused, the Prince-of-the-House directed a swift attack; hundreds of captives were brought back for sacrifice to Huitzilopochtli. Other neighboring lords were similarly coerced, provoked, and then attacked. Soon there was a regular levy of sacrificial victims from all conquered territories.

Tlacaellel also coerced the *pochteca*—traveling merchants—into serving as his spies in the outlying territories, and then sent ambassadors to each region, demanding that they worship and provide sacrificial victims for Huitzilopochtli; recognize Mexica sovereignty; and pay tribute. If the ruling lords complied, Tlacaellel permitted them to continue worshipping their old deities along with Huitzilopochtli. When they refused, the Mexica legions swept upon them without mercy, confiscating property, enslaving or sacrificing a significant part of the population, and burning their temples. All statues and other representations of the local gods were collected and brought back to Tenochtitlan, where there was a special prison for rival deities.

In 1440, with Itzcoatl's death and the succession of Montezuma I, Tlacaellel again strengthened the stranglehold of the Huitzilopochtli cult. He assumed the title of *Ciuhuacoatl*—"Vice-Ruler," but literally "Snake Woman"—and had a duplicate throne placed for himself next to Montezuma's. He now was supreme oracle of the empire. The chronicles read: "Nothing was done in the realm without his

*Huitzilopochtli, from Allain Manesson Mallet, Description de l'univers
(Paris: 1683), v. 5, p. 311 (fig. 135)*

orders, and thus he used the tiara and insignia of the king" (*Codice
Ramirez*, quoted in Padden, p. 31). One of Tlacaellel's first acts as
Ciuhuacoatl was to create a new ceremony called *motlatocapaca*,
literally "washing the feet in blood." Beginning with Montezuma,
each time a new monarch was elected, he was expected to personally

lead the army against some neighbor, in order to accumulate enough sacrificial victims for the public coronation ceremony. The king was then expected to begin the sacrificial slaughter with his own hands, and continue to tear out hearts until his feet were covered by the blood of Huitzilopochtli's victims.

Bit by bit, Tlacaellel insinuated Huitzilopochtli into nearly every ceremony in the elaborate Mexica sacred calendar, and so the demand for sacrificial victims quickly outpaced the supply. In addition, Tlacaellel argued that Huitzilopochtli demanded *fresh* victims, and the ever increasing distance to new imperial conquests made this difficult. His solution to this predicament was the *Xochiyaoyotl*, or "Flower Wars," which were prearranged military exercises that took place regularly, serving both to train young warriors and to provide captives for sacrifice. Tlacaellel told Montezuma:

> Our god will feed himself with them as though he were eating warm tortillas, soft and tasty, straight out of the oven.... And this war should be of such a nature that we do not endeavor to destroy the others totally. War must always continue, so that each time and whenever we wish and our god wishes to eat and feast, we may go there as one who goes to the market to buy something to eat... organized to obtain victims to offer our god Huitzilopochtli. (Diego Durán, *The History of the Indies of New Spain*, p. 242)

THE ATTACK ON THE HOLY GRAIL

Largely wed to materialist, "guns, germs, and steel" models of historical explanation, modern historians routinely make glib, dismissive statements about this episode of human depravity and carnage that should make us shudder and weep. For example, here is how one contemporary textbook concludes its review of these events:

> Aztec sacrifice, once perceived as a ruthless practice committed by a "tribe" seemingly obsessed with bloodshed, is now seen as no more or less brutal than what many imperial civilizations have done to "bring home the war." (2008 *World History Annual Editions*, McGraw-Hill)

We cannot—we must not—shrink from examining this holocaust that took place on this continent any more than we could or should turn away from confronting the holocausts of the twentieth century, or our own time. Very few contemporary historians assign much explanatory weight to Montezuma's fatalistic dread of Quetzalcoatl's return. In the case of the collapse of Maya civilization, materialist ecological explanations so dominate the scholarly discussion that there is little consideration given to the moral and spiritual dimension, which were of course the center of Maya life.

Images created by European artists of the god Huitzilopochtli invariably portray him with all the attributes of a demon—horns, cloven feet, bat wings, a devilish face staring out from his belly (see E. H. Boone, 1989). From our perspective a half millennium later, the Spanish appear as superstitious as the Mexica, wracked by fear of wholly imaginary entities. And yet we cannot ignore the stunning conclusion that the entire sacrificial system was dedicated to a single, bloodthirsty being. Would it not be helpful to know the true identity of that being the fifteenth- and sixteenth-century Mexica and their subject peoples called "Huitzilopochtli"?

The main reason that we cannot turn for the answer to the Mexica themselves is that, no matter how much they were still in a condition of consciousness that largely precluded rational, perspectival thought, *they were no longer clairvoyantly beholding the spiritual world.* Apart from the newly created imperial myths of Huitzilopochtli and other gods, there was a vast reservoir of authentic myth and legend that, as in other places around the world, gave true imaginative pictures of past spiritual realities. But by 1428— note that the establishment of the Mexica empire occurs just twice seven years after the advent of the cultural age of Pisces (called by Rudolf Steiner the age of the "consciousness soul") in 1414— the only individuals capable of clairvoyant communication with the spiritual world were the *tonalpuhque*, the priests. The original source of Tlacaellel's power was his claim to divine communication; one of the reasons that Tlacaellel could be so successful in inventing a suite of new deities is that only a handful of Mexica (principally the priests, who were initiated however by Tlacaellel, and thus under his sway) were able to communicate with the spiritual world, that is, the "third eye" was closed for the Mexica people, just as for the Europeans.

Cortés, Bernal Diaz, and their fellow conquistadores, and the Franciscan friars who followed them, all saw the religious practices of the Aztec as demonic, but our rightful indignation at the harsh measures of the Spanish has largely blinded us to the accuracy of this view. *The cult of Huitzilopochtli as practiced by the priests was a path of black magic initiation, centered on the act of ritual murder.* At first deep within the Earth, in the lava tube caves, but after 1428, in the rooms of the temples, the priests were given detailed instruction in how to carry out black magic murder. They were instructed that in ripping out the still-beating heart of their victims, the priests would become filled with vast spiritual knowledge, stolen from out of the spiritual world. The bond forged between murderer and murdered was so powerful that the murderer, still alive back on Earth, would be able to see and hear all the things that the murdered soul experienced in his journey through the upper worlds of the thirteen heavens. The initiates were also promised that by carrying out these murders, they could achieve a form of immortality. Tlacaellel, who lived to nearly one hundred, and whose vitality in old age was a constant source of amazement to others, illustrates the vampire-like quality of black magic initiation practices.

What was kept back from all but the most exalted members of the black magic order is that the spiritual effect of these murders was to drive the sacrificial victim's soul away from the Earth, with the intention never to return. These revolting mystery practices were thus ultimately aimed at creating an entire culture oriented toward fleeing the Earth.[33] Under Tlacaellel's supervision, the Mexica were well on their way to founding such a culture, before the arrival of the Spanish put an end to the widespread practice of black magic. Tlacaellel did not invent this system of black magic, but only stewarded the resurgence of an ancient practice. Fifteen hundred years before, centered in the same region, there had been a similar black magic mystery school, dedicated not to Huitzilopochtli, *but to Taotl and Quetzalcoatl*—and it is important here to note again the principle of inversion.

This is not an interpretation that can be found in the ethnological or historical literature; for this insight we must once again turn to the prophetic voice of Rudolf Steiner, who in 1916 delivered two lectures that both radically reorient the reading of the Mesoamerican past, and also suggest an extraordinary foretelling of the American present and near future, as it relates to the mystery of the end of the Maya Long Count calendar. According to Rudolf Steiner, there in the Valley of Mexico had once taken place the most grisly black magic practices:

> An ahrimanic, caricatured counterpart appeared in the West...[who] was called by a name that sounded something like Taotl. Taotl was thus an ahrimanic distortion of the "Great Spirit"—a mighty being and one who did not descend to physical incarnation. A great many men were initiated into the mysteries of Taotl but the initiation was of a completely ahrimanic character.... When a candidate had been initiated in the correct way, the teaching concerning the secrets of the cosmos was then imparted to him... [but] the wisdom was imparted to no one who had not previously committed a murder in a particular manner.... The one to be murdered was laid out on a structure that was reached by one or two steps running along each side. This scaffold-like structure, a kind of catafalque, was rounded off above and when the victim was laid upon it, he was bent strongly back. This special way of being bound to the scaffold forced his stomach outward so that with one cut, which the initiate had been prepared to perform, it could be cut out.... When the stomach had been excised, it was offered to the god Taotl, again with special ceremonies. (*Inner Impulses of Evolution,* p. 49)

The spiritual effect of these murders, according to Steiner, was that the sacrificial victim's soul was driven away from the Earth, into the realm of Lucifer—(see chapter 8). At the same time, the "initiate"—i.e., murderer—was bound to the victim, and could receive knowledge from the spiritual world, a knowledge which at the same time enabled the "initiate" to wield power over his fellow human beings.

These revolting mystery practices were thus twofold. On the one hand they were luciferically inspired by Quetzalcoatl in so far as they were ultimately aimed at creating an entire culture oriented toward fleeing the Earth. And on the other hand they were ahrimanically inspired by Taotl with regard to the execution of black-magic ritual murder bringing the "initiates" knowledge and power. These mystery practices that culminated in Mexico around the time of Christ offer a classic example of Lucifer (represented by Quetzalcoatl) and Ahriman (represented by Taotl) working hand in hand together to achieve their goals.[34] To prevent this from happening, another set of mysteries, with its own initiation practices, was established to counteract the Taotl/Quetzalcoatl mysteries:

> These were mysteries in which a being lived who did not come down to physical incarnation but also could be perceived by men gifted with a certain atavistic clairvoyance when they had been prepared. This being was Tezcatlipoca.... The teachings of Tezcatlipoca soon escaped from the mysteries and were spread abroad exoterically.... Another spirit was set up against [Tezcatlipoca] who, for the Western Hemisphere, had much in common with the spirit whom Goethe described as Mephistopheles. He was indeed his kin. This spirit was designated with a word that sounded like Quetzalcoatl.... Quetzalcoatl also never appeared directly incarnated. (ibid., pp. 51–52)

As if this story were not incredible enough, Steiner went on to tell how these suprasensory beings then worked through two historical individuals: He spoke first of a man called "Vitzliputzli," who had been born of a virgin, in the first year C.E. Hinting that he had researched this thoroughly in the Akashic record, Steiner further stated that at the same time, another man was born, who had in previous incarnations been an initiate in the Taotl/Quetzalcoatl mysteries, and who was thus "one of the greatest black magicians, if not the greatest ever to tread the Earth; he possessed the greatest secrets that are to be acquired on this path."

This black magician, at the age of thirty, had acquired a power so tremendous that he would have been able to detour human evolution. To prevent this, Vitzliputzli, the son of a virgin, after battling for three years against the unnamed black magician:

was able to have the great magician crucified, and not only through the Crucifixion to annihilate his body but also to place his soul under a ban, by this means rendering its activities powerless as well as its knowledge. Thus the knowledge assimilated by the great magician of Taotl was killed. In this way Vitzliputzli was able to win again for earthly life all those souls who, as indicated, had already received the urge to follow Lucifer and leave the Earth. Through the mighty victory he had gained over the powerful black magician, Vitzliputzli was able to imbue men again with the desire for earthly existence and successive incarnations. (ibid., pp. 53–54)

This crucifixion by Vitzlipuzli of the black magician had thus occurred *in 33, the year of Christ's Crucifixion at Golgotha.*

When Steiner told this remarkable story in 1916, archaeologists were still working out the chronological sequence of cultures in the Valley of Mexico. A great deal was of course known about the Mexica people as a result of their conquest after 1519 by the Spanish, but the peoples who had preceded them were a complete enigma. Even the Mexica, when they arrived in 1325 at Lake Texcoco and began to build their capital city of Tenochtitlan, were dumbfounded by the ruins at Teotihuacan, which had been abandoned centuries before. From the eyewitness accounts of the conquistadors, the world had long known of the Aztec empire's barbaric culture of death, of the "Flower Wars" waged against their neighbors in order to secure captives for sacrifice to the Sun God Huitzilopochtli (i.e., Steiner's "Vitzliputzli"). But the relationship of the Aztec, and the culture of heart sacrifice centered at their capital city of Tenochtitlan to the ruins of Teotihuacan—the "City of the Gods," just a couple of dozen miles away—was unknown. This was one of the principal questions that the pioneer Mexican anthropologist and archaeologist Manuel Gamio hoped to answer with his excavations in Mexico City, beginning in 1910.

In post-1428 *Aztec* myth, Huitzilopochtli was the god who instituted both the ritual of heart sacrifice and the imperial wars that they were designed to support. Quetzalcoatl was the god who spoke out *against* heart sacrifice and cannibalism. This is the *reverse* of that which is presented in Steiner's account concerning the collaboration between Quetzalcoatl and Taotl in the blood sacrifices practiced in ancient Mexico. Huitzilopochtli and the black magician inspired by Taotl were actually physically incarnated human beings, *but in Steiner's description the identity of Huitzilopochtli was the exact opposite of that familiar to us from the later Aztec myth.* Moreover, Steiner identified Tezcatlipoca, usually translated as "Smoking Mirror" (Aztec depictions of him show right foot as an obsidian mirror) as a "good god," whose qualities, however, are completely reversed in the later Aztec conception, where (according to Bernal Diaz, quoted earlier) Tezcatlipoca was the "god of hell." As in the case of Hitler, the black magician Tlacaellel was adept at the inversion of good to evil, which is the foundation of all black magic.

Returning to Steiner's description of the Mexican mysteries, it was well known from the accounts of the conquistadors that the Aztec had practiced *heart sacrifice*, and yet Steiner kept referring to the excision of the *stomach*. One more seeming discrepancy is that crucifixion was not known (and still is not) to be a form of sacrifice or torture found in Mesoamerica at this time. Steiner was not particularly well read in the history of Mesoamerica; his countryman Eduard Seler, who had never set foot in Mexico, was perhaps the leading authority on Mesoamerican myth, and Steiner had read some of Seler's work, but this narrative that he divulged was clearly read from the Akashic record, not from between the lines of contemporary scholarship. A few details of Steiner's story do fit what was known from Aztec myth: the principal gods named by Steiner— Huitzilopochtli, Quetzalcoatl, Tezcatlipoca—are those of the Aztec and pre-Aztec cultures of the region; Huitzilopochtli was born of a virgin, the goddess Coatlicue, who, in the myth, had conceived after being touched on the shoulder by a ball of feathers.[35]

Steiner made a very brief remark that linked the ancient culture of sacrifice with the more recent Tenochtitlan of the Aztec, when he said that the black magic mysteries of the first century C.E. were

> subsequently revived, however, and history tells of the fate suffered by numerous Europeans who went to America after the discovery of that continent. Many Europeans met their death at the hands of Mexican priest-initiates who bound

them to scaffold-like structures and cut out their stomachs with expert skill. This is a matter of historical knowledge, and it was an aftermath of what I have been describing to you. (ibid., p. 97)

In saying "aftermath," Steiner seemed to be suggesting that the black magic activities of the Aztec at the time of the Spanish arrival in Tenochtitlan (1519) were a true continuation of the earlier culture of black magic. Steiner saw a much deeper ancestry to both these episodes of black magic in America though, saying that they were "revivals" of the black magic practices that had developed in ancient Atlantean times and had ultimately brought that period of human history to an end.

Not all Toltecs accepted the Quetzalcoatl cult; opposed to it were individuals who were devoted to the being they knew as *Tezcatlipoca*. Once again, we must put aside the post-1428 myths of the "Smoking Mirror" created by Tlacaellel and seek the original myths. One of the most helpful indications is Tezcatlipoca's alternate name, *Yohualli Ehecatl*, usually translated as "Night Wind." One Nahuatl text describes Tezcatlipoca/Yohualli Ecatl as *can iuhqujn ioalli, i ehecatl*, which translates as: "he was invisible, like the night and the wind." The related Nahuatl word *ceoalli* means "just like a shadow," and both point to his nature as an invisible, etheric being, who communicated with his initiates just as Taotl and Quetzalcoatl did with their black magicians—through trained clairvoyance within the mystery practices. (M. Leon-Portilla, *Aztec Thought and Culture*, pp. 102–103)

At the center of the Tezcatlipoca mysteries was devotion not to heart sacrifice, but to *sacrifice of the heart*, that is, consecration of one's own inner self to the supreme god. Piety, chastity, purity of thought and deed—these were the core values of the Tezcatlipoca mysteries, which began to be adopted outside of the mystery centers, among portions of the Toltec people. While within the black magic schools novices gained power by inflicting pain and suffering, in Tezcatlipoca's school the novices adhered to the white magical principle that no power could be gained without the rigorous practice of selfless devotion. One could think of the Tezcatlipoca teachings as the "American Grail Mysteries," since the ideals and practices were so consistent with the Grail tradition that would develop in Europe in later centuries.

That the crucifixion by Huitzilopochtli of the black magician had occurred in the year of Christ's Crucifixion at Golgotha suggests that the activities of the spiritual being Quetzalcoatl and his human followers were intimately associated with the events that transpired half a world away, in Palestine, Jerusalem, and finally, at Golgotha, the Hill of the Skull, where Jesus Christ was crucified. It was as if Christ's adversary, unable to vanquish the Grail in the Old World, laid plans to crush it in the New World. Christ's central mission was to bring into world history the higher Self of humanity, and to offer with it a path of *inner sacrifice*, through the practice of Love. In the volcanic Valley of Mexico, the infernal powers bubbled up like magma to institute a culture based on a counter-image of Christ. This indeed is the hallmark of black magic, that always and everywhere it appears it is merely the *ape of God*, since it possesses no truly creative powers of its own.

This aping—the mendacious inversion of the Good, the True, and the Beautiful—is written all over the deeds of the Mexica empire. Tlacaellel stole and twisted the story of Huitzilopochtli's virgin birth; stole and twisted the story of Huitzilopochtli's vanquishing of the 400 Stars; stole Tezcatlipoca's preaching of a culture of love, and assigned it to the adversary, Quetzalcoatl. Incredibly, outrageously, Tlacaellel completely reversed the qualities and deeds of the gods and their earthly representatives—Quetzalcoatl, Tezcatlipoca, and Huitzilopochtli, and it is easy to see that Tlacaellel himself stepped into the role of the powerful Taotl black magician, with the difference that Tlacaellel served the ahrimanic caricature of Quetzalcoatl rather than the ahrimanic Taotl that his black-magic "colleague" had served some fourteen centuries before him. In the short space of a generation, aided by the coercive power of a cult of terror and backed by a militarist state, Tlacaellel turned white into black and black into white.

When Rudolf Steiner gave the lecture, "The Aftereffects of the Atlantean Mysteries in America and Asia," in which he made these revelations about the ancient Mexican mystery practices and their role in the events parallel to the culmination of Christ's earthly mission, his audience was so confused that he had to repeat its principle points a few days later. The day after this repetition, Steiner gave a lecture entitled "The Cosmic Knowledge of the Knights Templar," in which he characterized the Templar initiation practices and their resulting wisdom as luciferic, and said that their adversary Philip the Fair's attack upon them had been inspired by Ahriman.[36] In fact, Philip's burning desire for the Templars' gold, and his brutal interrogations of the Templars was itself a form of ahrimanic initiation that had given the French king the same order of knowledge as that engendered by the Mexican initiates in their practices of torture. Given earlier statements Steiner had made that black magic had brought on the Atlantean catastrophe, torture was clearly the perennial black heart of ahrimanic–sorathic magic.[37]

Steiner never again spoke of the first century magical battle in Mexico, and, especially within the context of these elliptical lectures with their far-flung themes and topics, it is difficult to fathom the reason for his having done so at that particular moment in 1916. Surely though, Steiner's revelation of the magical battle in ancient Mexico was made for a particular purpose. Taken alone, the implications of his brief narrative of the C.E. 33 crucifixion of the black magician were revolutionary: the synchronicity of the magical battle in Mexico with the events in Palestine drew the Western Hemisphere and its people into the Christian myth as critical historical actors, not centuries *after* the Mystery of Golgotha, but at the very same moment. Embedded as this story was within an epic historical sweep from Atlantis and Lemuria, through classical Greece and Rome, to Genghis Khan's thirteenth-century conquest of Asia, the fourteenth-century crushing of the Knights Templar, and fifteenth-century discovery of America, the story also called out to be heard as *present* reality as much as past event.

One constant of Steiner's teaching was that the human consciousness is the true plane upon which history unfolds, and that *all* outer deeds and events are the "footprints" of consciousness—and thus spiritual—evolution. Simultaneously aided and hindered by the suprasensory beings Lucifer and Ahriman, humanity had muddled through the middle of eternity to land in the twentieth century with the potential for vast new understandings. Yet, as was clear from this lecture series and many others given by Rudolf Steiner, humanity had repeatedly succumbed to the temptation toward black magic. In the fog-shrouded mists of ancient Atlantis, the Persian desert in C.E. 666 (Gondishapur), and the fields of southern France in 1332 (Knights Templars), The Beast had surfaced from the depths, finding human beings who were happy to unite themselves with him (see chapter 7). By telling this story of Huitzilopochtli's battle at the Turning Point in Time with Taotl and Quetzalcoatl, the "Feathered Serpent," Steiner consciously positioned America as a collaborator in the history of black magic, and for those who had ears to hear, that history was not over yet.

4. Redeeming Lucifer, Rediscovering Itzamna

> [With] the Itzas who settled Chichen Itza there ruled a great lord named Cuculcan, as an evidence of which the principal building [pyramid] is called Cuculcan. They said he came from the West, but are not agreed as to whether he came before or after the Itzas, or with them...and that after his return he was regarded in Mexico as one of their gods, and called Cezalcohuati [Quetzalcoatl]. In the Yucatán also he was reverenced as a god, because of his great services to the state, as appeared in the order which he established in the Yucatán after the death of the chiefs, to settle the discord caused in the land.
>
> —Fray Diego de Landa,
> *Yucatán Before and After the Conquest* (1566)

In our attempt to understand the true significance of the Maya calendar, we have wandered away from the Yucatán, to focus on events in the Valley of Mexico. Though Rudolf Steiner's revelations about the c.e. 33 spiritual battle between Huitzilopochtli and the black magician inspired by Taotl do not mention the Maya, they can help to identify the principal Maya deities, which in turn may allow us to understand the epic struggle between good and evil in the Yucatán region.

Of the many gods of Mesoamerica, none is more conspicuous than the "Plumed Serpent," Quetzalcoatl/Kukulkan. Even with all of the twisting that was done by Tlacaellel and the "Huitzilopochtli" cult (that is, the black magic cult dedicated to "Huitzilopochtli" in name only, but actually dedicated to the adversarial being Quetzalcoatl), the fundamental iconography of Quetzalcoatl shows that he was perceived as a *serpent*, just as he was clairvoyantly perceived in the ancient Abrahamic traditions. This clearly appears to be true of the Maya *Kukulkan* as well. The being called "Quetzalcoatl" by both the ancient Toltec and the modern Mexica, and "Kukulkan" by the Maya, was and is identical with the being known in Abrahamic traditions (Christianity, Judaism, and Islam) as Lucifer—Light Bringer; Morning Star; fallen Angel of overweening pride.

Lucifer's tale is told in various places in the Bible, and has been expanded upon in such canonical works of Western literature as Dante's *Inferno* and Milton's *Paradise Lost*. In the book of Isaiah Lucifer, who is referred to there as the Morning Star, is said to hold these words in his heart: "I will ascend to heaven; I will raise my throne above the stars of God; I will sit on the mount of assembly in the far north; I will ascend above the heights of the clouds, I will make myself like the Most High" (Isaiah 14:13–14). Lucifer seeks to encourage this sort of egotism in humans, approaching them from the will so forcefully that the powers of thinking are cut off completely. Lucifer is a "cosmic fantasist," who preys upon pious people who strive after the spiritual world, and for the good, but only out of egotism, and without the light of hard won knowledge. His influence was especially strong in the past, and since the age of the consciousness soul, he has been eclipsed by Ahriman.

The image that is used by Moses in the book of Genesis to describe Lucifer is the image of the serpent. This is the form in which Quetzalcoatl/Kukulkan is revered—the Plumed (Sacred) Serpent. There is perhaps no place better suited to explore Kukulkan's image than the ancient Maya city of Chichen Itza. The principle pyramid at Chichen Itza—known as "El Castillo" or the "Pyramid of Kukulkan"—has four stairways, each of which has at its base a pair of large sculptures of rattlesnake heads. These sculptures "come alive" each year at the vernal and autumnal equinox, when the setting sun transforms the pyramid's stepped sides into a slithering shadow cast upon the balustrade. Rattlesnake heads protrude from the four corners of "The Temple of the Jaguars," and feathered serpents adorn the columns and friezes. Feathered serpents are found on the sidewalls of the Ball Court, and the two large stone rings sport a pair of entwined feathered rattlesnakes. On the main wall of one of the temples adjoining the Ball Court, there is a magnificent feathered rattlesnake, flanked by a procession of priests. Snakes pour forth from the body of one priest, and another priest carries a bowl holding seven rattle-snake heads.

Of the many objects recovered from the Sacred Cenote—the "Well of Sacrifice"—at Chichen Itza, one of the most dramatic is "Disk H," a gold platter bearing a scene of heart sacrifice. Identical to Fray Diego de Landa's account, four men hold the sacrificial victim down across a rounded stone,

"Disk H"

and the priest—himself wearing a feathered headdress—pierces his chest with a stone knife. Above this gruesome scene hovers Kukulkan, who is presumably the recipient of the human heart.[38]

Just as in Christian tradition Lucifer is the "Morning Star," i.e., the planet Venus, Maya (and Aztec) myth, religion, and astronomy identify Kukulkan with the planet Venus.[39] At Chichen Itza, the Maya relationship with Kukulkan/Lucifer through the planet Venus is clearly seen in "El Caracol," the astronomical observatory. The outer doorways of the building are ten to twelve degrees out of alignment with the cardinal directions; archaeoastronomer Anthony Aveni (see *Skywatchers of Ancient Mexico*: University of Texas Press, 1980) demonstrated that the narrow slits built into the observation tower align quite accurately with the location of Venus along the horizon at the northern and southern extremes of its path through the sky. Aveni suggested that the observations of Venus recorded in the *Dresden Codex* (the most important Maya text to survive De Landa's destruction) may have been made at the Chichen Itza observatory.

Christ's promise that "I shall give you the Morning Star" suggests that sometime during human history, through the Christ impulse, Lucifer would be turned toward the good. Valentin Tomberg (1900–1973), in his "Studies on the New Testament," (in his book *Christ and Sophia*) notes that the conversion of Lucifer *began* at the Mystery of Golgotha; when Lucifer beheld the innocent Christ on the cross, he had an experience inwardly of thinking that he should be the one on the cross. Gradually over time, Lucifer will come to work with Christ. Some aspect of this can be seen in "New Age" teachings (see chapter 8).

Given the true identity of the Aztec deity Quetzalcoatl, it is rather dismaying to think that one of the most popular authors on the subject of 2012, Daniel Pinchbeck, has cast it as "the return of Quetzalcoatl." Pinchbeck's agenda is indeed aligned with Quetzalcoatl, in that he casts himself as a prophet of imminent consciousness expansion. This is the hallmark of Lucifer, to egotistically storm heaven and claim it as his own province. Pinchbeck has even claimed (in his book *2012: The Return of Quetzalcoatl*) to have had direct communication with the god Quetzalcoatl after ingesting the psychedelic brew *ayahuasca*.

The Maya Long Count—and John's Revelation, Zarathustra's *Bundahisn* tale of Ahura Mazda and Ahriman, and the Hindu *Satya Yuga*—clearly point to a return, *not of Quetzalcoatl, but of Christ!* The return of Christ in the etheric realm is actually the real event, of which the coming of Ahriman/Antichrist is merely the shadow, in the same way that the coming of Huitzilopochtli to the American continent two thousand years ago was the real event, and Quetzalcoatl's and Taotl's inspiration of the black magician and his followers was the shadow.

There are obviously many mysteries connected with the "American Golgotha" event of C.E. 33, whose full significance it will take much time to uncover. Rudolf Steiner brought this event to light in order to give us a picture of what needs to happen in relation to the impending incarnation of the Antichrist. The evil coming from Ahriman needs to be *bound* so as to be overcome. There are other sources of this image. In the Chinese tradition, Kwan Yin, the equivalent of Sophia, rides upon the back of a serpent, but in a fashion that implies a working together, not a hostile relationship. The redeemed and transformed serpent is also seen in the image of Moses raising the serpent upright; when the people of Israel walked in front of it, they were healed. The serpent power can be used as a healing force; the caduceus is another image of this.

Clothed with the Sun, the Moon under Her Feet

Each deed performed by Christ ripples eternally through time as an archetype for humanity's continual spiritual evolution, and as a representative of Christ in the Americas, Huiltzilopochtli's heroic deeds clearly served as a seed for the future. The myth of his birth, though twisted by Tlacaellel to serve ahrimanic aims, still preserves an important geographic detail—that Huitzilopochtli was born at Coatepec, "in the direction of Tula." Though on the surface this suggests that Coatepec is a location in a mythical-sacred geography, it is also a real place, and that place is quite possibly Tepeyac Hill, on the northern edge of the island city of ancient Tenochtitlan.

Twelve years after Cortés arrived in Mexico, on December 9, 1531, the feast day of the Immaculate Conception of Mary, an Aztec widower named Cuauhtlatoatzin—called "Juan Diego" by the Franciscans who baptized him—was walking to church when he heard from the top of Tepeyac Hill an extraordinary chorus of songbirds, and someone calling his name in Nahuatl. Running up the hill, he saw coming out of the mists a beautiful woman, dressed like an Aztec princess. Calling him *Xocoyte*—"little son"—she asked him in his native language where he was going, and he answered by saying that he was on the way to celebrate the Virgin's feast day. The woman asked Juan Diego to tell the Bishop of Mexico, Juan de Zumárraga, that she wanted a *teocalli,* a "sacred little house," to be built on the spot where she stood.[40]

Juan Diego went to the bishop as instructed, but the bishop, doubtful of the man's story, said that he needed some sign. Juan Diego returned to Tepeyac Hill and explained to the woman that the bishop did not believe him. After insisting upon his own unworthiness and begging the woman to use another messenger, Juan Diego was instructed to revisit the bishop and then to meet her on Tepeyac Hill in the evening of the next day. The following morning he returned to the bishop, but again the bishop was skeptical and demanded a sign.

On his return home Juan Diego discovered his uncle seriously ill. He cared for his uncle through the next day and missed his appointment with the Virgin. As the sun set the dying uncle requested a priest to hear his final confession. The following morning, concerned about his uncle's condition, Juan Diego tried to skirt around Tepeyac Hill, but again the woman stopped him, assuring him that his uncle would not die. The Virgin, as recorded later, announced herself as "Guadalupe." To the bewildered Juan Diego, filled with reverent awe, this may have sounded like "*Coatlaxopeuh*" (pronounced "Kwatlashupeh," the Nahuatl word means "who crushes the stone serpent" [41]). Perhaps this moment was a foretelling of the fulfillment of the sacred Nahuatl prophecy which lived in Juan Diego's heart. For the stone serpent was the image representing the god, Quetzalcoatl, whose *egregore*—called "Huitzilopochtli" by Tlacaellel and the Aztec—had demanded through the black-magic priests the blood of human sacrifice.[42] Amongst the Aztecs there had been premonitions that this would one day end and that there would be the return of a great god to the land of the Aztecs.[43] Perhaps these were the thoughts that lived in Juan Diego's heart as he humbly responded to the Virgin's bidding. The Virgin asked Juan Diego to climb the hill and gather flowers. Though it was December, when nothing would normally be in bloom, he found that the barren summit had been transformed into a garden, with roses of the kind found in the region of Castile in Spain, the former home of Bishop Zumárraga, not, however, native to Mexico.

The Virgin arranged the roses carefully on the outside of Juan Diego's native *tilma*[44] (cactus-fiber cloak) and folded the long front panels of the garment upwards, tying the lower corners around Juan Diego's neck. Thus the flowers were held basket-like within Juan Diego's outer garment. When Juan Diego unfolded his cloak before the bishop, the roses cascaded out, revealing impressed upon the cloth an image of the Virgin.

Upon seeing the rare Castilian roses, the bishop recognized in the image imprinted on Juan Diego's *tilma* the *Nuestra Señora de Guadalupe*, a famous representation of the Virgin from his native region of Castile. The image of the Aztec princess with the stars on her cloak, her olive-skinned face, the Angel at her feet, her hands folded in prayer—bearing features clearly intended for the Aztec people—brought the Spanish bishop to his knees.

Bishop Zumárraga was clearly a remarkable man. Unlike many of the Spanish who preceded him, who were his contemporaries, or who followed later, he had been horrified by the actions of the appointed Spanish administrators, who had exploited, enslaved, and killed thousands of the native peoples, even beating and killing the priests who tried to protect them. He had smuggled a message to King Charles V of Spain requesting a new council and in the meantime had prayed to the Virgin Mary for help, and had asked for Castilian roses as a sign that his prayers had been heard. It is understandable, then, that he immediately

Nuestra Señora de Guadalupe

recognized this apparition of the Virgin as divine. While the Virgin had appeared directly to Juan Diego, she appeared *indirectly* to the bishop through the miraculous vitality of the image on Juan Diego's *tilma*. There, the bishop beheld an image truly universal in scope, recognizable to all peoples.

The blue of the Virgin's mantle and the piety of her countenance would have been familiar to European Christians. Her covered hair worn parted in the middle is typical of the Holy Land. The glow of the nimbus around her and the crescent Moon below her gown are a reminder of "the woman clothed with the Sun, and the Moon under her feet" (Revelation 12:1)—a perpetual sign of virginity. The red, white, and blue on the feathered wings of the supporting Angel—familiar to the American flag, and interpreted as symbolizing faith, and fidelity—bear significance to both American and

European cultures. The Virgin appears standing on the Moon as a celestial queen with the hosts of Angels below, who serve as support for her heavenly and earthly dominion. Clothed with the flowers of the Earth and protected by a starry blue mantle, she appears as a timeless reminder of eternity and human immortality. Standing before us as the Virgin Mother bearing the pregnant promise of the future of humanity, she wears the *cingulum* (sash) of the Aztec, worn by unmarried virgins as a symbol of chastity.

In the activity of "reading the images," we can seek for meaning through the use of *symbolist logic* as a "sacred science" which uses the language of verbal analogy, visual harmony, and correspondence. To the degree that this activity requires us to think in words, we must also remember that that which is living in the icon bears an essence, vitality, and essential meaning existing independent of those words. For example, the whiteness of the Virgin's ermine fur depicts purity as a divine status of royalty, just as the eight-pointed star-flowers on her mantle represent the spiritual "crowning" of baptism and regeneration.

But most important to grasp is that the Virgin of Guadalupe's appearance was immediately recognizable to the Aztecs who, having no written language, were adept at reading the language of images. Standing in front of the Sun, the Virgin of Guadalupe was therefore greater than the Sun God Huitzilopochtli. Her skin was the color of a native Mexica; her blue-green mantle was the color once reserved for the divine couple of Aztec myth—Ometecuhtli and Omecihuatl; the white fur at her neck and sleeves and the gold border were marks of royalty for the Aztecs; the broach at her throat bore the same black cross carried by Cortés and the Spanish friars; the sash at the Virgin of Guadalupe's waist was worn by pregnant women in Aztec culture.

Flowers represented for the Aztecs the experience of the divine and are central to understanding this sacred icon. The single four-petalled, cross-shaped flower over her womb represented the *ollin,* the familiar Aztec glyph for the present era; it also signified the sacred *quincunx* or center of the universe, the Flower of the Sun, signifying abundance for our age. The cross-shaped flowers on her garment were the *mamalhuaztli,* signifying new life. The large tri-angular flowers depict the Mexican magnolia; nine in number, they represent the nine levels of the Aztec underworld. Worn by the Virgin, she becomes Our Lady who bears our pain. The triangular flower on her womb reminds the viewer of the sacrifice of the Virgin's own son and thus sounds the end of human sacrifice.[45]

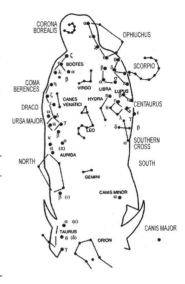

Much has been made of the seemingly supernatural, or at least inexplicable, qualities of the *tilma* image—the method by which the image is imprinted into the fibers, mysteriously preserved over such a long period; the remarkable discovery through the modern technology of computerized digital analysis of high resolution photographs of the reflection in the Virgin's eyes of the room and the entire group present at the revelation—the bishop, his attendants, etc.; and the survival of the *tilma* after an anarchist exploded a bomb hidden in some flowers placed underneath its protective case in 1921.[46]

In addition, modern technology has revealed the recording of *natural* phenomena on the image that prove equally stunning. Depicted on the Virgin's cloak is an accurate star map for 10:30 a.m. local time on the day that the image appeared on Juan Diego's *tilma*. In 1531 the Julian calendar was still in use, differing by ten days from the Gregorian calendar that was later introduced (in 1582), so the winter solstice took place on that day, Tuesday, December 12. The main constellations of the northern sky are laid out on the right of the mantle; on the left are shown the southern constellations that can be seen from Tepeyac Hill in winter at dawn.[47] The top of the *tilma* indicates the geographical position of the East—as in Aztec tradition, East is at the top of the map. The image thus bears a topographical relationship to the map of Mexico. For example, the flowers on her tunic are depicted in correspondence with actual geographical locations of their native growth.

The image is even dated according to Aztec practice—the three stars at the foot of the Virgin's tunic represent the Aztec date of 13 Acatl, relating to the year 1531.[48] All things considered, the stars retain their corresponding "positions in the sky." This is one of the most compelling aspects of the interpretation of the icon. The stars are literally a script to be read, and with deeper contemplation the images even point to an interpretation relating to the Apocalyptic image in chapter 12 of Revelation : the Corona Borealis (Northern Crown) rests upon the Virgin of Guadalupe's head; Virgo, the Virgin, is on her breast near her hands; Leo, the Lion, marks her pregnant womb, pregnant with the "Lion of Judah" marked by Leo's main star Regulus, "the little king"; Gemini, the Twins, are in the region of the knees; the supporting Angel gazes up toward Orion, according to the Egyptians the home of Osiris, who was seen by them as a pre-incarnatory manifestation of Christ. Following the Angel's upward gaze, the Angel serves as "mage" heralding the birth of a new star. The viewer's conscious beholding moves from below to above, following the unfolding of the ancient Aztec legend. Viewed in this way it could be seen that the Virgin of Guadalupe's appearance heralded the return of Christ to the Americas as a fulfillment of the Aztec legend concerning the return of Quetzalcoatl or, according to some interpreters of the legend, the return of Huitzilopochtli.

Before the Spanish conquest, Tepeyac Hill had once born a temple dedicated to the Aztec lunar goddess Tonantzin, who originally did not ask for human sacrifice. Later the hill became a sacrificial site still dedicated to Tonantzin, who was variously referred to as "Little Mother" (the patron of childbirth), "Goddess of Sustenance," and "Honored Grandmother." No doubt in some uncorrupted pre-Aztec form, Tonantzin had been a sustaining, nurturing, loving being, but in the inverted teachings of the post-Tlacaellel Aztec priests, she had come to be known as a devouring, vengeful Spider goddess who ate her own children. Her fate had followed that of Huitzilopochtli and Tezcatlipoca—her gifts having been inverted by black magicians in service of the adversaries of the true Sun Spirit. The wisdom of Our Lady of Guadalupe's appearance to Juan Diego on Tepeyac Hill can be understood in coincidence with this ill-fated myth of the lunar goddess Tonantzin and thus recognized by the Aztec culture as a signal of redemptive love pouring into this blackened region of the world.

Within weeks after the occurrence of the miracle—in the rhythm of the return of the Sun after the darkest hour of the Winter solstice— Bishop Zumárraga ordered a shrine to be built where the Virgin had indicated. He entrusted the cloak with its miraculous image to Juan Diego, who moved into a small hermitage near the spot of the Virgin's appearance. Juan Diego cared for the chapel and the first pilgrims who came to pray there, until his death in 1548.

Only a short decade before Juan Diego's death, seven years after the Virgin of Guadalupe's appearance, eight million Mexican natives had been converted to the Christian faith, whereas before the incident at Tepeyac Hill, the Franciscan and Dominican friars had been notoriously unsuccessful in their evangelization. This conversion came at a time when the Spanish were on the brink of losing the Americas due to their torture and cruelty to the indigenous peoples. Even so, the hungry gods invoked through the black magic practices of the corrupted Aztec priests persisted, resulting in native rebellions which racked the countryside, and in the farther reaches of the old Aztec empire, heart sacrifice still continued.

Perhaps the original myth of a future return of a god to the Valley of Mexico had been true after all. That the myth centered on Huitzilopochtli and not Quetzalcoatl is a controversial interpretation.[49] Huitzilopochtli was the New World emissary and ally of Christ, the Old World God-Man who came to *end* human sacrifice. Huitzilopochtli's mission had been to institute a culture of *inner* sacrifice of one's heart to the Divine. Perhaps this myth, before Tlacaellel took hold of it and twisted it, *had* specified a return in a 1 Acatl year. If so, Hernan Cortés truly did fulfill the prophecy, at least in part. Montezuma's sister, Princess Papantzin, lapsed into a coma in 1509. The Aztecs laid her in a tomb, believing she was dead, but almost immediately, reports of the day claim that she cried out to be released. She related a dream, in which a luminous being led her to the shore of the boundless ocean, and several large ships appeared with black crosses on their sails similar to that on her guide's forehead. The princess was informed that the men in the ships came from a distant land and would conquer the country and bring knowledge of the true God. Possibly the superstitious Montezuma was influenced to read

*Frederick Catherwood's drawing of the temple ruins at Tulum,
from John L. Stephens's Incidents of Travel in Yucatán (1843)*

the doom of his empire in this dream.[50] Cortés landed in Mexico on
the very day predicted by the ancient prophecy. The final fulfillment
of the prophecy, however, came only with the Virgin of Guadalupe's
appearance at Tepeyac Hill, and the spreading of her protective mantle of stars over the Mexican people.

Like the Virgin Mary, Our Lady of Guadalupe is a manifestation
of an aspect of Divine Sophia, who continually works with Christ
in guiding spiritual and human evolution. Though North Americans
have begun to come into relationship with Sophia only in recent years,
we may take great comfort in knowing that our Mexican brothers and
sisters have maintained an extraordinary devotion to Sophia's manifestation in the Virgin of Guadalupe since her appearance in 1531 at
Tepeyac Hill.

Reported through the eyes of visiting beholders, the Virgin of
Guadalupe's image remains a compelling experience. Pope John
Paul II, upon visiting the icon in the year 2002, before a crowd of
twelve million people proclaimed Juan Diego a saint and emphasized
the importance for this continent of Our Lady of Guadalupe as the

Mother of the Americas.[51] This came at a most significant moment in time: that of the surfacing of the "beast" of Revelation 13, whose head suffered a "mortal wound" on September 11, 2001—as discussed in chapter 9. Seen in this light, not only was the 1531 miraculous appearance of the Virgin of Guadalupe a Sophia manifestation to set her seal on the overcoming of the Aztec black-magic practice of human sacrifice, but also to set her seal of protection on the Americas in view of the twenty-first century surfacing of The Beast

The "Descending God"
over the central entrance to
the main temple at Tulum

and his prophet to establish the world empire of the Antichrist, during which time not only the Americas but also the whole world is in need of the protecting influence of Sophia manifesting from celestial heights through Our Lady of Guadalupe.[52] Herein lies the deeper significance of the pope's 2002 visit to her shrine and his emphasis upon the Virgin of Guadalupe as the Mother of the Americas.

THE "DESCENDING GOD" AT ZAMA

In the Valley of Mexico, the home of the Aztec, there is evidence that both Christ and Sophia have been active in the ancient and recent past. Is there evidence that Christ and Sophia were also active among the ancient Maya? One possibility is at Tulum, on the east coast of the Yucatán Peninsula, south of Cancun and Cozumel. Originally called *Zama* ("dawn"), the Maya ruins at Tulum are not of a city, but a temple complex, devoted to what some anthropologists have come to call the "Descending God."

The main temple ("Castillo") in Tulum has three large niches over the three doorways into the temple. In the niche above the center doorway is the "Descending God." In the right-hand niche there is a sculpture of the Father God, Hunab Ku, and to his left there is an empty niche which clearly never bore an image. It is tempting to imagine that this empty niche was included by the builders of the temple to receive the being whom we would identify with the Holy Spirit.

Could it be that this image of a god who seems to be diving toward the Earth is *Itzamna*, who is usually thought as the son of Hunab Ku? Patron of the day Ahau, last of the twenty Maya days, *Itzamna*'s day sign means "emperor" or "great lord," and is sometimes called "the first priest/shaman" in colonial Maya sources. Though there is still a great deal of mystery about Itzamna, Linda Schele has brought interesting linguistic evidence to bear on Itzamna's identity:

> The *itz* of *yitz ka'an,* the blessed substance of the sky, which flows through the portal represented by the hanging sky platform on the shaman's altar (literally, "its blessed substance, the sky"), is the *itz* of *itzamna. Itzam* (literally, "one who does *itz*" or an *"itz-er")* is the term for shaman: the person who opens the portal to bring *itz* into the world. What is *itz?* For the Maya it is many things: the milk of an animal or a human; the sap of a tree, especially copal, the resin used as incense; it is the sweat from a human body, tears from a human eye, the melted wax dripping down the side of a candle, the rust on metal. These substances are secreted from many kinds of objects. Many of them—like milk, tree resins, and candle wax—are considered precious substances that sustain the gods. *Y-itz ka'anil* is the magic stuff the shaman brings through the portal from the Otherworld. As an *itz-er,* the shaman is the direct analog of Itzamna, the greatest *itz-er* of them all. When the village shaman opens the portal from this side, Itzamna opens it from the other and sends the precious *itz* through to nourish and sustain humanity in all its diversity. Obviously, a reciprocity is at work here.[53]

"The greatest *itz-er* of them all" is suggestive of Christ or of his servant Huitzilopochtli, for both made themselves vehicles of divine power to preserve and protect humanity.

The Mayan *itz* seems to be analogous to the Nahuatl word *ihiyotl*, which was identified by the Aztec with the liver, and was implicated in the magical practice of the evil eye. The *ihiyotl* was known to be a source of energy which could be used for one's own benefit or for others. A headache could be cured with the *ihiyotl* in the breath; likewise, applying *ihiyotl* with the hand brought strength. But its promiscuous release, or its use with malicious intent, could cause catastrophic damage. Sorcerers breathed *ihiyotl* on their victims to bewitch or destroy them. If we were to equate *itz* and *ihiyotl* with a modern term from the vocabulary describing the human subtle body, it is the "etheric."[54]

The etheric is both the realm in which Christ is now to be found, and, because of this, *the realm that Ahriman seeks to possess.* Ahriman's ambition is to mechanize everything by taking hold of the Earth's etheric forces—genetic engineering is the most spectacular expression of this ahrimanic activity, along with ideas of advanced technology to manipulate the natural electromagnetic circuit of the Earth (such as in HAARP, the High Altitude Auroral Research Program). The laws of the etheric realm have been communicated through eurythmy, which is a tool available for humans to work with the laws of etheric movement. Through the practice of eurythmy, human movements come into accord with the laws of the etheric body. Thus, through eurythmy it is possible to establish an "Ahriman Free Zone." The centuries of human heart sacrifice upon the pyramid temples of Mesoamerica helped to build a "receiving vessel" for Ahriman. Today this can be counterbalanced by consciously connecting with the Etheric Christ through performing eurythmy, whose prayers and mandala-like movement forms heal and nurture the etheric realm in these same locations.[55] This is the true imagination whose prophecy awaits realization in America—the image of Christ, not Kukulkan/Quetzalcoatl, standing in glory at the top of the pyramids.

5. Recognizing Evil, Manifesting the Good

The remarkable persistence of the principle Mesoamerican deities, and the tortured history of their deeds and inspirations, holds a critical lesson for contemporary Americans, who only recently—and even then, quite reluctantly—have been willing to consider themselves as subjects or agents of an empire. The American myth has for too long been that our nation's projection of economic, political, and military power was wholly without self-interest, a benevolent extension of our founding ideals of liberty to the entire globe. In 2003, this myth allowed the Bush administration to deceive the American people into supporting the invasion and occupation of Iraq; even today, after abundant evidence of the extent of that deception, almost half of the American public seems to actively reject this evidence. It is now commonplace to call the Iraq War a "mistake," a word which allows Americans to continue to delude themselves about this cynical and catastrophic imperial act of aggression.

Over five hundred years ago, the words of an Aztec poet living in Tenochtitlan around C.E. 1500—"Who could shake the foundations of heaven?"—rang out as a triumphal boast of empire. Within a couple of generations, the boast would ring hollow, as Tenochtitlan's sacrificial pyramids were replaced by Spanish cathedrals. No one—Spanish or Mexica—who lived at the time of the Spanish conquest doubted that the Earthly battle between empires was also a heavenly one, ordained and ordered by gods. Today, as the upstart American empire flounders, there are few—save fundamentalist Christians—who conceive of unfolding events as part of a titanic spiritual battle. The prophetic calendars of the past—Maya, Christian, Persian, and Hindu—suggest otherwise, in their stunning coincidence of chronological focus upon the time in which we are now living.

In 1519, Montezuma—himself the supreme priest-astronomer of the Aztec empire, and thus the one believed by his people to be the most qualified to interpret prophecy—made a fatal mistake of recognition when Hernan Cortés appeared on the eastern shore of the Aztec empire. From one perspective, we could say that Montezuma (and his subjects, up until the moment that they finally shook themselves loose from their collective illusion, and attacked the Spanish) mistook as good that which was evil. Mistaken as Quetzalcoatl, the god whom Aztec myth identified as a culture-inspirer, Cortés turned out to be a culture-destroyer.

So often in history, the greatest forces of evil have appeared in the guise of the good. It could not be otherwise, given that leaders are always and everywhere *created* by the people who choose them. If a people turn away from their destiny, they are almost guaranteed to manifest evil in themselves and in their leaders. For most of human history, leaders claimed that divine providence supported their decisions and actions; the last century has seen a procession of empires claiming secular, rather than sacred, sanction, with equally devastating results.

Half a millennium ago, the Aztec, Maya, and the other native nations of the American continent had scores of soothsayers, only a handful of whom possessed the skills and talent requisite for the difficult task of prophecy. Aside from the indications of Rudolf Steiner and the calendars discussed here, are there contemporary, "indigenous" prophets who can speak to the destiny of twenty-first century America?

At 2 a.m. on February 5, 1962, amidst a rare "stellium" (cluster) of the seven classical planets (plus Chiron) in the sign of Capricorn, there was a total eclipse of the sun whose path of totality passed over Indonesia, New Guinea, and the eastern Pacific Ocean. At 7:17 a.m., as she readied herself to greet the rising sun by reciting the twenty-third Psalm, American psychic Jeane Dixon beheld this picture:

> The bare-limb trees of the city had given way to an endless desert scene, broiled by a relentless sun. Glowing like an enormous ball of fire, the sun had cracked the horizon, emitting brilliant rays of scintillating light, which seemed to attract the

Earth like a magic wand. The Sun's rays parted, facilitating the appearance of the Egyptian Pharaoh Akhenaten and Queen Nefertiti. But my eyes were drawn to the new-born-child she tenderly cradled in her other arm. He was wrapped in soiled, ragged swaddling clothes, in stark contrast to the magnificently arrayed royal couple. I then became aware of a multitude of people that appeared. I witnessed Nefertiti hand the child to the people. Instantly rays of sunlight burst forth from the little boy, which blended with the brilliance of the sun. My eyes once more focused on the baby. By now he had grown to manhood, and a small cross, which had formed above his head enlarged and expanded until it covered the Earth in all directions. Suffering people, of all races, knelt in worshipful adoration, lifting their arms and offering their hearts to him.[56]

Jeane Dixon—whose elegant Washington, DC, townhouse was less than a mile from the White House—looked over at her bedside clock to see the time, and then recorded her waking vision. Her first impression was that she had witnessed the birth of a great king who would revolutionize the world. At the end of her vision, however, she saw that while most people followed the man, a small group followed a narrow path away from him. By 1969, when she published *My Life and Prophecies*, the "Washington Seeress" had concluded that the man in the flowing robe was the Antichrist, who would "form a new all-embracing doctrine based on his almighty power."

Though the February 1962 vision was interpreted by Jeane Dixon as that of a child born in the Middle East, Dixon had other visions connecting this individual to America:

I have seen a "government within a government" develop in the United States within the last few years.... I see this "government within a government" being controlled and financed by a well-oiled political "machine" of one of our leading political families. With their eye on the White House, I see them discredit any man who occupies it without their approval, no matter how good his political programs may be.

They will—through political intimidation, propaganda, and illegal sixth-column activities—make every effort to show the nation that only their man, the one who heads their "machine," has the sole right to occupy the White House. Their campaign is going to cause great harm to our nation both here and abroad.

I "see" this group succeed in taking over de facto control of the country. They will give rise to an upheaval in our social structure as never before seen. They will bring about increased social unrest and great discontent. Foreign subversive elements will—as they did in the 1960s—infiltrate the unruly factions and cause renewed fighting on the nation's campuses and in racial ghettos.

All of the evil in the masses will be swept toward an unknown frenzy by this "machine"...[57]

The daughter of a wealthy Wisconsin lumber baron, Dixon had married a successful businessman who after World War II had become a D.C. real estate tycoon; she served as secretary/treasurer and later CEO of the realty company. As a Washington socialite who frequented diplomatic functions and parties at the homes of capitol city power brokers, Jeane Dixon was a member of the D.C. establishment. A devout Catholic, her politics were right-wing Republican; she maintained close friendships with FBI director J. Edgar Hoover, Senator Strom Thurmond, and President Ronald Reagan and his wife Nancy. The book that recounts her 1962 vision is filled with bitter polemics against civil rights and anti-war activists, whom she believed were unwitting tools of Soviet agents. Dixon's fervent patriotism makes her declaration of a dark governmental conspiracy with the Antichrist all the more striking:

> His disciples...will have the power and the propaganda machine of the United States backing them, advancing his cause beyond anything ever thought possible.
>
> Like Christ, the Antichrist will center his work at the city of Jerusalem. I get the distinct feeling that the religions of the world will somehow merge with the philosophies of the East. I see the youth flock to him and partake of his wisdom.[58]

As a devoted Bible student, Jeane Dixon interpreted her visions through the lens of John's Revelation:

And I beheld another beast coming up out of the Earth; and he had two horns like a lamb, and he spake as a dragon. And he exerciseth all the power of the first beast before him, and causeth the Earth and them which dwell therein to worship the first beast, whose deadly wound was healed. And he doeth great wonders, so that he maketh fire come down from heaven on the Earth in the sight of men, And deceiveth them that dwell on the Earth by the means of those miracles which he had power to do in the sight of The Beast; saying to them that dwell on the Earth, that they should make an image to The Beast, which had the wound by a sword, and did live. And he had power to give life unto the image of The Beast, that the image of The Beast should both speak, and cause that as many as would not worship the image of The Beast should be killed. (Revelation 13:11–15)

Verse-by-verse, Dixon found correspondence between John's prophecies and the content of her visions. She saw these passages from chapter 13 as pointing directly to the "False Prophet" whose mission had been prepared by the "government within a government":

The social and religious chaos generated by this political machine throughout the United States will prepare the nation for the coming of the prophet of the Antichrist. This political unit of the East will be the tool of the serpent in delivering the masses to him.... With teaching and propaganda the prophet will cause people not merely to accept the Antichrist but rather to desire him with positive enthusiasm to create the conditions of his coming and to participate in organizing the frightful and terrifying despotism of his World Empire.[59]

Dixon's scenario was nuanced rather than literalistic, saying that the miracles, signs, and wonders that Revelation attributed to the Antichrist and his prophet would not be supernatural events but "the prodigies of science and human achievements." She pointed particularly to the "fire from heaven" spoken of by John, which she saw as the ultimate symbol of the conquest of Nature. "The ideological and falsely scientific prophet" would advance an anti-Christian science perfectly tailored to modern materialism. Finally, she anticipated a full victorious reign of the Antichrist and his prophet, who would be *"specific and identifiable persons!"*[60]

Dixon's celebrity had always been based on the fact that the "specific and identifiable persons" in her visions were almost always noteworthy national and international figures, usually from the world of politics. She gained her initial fame for having successfully predicted the assassinations of Mahatma Gandhi, John and Robert Kennedy, and Martin Luther King, Jr. and the death of Secretary of State John Foster Dulles. Even in her own lifetime, however, Dixon was as widely known for her many wildly inaccurate statements about the future. She predicted: the outbreak of World War III in China in 1958; that labor leader Walter Reuther would run for President in 1964; that the Russians would land the first man on the moon; that a comet would strike the Earth in the middle of the 1980s; also that there would be the first woman President of the United States in the 1980s; that warfare would break out in 1999; and that Chinese and Mongol troops would invade the Middle East in 2000.[61] It became a national journalistic sport to tally up Jeane Dixon's predictions at year's end, with the misses sometimes outnumbering the hits. A Temple University mathematician coined the phrase "the Jeane Dixon effect," to describe the tendency of a gullible media and public to proclaim a few accurate predictions while overlooking the much larger number of incorrect forecasts.

Believing her faculty of prophecy to have been given by God, Dixon attributed any errors to her own mistakes in interpretation. Indeed, her conservative politics always colored her public predictions, and these can be seen to have been the most erroneous. Calling her perceptions "revelations from God," she claimed to hear the voices of Christ and Angels, but she never claimed to be able to call up her gift of prophecy at will. The "Jeane Dixon effect," however apt it may be in describing one aspect of Dixon's proclamations, does not explain the many documented cases in which Dixon described important future events in uncanny detail. Though she made considerable effort to discern it, the most important detail—the actual timing of the Antichrist's appearance—eluded Jeane Dixon. Believing that she had witnessed his birth in 1962, she thought that the Antichrist would appear in 1992, as a Satanic echo of the fact that Christ's ministry began in his thirtieth year.

In Jeane Dixon's vision, she interprets that the Egyptian Pharaoh Akhenaton and Queen Nefertiti are the ancestors of the child who shall become the Antichrist. This may suggest that the child is a very special person, perhaps someone who was a good person in the past, and whose consciousness is taken over by an adversarial being. An example from the past is that of the sixteenth century ascetic Spanish Franciscan saint and mystic Peter of Alcantara, who was actually a very high being, as is evident from miraculous stories about him and also from the report of Teresa of Avila that at the death of Peter she saw his soul in light-illumined form soar toward heaven.[62] In his subsequent incarnation in the nineteenth century as the brilliant German philosopher Friedrich Nietzsche, according to Rudolf Steiner when Nietzsche had his mental breakdown he became possessed by Ahriman and—while possessed—wrote the strongly anti-Christian book *The Antichrist* in which the concept of the will to power plays such a prominent role.[63] The idea of the will to power became central to Nazi ideology, and thus a direct line is evident by way of Ahriman's possession of Nietzsche to Hitler's bid for world dominion as a forerunner of the Antichrist.

Another prophetic voice—the Russian philosopher, poet, and founder of Russian Sophiology, Vladimir Solovyov—wrote of a similar scenario in his *War, Progress, and the End of History: Three Conversations Including a Short Story of the Anti-Christ*.[64] Finished on Easter Sunday, 1900, just a few months before he died, the book is a series of dialogues between five members of the Russian intelligentsia, held in the garden of a villa in the Alps. Solovyov's prefatory question sets the tone for the book: "Is *evil* only a natural *defect*, an imperfection disappearing by itself with the growth of good, or is it a real *power*, *ruling* our world by means of temptations, so that to fight it successfully assistance must be found in another sphere of being?" The way that Solovyov describes it, the individual who becomes the Antichrist writes a bestselling book—*The Open Way to World Peace and Welfare*. He is a good person, a very high being, when he writes this book, but then he goes for a walk one night, and a presence promises him that he can become world ruler. Something like this happened to twenty-nine-and-a-half-year-old Adolf Hitler, who became possessed after losing consciousness in a trench on the frontline at Ypres in October 1918 after a mustard gas attack. Temporarily blinded by the mustard gas, Hitler recovered in a German military hospital and then discovered that through the power of the word he could mesmerize people.[65]

As mentioned in chapter 2 of this book, Revelation 13 says that the Antichrist shall reign for "two and forty months." According to astronomical research, in particular on account of the longest solar eclipse of the century occurring on that day, it is possible that the starting date for this reign could fall on or around July 22, 2009, when Pluto will be at 6½° Sagittarius, just 2½° from its location at the last temptation of Christ, which signified the opening of the gates of hell. Most provocative of all, the July 22, 2009 position of Pluto will be just ½° away from where it was at the historical event of the baptism in the Jordan on September 23, C.E. 29 (6°53' Sagittarius), thus mimicking Christ's incarnation at the Baptism. Accordingly, July 22, 2009 may be the counter-image of the Baptism, the solar eclipse presenting the possibility that Ahriman, as prophesied by Steiner,[66] will descend into a human being, just as Christ entered into Jesus of Nazareth. Ahriman's three-and-a-half-year "ministry" would then begin and would last until December 21, 2012—the end of the Maya calendar.

If July 22, 2009 truly marks the beginning of the Antichrist's three-and-a-half-year rulership, and he is preceded by the "false prophet," it seems almost certain that he will come on the world stage very soon, if he is not already present. Along with Revelation, two other books of the Bible—the Second Epistle to the Thessalonians and the book of Daniel—describe the false prophet as speaking pompous words. Revelation and II Thessalonians attribute to him "miraculous signs" and say that he will deceive the people and lead them into idolatry. The book of Daniel agrees with Revelation about the three-and-a-half-year period, suggesting that the false prophet will be destroyed at the return of Jesus Christ. All three books suggest a person of great political power and religious influence, and all point to events of global significance.

A clue as to the identity of the false prophet of the Antichrist lies in the Gospel of Luke. There it is described how, at the Annunciation, the Archangel Gabriel appeared to the Virgin Mary and told her that "the Holy Ghost shall come upon thee," to conceive the Son of God. Gabriel also informed Mary that her cousin Elizabeth, formerly childless, was already six months pregnant. Mary visited Elizabeth in Judea, and when Elizabeth, the mother of John the Baptist, heard Mary's voice, her baby leapt in her womb; this is often seen as John's first act of prophecy. Following the principle that Satan is the "ape of God," it is possible that the false prophet was born six months before the Antichrist, that is, on or about August 5, 1961.

America, like so many nations, has a long tradition of mistaking as good that which is very evil. Even as it seems that at this moment we are as a nation wiser, less gullible, more capable of choosing a leader, we must be cautious in light of our long history of following false prophets. The individuals who most readily come to mind—Cotton Mather, Jonathan Edwards, William Miller, Joseph Smith—were religious reformers, but the twentieth century saw the prophetic mantle transferred to more secular figures—William Dudley Pelley, founder of the fascist Silver Legion; anti-Communist crusader Joseph McCarthy; economist Leo Strauss, who birthed the Neoconservatives. Apart from individual messiahs, it can be said that America has been continually possessed by a collective messianism, whether the Puritan conception of its colonial experiment as a shining "City on a Hill," the nineteenth century belief in manifest destiny, or a more recent rhetorical stance as the bringer of democracy and world-protector against the "Axis of Evil." Our national self-delusion has proved remarkably persistent, regardless of the political party in power.

At this moment, much of America stands expectant once again, having elected as president a man who embodies and expresses the exuberance of the nation, even as it struggles with extraordinary challenges at home and abroad. Few modern American presidents have had as much hope invested in them as President Barack Obama. Having mobilized millions of new voters, many are already wondering if he can and will act to fulfill their hopes.

"By their fruits you shall know them" (Matthew 7:16). This—the fruits—is what is decisive as far as Christ is concerned. In other words, ultimately it is deeds that count. During the eight year-presidency of George W. Bush, America became embroiled in two costly and devastating wars waged in Muslim countries, Afghanistan and Iraq, with many hundreds of thousands of men, women, and children dead, and many millions of people displaced. During this time, the country's debt grew to more than $10 trillion. In 2008 the United States was plunged into financial crisis through the reckless actions of bankers who fueled the housing bubble that led to the subprime mortgage crisis. While George W. Bush cannot be held entirely responsible for the financial crisis, its occurrence during his presidency does reflect something of the lack of care and oversight from the highest government levels regarding the overall structure, direction, and operation of the U.S. financial system.

"By their fruits you shall know them." America's destiny under a new President could be more of the same or be a wind of change blowing through the U.S. to reveal and bring forth fruit worthy of the name of Christ and in the spirit of Christ, who taught humankind the Mystery of Love expressed in the three commandments: 1) Love the Lord your God with all your heart, and with all your soul, and with all your mind, and with all your strength: this is the first commandment (Mark 12:30); 2) love your neighbor as yourself (Matthew 22:39); and 3) love your enemies and pray for those who persecute you (Matthew 5:44). Of these three, the third is the most difficult. At the time of Christ the traditional attitude was expressed in the words spoken immediately prior to the giving of the third commandment: You have heard that it was said, "You shall love your neighbor and hate your enemy" (Matthew 5:43; Moses spoke the former part—Leviticus 19:18—and the scribes added the latter.) However, Christ was quite clear that one should not only love one's enemy but also not fight against one's enemy: All those who take up the sword shall perish by the sword (Matthew 26:52).

Though Jeane Dixon did not see the final outcome of her vision of the Antichrist's life, we find in the Zoroastrian tradition through the teachings of Zarathustra a remarkable account that helps to fill in the end scenario. In the Zoroastrian *Bundahisn* account, Ahriman tries to seize his chance, and seems to be winning. Then Ahura Mazda (the pre-incarnatory being of Christ) speaks the *Ahunvar* prayer, and as he speaks it, Ahriman falls into a stupor, seeing that his efforts are fruitless.[67] There is no way to go against the divine plan. Seeing this vision, he is defeated.

The impending incarnation of Ahriman is indeed part of the divine plan, since Christ revealed it to John, as described in Revelation 13. Ahriman's ambition and method is earthly power, power *over*. In the final days of the sojourn in the wilderness, the tempter promises Christ vast rewards: "All the kingdoms of the world I will give you, if you will fall down and worship me" (Matthew 4:9). This temptation still lives in today's world. With the interweaving of financial concerns, we as a nation find ourselves at the very threshold of "One World." Will we choose to direct the sword of world leadership through dominance and power? Or will our hearts hearken to the divine accord of cooperation and dynamic creativity through the synergy and abundance of the interweaving qualities of the gifts of various cultures? And will we choose perspectives which enrich the tapestry of humanity, manifesting love of Christ and the wisdom of Sophia?

Christ's response to this temptation, "You shall worship the Lord your God and him only shall you serve," can be our response as well. We all may freely choose true power, by doing the will of God. As Christ said, if you do these things in my name you will be able to move mountains (paraphrasing Mark 11:23). He also said: "He that believeth in me, the works that I do shall he do also; and greater works than these shall he do; because I go unto my Father. And whatsoever ye shall ask in my name, that will I do, that the Father may be glorified in the Son. If ye shall ask anything in my name, I will do it" (John 14:12).

Another name for true power is white, or sacred, magic. The essence of sacred magic is expressed in the words: "Not my will...but thy will be done" (Matthew 26:39–42). Two thousand years ago, Huitzilopochtli and his allies exercised true power, in repulsing the influence of Quetzalcoatl and defeating the black magician inspired by Taotl. Before they could manifest true power, they had to *recognize* false power, the power over humanity that was being wielded by the black magicians who held sway over their civilization. Though we live in an age when magic seems to be in eclipse except in the realm of fantasy literature, we need not be Muggles. If we take it upon ourselves to recognize and call out falsehood when we encounter it; if we cultivate equanimity in the face of fear; if we choose love over hate, we begin to practice sacred magic and, like Huitzilopochtli, help fulfill the divine plan.

Part II:

Penetrating the Mysteries of Time

by Robert Powell

6. Dating Kali Yuga in Relation to the Maya Calendar

From Rudolf Steiner's lecture of January 27, 1910, it is possible to gain an overview of the Hindu cycle of *yugas*, or epochs.[68] The first, *Satya Yuga*, or *Krita Yuga*, was later called the Golden Age,[69] and during this yuga the power of clairvoyance of human beings had access to the highest regions of the spiritual world. Then followed the *Treta Yuga*, later called the Silver Age, during which the power of clairvoyance diminished but was still able to cognize the influences of the spiritual world upon human beings. After the Silver Age came the Bronze Age, or *Dvapara Yuga*, during which the primal clairvoyance diminished even further and human beings had only a weak connection with the spiritual world—which was sufficient, however, to convince them of the existence of spiritual reality.

Then came the fourth yuga in the cycle, *Kali Yuga*, also known as the Iron Age, or the Dark Age, during which the ancient clairvoyance disappeared and, correspondingly, the portal to the spiritual world gradually closed altogether. The positive side to this was the development of "I"-consciousness. In his dating of the *Kali Yuga* (the tabulation below gives an overview of his dating of the whole yuga cycle), Steiner agrees with the classical Hindu date of 3102 B.C.E. for the start of *Kali Yuga*. Where he differs from the Hindu tradition, however, is that he spoke of *Kali Yuga* lasting for five thousand years, from 3102 B.C.E. (this is -3101 for astronomers) to C.E. 1899, whereas the Hindu tradition indicates that *Kali Yuga* will last for 432,000 years. During this Dark Age the great event of Christ's incarnation took place. According to Steiner, if this had not taken place, human "I"-consciousness would have developed solely in an egotistical direction. In relation to the end of *Kali Yuga* in 1899, Steiner spoke of a New Age (*Satya Yuga*, a new Golden Age) beginning, which lasts for

2,500 years until 4399, during which a new faculty of clairvoyance—what he called "etheric vision"—is arising, enabling human beings to behold Christ within the etheric aura of the Earth. It is the return of Christ—not in a physical body, but in an etheric body—which is what underlies the New Age.

From this synopsis of Steiner's lecture, those who are familiar with the traditional Hindu chronology of the yugas will know that the traditional date for the close of *Kali Yuga* is very different from that indicated here by Rudolf Steiner. According to the *Laws of Manu* (*Mânavadharma Shâstra*), the yugas are very long periods of time:

1. Satya Yuga, or Krita Yuga: 1,728,000 years
2. Treta Yuga: 1,296,000 years
3. Dvapara Yuga: 864,000 years
4. Kali Yuga: 432,000 years

The cycle of four yugas lasts for a total of 4,320,000 years, known as a *mahayuga*. According to mainstream Hinduism, which acknowledges 3102 B.C.E. as the start of *Kali Yuga*, there are still some 427,000 years of *Kali Yuga* left! The question is this: Did any other sources support Steiner's view that *Kali Yuga*, or Dark Age, lasted only five thousand years, from 3102 B.C.E. to C.E. 1899?

An alternate view of the yuga cycle and its timescale was taught by the Indian yogi Sri Yukteswar (1855–1936). His disciple Yogananda moved to America in 1920 and founded the Self-Realization Fellowship, with its ashram located about twenty-five miles north of San Diego. Through Yogananda, Sri Yukteswar's teachings on the yuga cycle, presented in his 1894 book *The Holy Science*, became more widely known. According to Sri Yukteswar, the lengths of the yugas given in *The Laws of Manu* are all too long by a factor of 360, and therefore he divided these figures by 360 to arrive at the following: the descending phase of *Satya Yuga* lasts 4,800 years; that of *Treta Yuga* lasts 3,600 years; that of *Dvapara Yuga* lasts 2,400 years; that of *Kali Yuga* lasts 1,200 years. The ascending phase of *Kali Yuga* then begins, also lasting 1,200 years; this is followed by the ascending phase of *Dvapara Yuga*, lasting 2,400 years; and so on. According to Sri Yukteswar, the ascending phase of *Kali Yuga* began in September of C.E. 499. He added 1,200 years to this to arrive at 1699 as the end of *Kali Yuga*, and stated that, since September 1699, we have been in the ascending phase of *Dvapara Yuga*.

A further refinement to these dates was explained by Sri Yukteswar. He indicated that each yuga has a cusp at its beginning and its end, the cusp being a period of transition and lasting for one-twelfth of the yuga. According to this idea, the 4,800 years of *Satya Yuga* are made up of 400 + 4,000 + 400 (400 being the length of the cusp of *Satya Yuga*). Similarly, the 3,600 years of *Treta Yuga* comprise 300 + 3,000 + 300. Further, the 2,400 years of *Dvapara Yuga* = 200 + 2,000 + 200, and the 1,200 years of *Kali Yuga* = 100 + 1,000 + 100. Taking C.E. 1699 as the end of the ascending phase of *Kali Yuga* and adding 200 years as the cusp of *Dvapara Yuga*, leads to 1899 as the date for the main phase of the ascending *Dvapara Yuga*, which, according to Sri Yukteswar, signifies a time (since 1899) of great spiritual progress for humanity.

Here it is evident that the date 1899 is emphasized as an important point of transition in humanity's evolution, against the background of the yuga cycle, but that this date is attributed a quite different significance within the yuga cycle than that given to it by Rudolf Steiner. Nevertheless, it is interesting that two spiritual teachers, working from their respective grasp of the yuga cycle, both arrived at 1899 as a date of great importance.

More recently, David Hedges, writing for AboutHinduism.com, also refers to a 5,000-year period.[70] He draws upon a discourse of Krishna to Ganga Devi in the *Brahma-Vaivarta Purana* speaking of a Golden Age lasting 10,000 years that will come 5,000 years after the start of *Kali Yuga*. This idea offers a bridge between Steiner's dating of *Kali Yuga* and the traditional Hindu dating, but again it differs from Steiner's perspective, who speaks of the New Age (the new *Satya Yuga* or Golden Age) lasting for 2,500 rather than 10,000 years. What is of interest here is that David Hedges also draws a parallel with the Maya calendar, pointing out that there is only a twelve-year difference between the start of the Hindu *Kali Yuga* and the Maya calendar—a fact that also caught my attention several years ago. Then, however, instead of drawing the conclusion that Steiner came to regarding the significance of the year 1899 as the start of the new yuga, David Hedges lengthens the 5,000-year Krishna indication from the *Brahma Vaivarta Purana* to 5,113 years in order to arrive at 2012 as the start of the new Golden Age. He concludes that the 10,000-year Golden Age prophesied by Krishna to take place during *Kali Yuga* could begin in 2012.

Another spiritual teacher who refers to 1899 is Helene Petrovna Blavatsky (1831–1891), sometimes referred to as H.P.B. She stated: "We are in *Kali Yuga*—the Black Age—and the restrictions in this cycle, the first 5,000 years of which will expire in 1897, are great and almost insuperable."[71] Since H.P. Blavatsky acknowledged the traditional Hindu date (3102 B.C.E.) of the beginning of *Kali Yuga*, it is clear that in her statement she really meant the year 1899 (and not 1897). Thus, in fact, she was indeed pointing to the year 1899, but erroneously stated 1897 instead.

Moreover, in a letter written by H.P. Blavatsky in 1890, she elaborated upon her role as the bringer of the teachings of theosophy, and of the significance of the founding of the Theosophical Society in 1875. She then refers to the importance of the last quarter of the century as a time of great importance in each century, alluding to her own significance in terms of the spiritual revelation she was bringing, indicating that "there remains but a few years to the last hour of the term—namely, till December 31, 1899. Those who will not have profited by the opportunity (given to the world in every last quarter of a century)... will advance no further than the knowledge already acquired."[72]

Here again H.P. Blavatsky was pointing to the year 1899, but actually in a very different sense than Rudolf Steiner, who indicated that 1899 would be the *beginning* of a New Age rather than the end of a term of grace of the spiritual revelation of theosophy through H.P. Blavatsky. Steiner's conception of the New Age, as outlined above, is of a period of 2,500 years of humanity's development of etheric vision and that, through this new faculty, an increasing number of human beings will behold Christ in the etheric realm.

To the best of my knowledge, Steiner was the first person to speak of the New Age, a term that is now widely accepted to relate to the new spiritual faculties that are arising among human beings in the twentieth and twenty-first centuries. However, the popular use of the expression New Age at the present time does not usually have the connotation of a new yuga (*Satya Yuga*) as indicated by Rudolf Steiner, and is generally not seen in relation to Christ's Second Coming, his reappearance in the etheric realm. More often than not the New Age is identified with the Aquarian Age which, however, does not start until the vernal point (on account of the precession of the equinoxes) enters Aquarius in C.E. 2375. At that time, the vernal point will be at 0° Pisces (= 30° Aquarius) and will then regress through the sign of Aquarius for 2,160 years until 4535, when it will enter Capricorn.[73] In contrast to the generally vague ideas concerning the New Age that currently prevail, Rudolf Steiner gave the term New Age a very specific meaning. He agreed with the traditional Hindu view—not accepted by all, but by some exponents of Hinduism—that after the end of *Kali Yuga*, a new *Satya Yuga* begins. Steiner referred to this new *Satya Yuga*, lasting 2,500 years from 1899 to 4399, as the Age of Light. Obviously there is much more that could be said on this theme of the cycle of yugas. To my way of understanding, the exposition by Rudolf Steiner is the most plausible and meaningful—that the New Age began in 1899 and has to do with the return of Christ in the etheric, and will last for 2500 years.[74] This conception of the New Age as the *Satya Yuga*—the new yuga—sheds light on the Maya calendar.

Before turning our attention to the Maya calendar, it is helpful to consider the following, which summarizes Rudolf Steiner's perspective on the cycle of yugas.

Tabulation of the Golden Age, Silver Age, Bronze Age

The Golden Age—*Krita Yuga* =	about 20,000 years
The Silver Age—*Treta Yuga* =	about 15,000 years
The Bronze Age—*Dvapara Yuga* =	about 10,000 years
The Dark Age—*Kali Yuga* =	about 5,000 years
New Age (*Satya Yuga*) =	about 2,500 years

This tabulation is from footnote 72 in the lecture cycle *Foundations of Esotericism*. It refers to Rudolf Steiner's mention of the Golden Age, Silver Age, and Bronze Age in lecture 26 (October 28, 1905) of this cycle.[75] The fact that this is a footnote signifies that it is not known with certainty whether these figures derive from Rudolf Steiner or whether they were tabulated by someone else. In any case, what is apparent from this tabulation is that for the first four yugas the same time ratio is preserved as in *The Laws of Manu* and in Sri Yukteswar's *The Holy Science*. The four yugas are in the ratio: 4:3:2:1, meaning that *Krita Yuga* is four times the length of *Kali Yuga*, *Treta Yuga* is three times the length of *Kali Yuga*, and *Dvapara Yuga* is twice the length of *Kali Yuga*. What is new here is that it emerges that the New Age—the new *Satya Yuga* following *Kali Yuga*—is half the length of *Kali Yuga*. From these dates it is possible to arrive at a dating of the sequence of yugas:

The Golden Age, *Krita Yuga*	48102—28102 B.C.E.
The Silver Age—*Treta Yuga*	28102—13102 B.C.E.
The Bronze Age—*Dvapara Yuga*	13102—3102 B.C.E.
The Dark Age—*Kali Yuga*	3102 B.C.E.—C.E. 1899
New Age (*Satya Yuga*)	1899—4399

According to this, the New Age is the fifth age, and it is here where there is an interesting overlap with Maya and other Mesoamerican cosmologies, which typically placed themselves in the period of the Fourth or Fifth Sun. This chronology has been carried into the present by some Mayans; Guatemalan researcher, historian, and anthropologist Carlos Barrios states that contemporary Mayans believe that the year 2012 marks the *end* of the Fourth World, and the *start* of the Fifth World, and it is here where there is some agreement with Steiner's view concerning the five yugas.[76]

We are no longer in the World of the Fourth Sun, but we are not yet in the World of the Fifth Sun. This is the time in between, the time of transition. As we pass through transition there is a colossal, global convergence of environmental destruction,

social chaos, war, and ongoing Earth changes. All this was foreseen via the simple, spiral mathematics of the Maya calendars.
Everything will change.[77]

I am not the first author to suggest that there is a relationship
between the Maya Long Count calendar (3114 B.C.E.–C.E. 2012) and
the *Kali Yuga* (3102 B.C.E.–C.E. 1899) (Steiner's dating). An interpretation along these lines has been suggested by Gene D. Matlock in his
article "Will the Mayan Prophecy Really Happen?" Again, in quoting
here from Matlock's article, it is a matter of drawing upon a "New
Age" perspective of the year 2012, whereby his point of view is only
one of many. (It is not possible here to explore these various perspectives, interesting though they may be).[78] The following quote from
Matlock's article offers a viewpoint that is shared by many at the
present time:

> One day in Brahma's life is called a *Maha Yuga* (Great Age),
> consisting of four Ages (Yugas) named *Satya*, *Treta*, *Dvapara*
> and *Kali*. A *Maha Yuga* is 4,320,000 of our years. At the end
> of this time, everything in this cycle becomes destroyed by a
> cosmic fire.
>
> After the day of Brahma, there will be a brahmic night of
> equal length. After that night is over, another Brahmic day
> dawns, called *Satya Yuga*. The *Satya Yuga* will be an undreamed
> of paradise for the new humankind emerging from the previous
> brahmic night. A *Kali Yuga* lasts for 432,000 of our years. The
> ratios between the *Satya*, *Treta*, *Dvapara* and *Kali* years are
> 4:3:2:1. In other words, the *Satya Yuga*, which consists of full
> righteousness, decreases by one fourth to *Treta Yuga*, one-half
> in *Dvapara Yuga*, and last of all, three fourths in *Kali Yuga*.
>
> Life for humanity will descend in quality until the end of
> *Kali Yuga* arrives. After that comes the brahmic night and the
> beginning of another *Chatur* (Four) *Yuga* (Ages) the follow-
> ing dawn.... Those of us who have studied the *Chatur Yuga*
> carefully, previously thought that we ended the *Kali Yuga* a
> few years ago, in approximately C.E. 2000. We thought we
> would just phase out slowly. But not being as knowledgeable
> of astronomy as the Meso-American Maya wisemen and their
> forefathers, the Maya in India, we did not calculate correctly.

Our Meso-American Mayans say that the end of the *Kali Age*
will occur in C.E. 2012.[79]

There is a problem with the above interpretation by Gene D.
Matlock, and that is that he ignores the universally acknowledged
date of 3102 B.C.E. as the start of *Kali Yuga*. If one accepts this date
as the start of *Kali Yuga*, and if the length of *Kali Yuga* is assumed to
be 432,000 years, as indicated in *The Laws of Manu* (and in Gene D.
Matlock's article), then *Kali Yuga* is not scheduled to end for another
427,000 years. Nevertheless, Gene D. Matlock's article is indicative of
something real, namely the sense that the end of *Kali Yuga* falls in our
time—first he thought in C.E. 2000, and then in C.E. 2012 as indicated
by the Maya calendar.

It is here where the research presented in this book can shed light
on the question of the parallel between the Hindu yugas and Maya
cosmology, in particular between the fourth yuga, *Kali Yuga*, and the
Maya Long Count calendar ending in 2012, which Barrios and other
Maya researchers suggest indicates the period of the Fourth World—
the world that gave birth to the "dark power of materialism."[80] What
is clear to everyone is that the two calendars—the Hindu and the
Maya—both start more or less at the same time, a little before the
year 3100 B.C.E., and that their starting dates are only twelve years
apart. If Steiner's dating of *Kali Yuga* is accepted, the end of *Kali
Yuga* in C.E. 1899 is 113 years prior to the end of the Maya calendar
in 2012. Could it be this period that Carlos Barrios means when he
says, "This is the time in between, the time of transition"? In other
words, the time of transition means that the dawning of the New Age
(*Satya Yuga*) was in 1899, and that the sunrise of this New Age will be
in 2012. If this interpretation is correct, it is not surprising to witness
a colossal struggle on the part of the "dark power of materialism" to
maintain its hold and not give way to the New Age, *Satya Yuga*, that
is seeking to come to expression.

The central thesis that is put forward in this book—in light of the
Apocalypse Code discussed in chapter 2—is that the culmination of
this colossal struggle takes place in the three and a half years preceding 2012 in the shape of the conflict between Christ, who is ushering

in the New Age of Light, and the Antichrist, who is the motivating force behind the "dark power of materialism." It is clear that this struggle has been underway throughout the twentieth century and is now reaching its climax in the twenty-first century. Against this background, the primary event of our time is not the coming of the Antichrist forecast in relation to the solar eclipse on July 22, 2009, almost exactly three and a half years before the end of the Maya calendar in 2012. The coming of the Antichrist simply represents the shadow side of Christ's coming in the etheric realm, and a new level of inflow of Christ in the etheric realm can be expected to begin in the year 2009 as the most powerful source of help and assistance in the coming time of three and a half years leading up to the sunrise of the New Age at the winter solstice in 2012.[81] This is the *most important event of our time* or, to use Rudolf Steiner's expression, it is the *greatest mystery of our time.*

7. The Rhythm of 666 Years

The Apocalypse of John states: "The name of The Beast or the number of its name...is 666" (Revelation 13:17–18). As described in chapter 2 of this book, the "beast" is the being known in esoteric teaching as Sorath, whose name in Hebrew is composed of the four letters *Samech-Vau-Resh-Tau*. Every letter in the Hebrew alphabet also signifies a number, and the numerical value of these four letters—*Samech* (60), *Vau* (6), *Resh* (200), *Tau* (400)—is 60 + 6 + 200 + 400 = 666. To the best of my knowledge, Rudolf Steiner was the first to reveal the meaning of the number 666 as the number of the Sun Demon, Sorath[82]; previously all kinds of speculation surrounded the number 666. For example, various authors speculated that the letters of the name N-e-r-o, when converted to numerical values, add up to 666. This depends of course upon how numerical values are assigned to letters of our alphabet (in contrast to the Hebrew alphabet, where the letters are simultaneously numbers, and so there is no ambiguity regarding the numerical value of the letters comprising Hebrew words).

In addition to revealing the mystery of the name of The Beast whose number is 666, Rudolf Steiner also referred to the time rhythm of 666 in connection with the rhythmic intervention of Sorath historically. As indicated in chapter 2, since the coming of Christ three such interventions have taken place: in 666, in 1332 (= 2 x 666), and in 1998 (= 3 x 666). Given the significance of this third date for human beings living now, it is important to have a clear grasp of this rhythm and its relevance to our time. On this account the following overview of Rudolf Steiner's principle statements concerning the historical rhythm of 666 years are reproduced here:

> The year 666 was intended [by Sorath] to deluge humanity with
> a knowledge and a culture which the primal gods had intended

for human beings only during the third millennium. It cannot be conceived—need not be conceived—into what situation the so-called civilized world would have come if it had been deluged with this wisdom in the year 666. With their lack of self-discipline people would have come utterly to grief.... Whatever would have become of them had they been deluged with all this wisdom of The Beast?[83]

Here, when Steiner speaks of the "primal gods," he means the Elohim and other guiding beings of humankind's evolution referred to in the Bible.[84] These guiding beings operate according to a divine plan for the evolution of the Earth and humanity, whereas the interventions of Sorath and Ahriman (Satan) are intended to preempt the divine plan by bringing in the future prematurely. This, according to Steiner, was Sorath's plan around the year 666. How did he intend to realize this plan?

The aim of the being who hoped to intervene in 666 was to make himself God... The intention of the being who wanted to appear in 666 was to cut off the possibility of all future earthly evolution.... Very little is said about the academy of learning at Gondishapur....[85] An impressive world outlook developed in Gondishapur during the seventh century...it was in Gondishapur that the teaching I spoke of yesterday [the teaching of Sorath] was given.... It would have made of human beings mere creatures of the Earth and would have shut them off from their true future evolution into the spiritual world...Whoever has an inkling of the wisdom of Gondishapur will indeed regard it as in the highest sense dangerous for humanity, but also as a phenomenon of great power. And the intention was to deluge with this learning not only the immediate vicinity but the whole of the then known civilized world.... Through the appearance of Mohammed and his visionary religious teaching, there was a deadening [blunting] of the influence that was meant to go out from Gondishapur.... Mohammedanism was destined to deaden [blunten] the Gnostic wisdom of Gondishapur, to take from it the strong ahrimanically seductive force that would otherwise have been exercised upon humankind.[86]

Most people have probably never heard of the Academy of Gondishapur, often referred to today as the Gondishapur School of Medicine.[87] Given Rudolf Steiner's strong words of warning, it is remarkable to consider that the leading physicians of the Gondishapur School for more than two centuries were from the Christian-Iranian Buhktishu family (in Syriac Buhktishu means "Jesus has saved").[88] The Christian physicians at Gondishapur were primarily Nestorians. The Nestorian Christians had been driven into exile in a series of purges directed against them in Edessa and Nisibis and—together with exiled pagan Greek philosophers from Athens and Syriac-speaking Christians fleeing religious persecution—had gone to Gondishapur. Here we cannot go into the complex history of Nestorius and his teachings (such as the "Nestorian heresy") or the intricacies of the various influences in the Gondishapur School. One nevertheless wonders whether the "eminent teacher" of the Gondishapur School of Medicine mentioned by Steiner was from the Buhktishu family? "The eminent teacher, whose name is unknown, but who was the greatest opponent of Jesus Christ, failed to achieve his purpose—the purpose of the teaching he gave to his pupils at Gondishapur."[89] If yes, we have a paradox: Someone who was explicitly Christian was "the greatest opponent of Jesus Christ."

This eminent teacher, who lived in the seventh century (connected with the year 666, including the decades immediately preceding and following this date), was evidently the focus of Sorath's inspiration to bring a teaching that would work upon humanity so as to preclude the future spiritual development of human beings. Based upon a new understanding (by way of the Apocalypse Code) of Revelation 13, this book suggests that the prophet of the Antichrist is a human being who is the central focus of the inspiration of Sorath in our time, whose mission will occur in the decades immediately preceding and following the year 1998 (3 x 666).

Before discussing the year 1998, it is important to consider some further statements made by Rudolf Steiner concerning 666. These statements qualify his initial portrayal quoted above: "Through the appearance of Mohammed and his visionary religious teaching, there was a deadening [blunting] of the influence that was meant to go out from Gondishapur." Under Caliph Umar (sometimes spelled Omar, who was caliph from 634 to 644) Muslim armies conquered Gondishapur in the year 638, destroying the academy and burning the library. This, clearly, was something that blunted the influence of the academy. Nevertheless, the Gondishapur School recovered and persisted under Muslim rule for several centuries. When the caliphs Harun al-Rashid and his son al-Ma'mun founded the House of Wisdom in Baghdad in the ninth century, it was staffed with graduates of the older Academy of Gondishapur. From this time onward the significance of the Gondishapur School gradually declined, and the House of Wisdom became the unrivalled center for the study of humanities and the sciences, including mathematics, astronomy, medicine, chemistry, zoology, and geography, ushering in the golden age of Islamic science.

As Steiner noted on various occasions, Islamic science shaped the development of Western science—in particular, its penchant for abstract thinking—and exerted an influence that ultimately derived from the Gnostic wisdom of the Academy of Gondishapur, notwithstanding the blunting influence of Islam upon the Gondishapur School. Here he gives the example of the highly influential Muslim philosopher, theologian, and polymath Averroes, "The founding father of secular thought in Western Europe."[90]

> The thoughts of human beings such as Averroes, who had acquired the Gnostic wisdom of Gondishapur in its deadened [blunted] form, were focused upon this.... "When a human being dies, it is only the substance of the soul that flows into the universal spirituality. The human being has no personal individuality. All that is soul in separate human beings is merely a reflection of one universal soul." Why did he say this? He said it because it is part of the Gondishapur wisdom, which told people not that each individual is to develop the consciousness soul, but that the wisdom of the consciousness soul was to come to them as a revelation from above. Then it would have been an ahrimanic revelation...with the individual consciousness becoming merely semblance.[91]

In his final discussion of Sorath and the mystery of 666 just six months prior to his death, Steiner did not then refer to Gondishapur but simply to Arabism—meaning the influence of thinkers such as Averroes. He identified Arabism with the teaching of the Sun Demon, Sorath. "What would happen if Arabism, the teaching of the Sun Demon, were to be entirely victorious?"[92] Let us recall that Rudolf Steiner spoke these words in 1924, long before the event of September 11, 2001, which led to the War on Terror that plunged the United States into two protracted wars waged in Muslim countries, Iraq and Afghanistan. In writing this, I am very conscious of the danger of over-generalization and of the risk of demonization of whole peoples, which is very far, indeed, from my intention. Also, to label Islamic thought in general as Arabism and, consequently, simply to identify it with Sorath's teaching is also clearly too simplistic. Rather, it is a matter of identifying trends, which, it seems, was also Steiner's concern. Moreover, I am conscious of the fact that it is impossible to do justice to this sensitive theme in the space of this short book, and so I trust that the reader will not interpret the discussion here in any way as "anti-Islamic," but rather as an attempt to contribute to a deeper understanding of the "clash of civilizations" between the Western world and Islam. Let us continue further with the statements by Rudolf Steiner in 1924, some six months before his death.

> The number 666 was there in one instance at the time when Arabism was flowing into Christianity in order to impress the seal of materialism on to Western culture. But it was there for a second time after a further 666 years had passed, in 1332, in the fourteenth century. At that time once again The Beast rose up out of the waves of world events. To one whose vision is like that of the apocalyptist [the writer of Revelation], world events appear as continuous waves of time spans measuring 666 years. The Beast rises up to threaten Christianity in its search for true humanity.... In the fourteenth century we see Sorath, the adversary, rising up once again....
>
> It is of course difficult now to consider what might have become of European civilization if that powerful...Order of the Knights Templar—their riches were confiscated, as we know— had been able to achieve its goals. But in the hearts and souls of those who could not rest until the Order had been destroyed

in 1312 and until Jacques de Molay [grandmaster of the Order] had met his death in 1314, in the hearts of those who were the adversaries of the Christ who looked to the cosmos, in these hearts Sorath lived again. [93]

Rudolf Steiner put forward that the Templars cultivated a form of Christianity in which they "looked to the cosmos," in particular to the Sun in connection with Christ, whom they—as did many of the early Christians—regarded as the Spirit of the Sun, a theme which we shall return to below. King Philip IV, commonly referred to as Philip the Fair (Philippe le Bel), was born in 1268, one hundred and fifty years after the formation of the Knights Templar. Philip was King of France from 1285 to 1314, the year in which the Order's leader Jacques de Molay was burned at the stake through the machinations of Philip. In contrast to his appearance ("the Fair" was a reference to Philip IV's handsome appearance: tall, with long blonde hair and blue eyes), Philip the Fair was a cold and secretive man whose greatest wish was for France to be the dominating power of the empire, with himself at its head. This wish was inculcated in him by way of Sorath's inspiration. Requiring great financial resources to accomplish his plan, Philip sought to acquire the Templars' substantial fortune of gold.

Philip also engaged in aggressive conflict with Pope Boniface VIII, since he needed a weak and subservient papal throne. At one point Philip publicly burned Boniface VIII's papal bull *Unam Sanctam,* the document that gave the pope absolute supremacy over everyone. Then, when Pope Clement V was elected pope in 1305, Philip found a weak personality who actually moved the papal court to Avignon in France, effectively placing himself under Philip's jurisdiction. Complying with Philip's wish, the pope officially disbanded the Templar Order, and Philip the Fair, as king of France, launched a persecution of the Templars in a fake trial with trumped-up charges and false confessions extracted under torture, enabling him to expropriate their wealth and sentence Jacques de Molay, their grandmaster, to be burned at the stake.

In his quest for more and more money and power, Philip was possessed by Sorath. When he became aware of the accumulated gold of the Knights Templar, he was inspired by Sorath with the idea of stealing their vast wealth in order to realize his political agenda. Pope Clement V became an unwitting tool in bringing this greedy and despicable plan to realization. It is said that Jacques de Molay pronounced from the flames a divine prophecy calling Philip and Clement to judgment within the year; this came to pass. Philip the Fair died just eight months after the death of Jacques de Molay. Pope Clement V died that same year (1314), just one month after Jacques de Molay.

In light of the activity of the Academy of Gondishapur, one can see Sorath's intervention in the year 666 as directed at human intelligence, whereas the intervention associated with the year 1332 was more of an attack on the level of egotistical feeling, fired by an obsession with power and with gold, the metal traditionally associated with the Sun (and thus susceptible to the sphere of influence of Sorath, the Sun Demon). In both cases it should be noted that the dates 666 and 1332 are only approximate, since the culmination of the Gondishapur School must have been prior to the year 638, when the Muslim conquest of the city of Gondishapur took place (638 being twenty-eight years before 666), and the trial and destruction of the Knights Templar took place in the period prior to the death of Philip the Fair in November 1314 (thus at least eighteen years before 1332). As we see from these two examples, when speaking of the rhythm of 666 years, one has to look at the whole time span of a few decades immediately preceding or following the exact date.

Now we come to the intervention of Sorath associated with 1998 (again, only an approximate date). For Steiner, speaking in 1924, the year 1998 lay in the future:

> During the first 666...Sorath was still hidden away inside the evolutionary process of events. He was not seen in any external form, for he lived within the deeds of Arabism.... When the second 666 years had passed, he showed himself in the thinking and feeling of the tortured Templars.[94] And before this century is out, he will show himself by making his appearance in many humans as the being by whom they are possessed.... At the end of this [the twentieth] century, Sorath will be on the loose again, so that the intention to sweep away anything spiritual

will be deep-seated in large numbers of earthly souls, just as the apocalyptist has foreseen in The beast-like countenance and the beast-like strength that will underlie the deeds of the adversary against the spiritual.... The entry of [the Archangel] Michael into the spiritual evolution of humanity at the end of the nineteenth century and the appearance of the Etheric Christ during the first half of the twentieth century are events that will be followed by the arrival of the Sun Demon before this century comes to an end. [95]

Steiner is speaking in terms of a general anti-spiritual impulse associated with the emergence of Sorath. Based on my research, I see this third intervention very much against the background of Revelation 13, where the coming of the false prophet is described: "Like a lamb, and it spoke like a dragon" (Revelation 13:11). In other words, just as there was a human focus, the "eminent teacher," associated with the first intervention of Sorath, and also a human focus, Philip the Fair, associated with the second intervention of Sorath, so also there will be a human focus for the third intervention of Sorath, and this human being will be the prophet of the Antichrist spoken of by Jeane Dixon in her vision of the coming of the Antichrist. In her vision she beheld the Pharaoh Akhenaton together with his beautiful wife Nefertiti.

Glowing like an enormous ball of fire, the Sun had cracked the horizon, emitting brilliant rays of scintillating light, which seemed to attract the Earth like a magic wand. The Sun's rays parted, facilitating the appearance of an Egyptian Pharaoh [Akhenaton] and his queen. I immediately recognized her as Queen Nefertiti.... My eyes were drawn to Nefertiti and the child she tenderly cradled in her other arm...wrapped in soiled, ragged swaddling clothes...in stark contrast to the magnificently arrayed royal couple.... I then became aware of a multitude of people that appeared.... I witnessed Nefertiti hand the child to the people. Instantly rays of sunlight burst forth from the little boy, carefully blending themselves with the brilliance of the Sun. [96]

The extraordinary thing about this vision is that Ahkenaton's death occurred in (or close to) the year 1332 B.C.E., which is 2 x 666 years before the coming of Christ. It is known that Ahkenaton was focused on a god whom he called Aton, after whom he renamed himself shortly after he became pharaoh (he was originally called Amenophis IV), and he identified Aton with the disk of the Sun—the physical splendor of the Sun rising across the eastern horizon, for example, or the setting of the Sun on the western horizon (in the case of Jeane Dixon's vision it was the *rising* Sun that she beheld at the time of the vision).

Whereas Rudolf Steiner did not speak about interventions of Sorath prior to Christ's coming, the possibility of such interventions, in keeping with the rhythm of 666 years, are worthy of consideration, and in this connection the life of the Pharaoh Akhenaton offers food for thought. Akhenaton was determined to bring radical change to the Egyptian people, who were part of a mighty empire when he ascended to the throne. Part of this radical change was to break completely with the tradition of the past—the central focus of the Egyptian religion up to that time having been upon Osiris, Isis, and Horus. As I have described elsewhere, Osiris and Isis were manifestations of Christ and Sophia in their pre-incarnatory forms.[97] Moreover, Horus for the people of ancient Egypt was a kind of premonition of the coming of the Christ child. As Steiner pointed out, the *Sistine Madonna,* the famous painting by Raphael, expresses this in a beautiful way. "Raphael's wonderful picture of the Madonna [and Child] succeeds so well in leading us back to the realms to which the old figures of Isis belong...Isis who transmits her force to Horus."[98]

In the sense that Akhenaton broke with the religion of Osiris, Isis, and Horus (the religion of Christ and Sophia in their pre-Christian forms, preparing for the coming of Christ) and substituted a new religion focused upon Aton, represented by the disk of the Sun, we are offered a striking example in humankind's spiritual history of radical change and break with the past. As Jeane Dixon points out in her vision (if it does in fact come true), something similar to what took place with the one she calls the "heretic pharaoh"[99] will be repeated by the prophet of the Antichrist—and by the Antichrist himself—who will bring a new kind of "religion" in our time.

Egyptologists generally agree that, although there were a multitude of gods in the religion of ancient Egypt, ultimately the central god was Osiris—and, together with him, Isis and Horus. Further, it is evident that the devotion to Isis and Osiris was introduced to Egypt by the great teacher of the Egyptian mysteries Hermes Trismegistus, who occupied a similar position in ancient Egypt to that of Moses in ancient Israel. It emerges from my research that Hermes lived around 2500 B.C.E., the Pyramid Age of the fourth dynasty when the great pyramid at Giza was constructed. Through the inspiration of Hermes, texts concerning the death and resurrection of Osiris, his conflict with his evil brother Seth,[100] and his son Horus, aided by Isis, taking up this conflict were inscribed inside some of the smaller pyramids constructed at Saqqara during the fifth and sixth dynasties, approximately 2350 to 2150 B.C.E. These pyramid texts were discovered in 1880 and published in English in 1910.[101] In English translation, they are presented as utterances addressed primarily to the pharaoh. These hieroglyphic inscriptions were found in five pyramids. The most extensive and best-preserved come from the pyramid of Pharaoh Unas (c. 2356–2323 B.C.E.), who lived some 150 years after the time of Hermes. The pyramid texts, inscribed around 150 years after they were given orally through Hermes to the Egyptian priests, constitute the essence of the ancient religion of Osiris that Hermes introduced into Egypt. They comprise a well-developed theology and mythology, and were used specifically for royal ceremonies and rites during the great Pyramid Age.

From Rudolf Steiner's descriptions, it is apparent that Hermes was a great initiate and that his primary mission was to introduce the religion of Osiris into Egypt by way of preparation for the coming of Christ. This makes sense only if it is understood that Osiris was a pre-incarnatory form of Christ, who at that time was approaching the Earth from celestial heights.

The pyramid texts refer to the constellation of Orion as the abode of Osiris. What does this tell us? The significance of this can be grasped now against the background of a modern astronomical understanding of our Milky Way Galaxy. From an image of our galaxy (page 107), it can be seen that our Sun is located on the Orion arm situated between the Sagittarius and Perseus arms, which are two of the four main spiral arms extending out from the Galactic Center. Our local part of the galaxy, to which our Sun belongs, is a side arm called the Orion arm, because when we look up to the constellation of Orion we are looking toward the center of the Orion arm. The teaching of Hermes linking Osiris to Orion can be interpreted as an indication of the incarnation of a sublime being, originating from the center of our galaxy, uniting with the Orion arm as one of the stages on the path of incarnation of this being.[102] A later stage on the path of incarnation was when this being united with our Sun, and the last stage was that of descending into the human being, Jesus of Nazareth, at the time of his baptism in the River Jordan by John the Baptist, who acted as his prophet.

Against this background, it can be understood why on the one hand the Egyptians saw Osiris in relation to the constellation of Orion, and on the other hand in connection with the Sun. Orion (or, rather, the Orion arm) and the Sun are two of the stages of the incarnation of the great being whom the Egyptians called Osiris (and whom we call Christ)—and, further, we can comprehend why many of the early Christians identified Christ as a Sun being.

This cosmological background is important to understand what took place through Akhenaton, who came forth with his own solar religion—not the Osiris religion revealed in ancient Egypt by Hermes, but a religion oriented to the solar disk, whom he called Aton. In the words of Jeane Dixon:

> It was a proud and stately procession that moved slowly down the King's Way. It was sunrise and time for Ahkenaton's worship of Aton, the god of the Disk of the Sun. His ceremonial walk in the temple procession, surrounded by his priests and accompanied by his wife, the beautiful Nefertiti, was a journey of victory. Son of Amenophis III, the most illustrious monarch of Egypt's eighteenth dynasty who formed historical and far-reaching alliances with the kings of Babylonia and Assyria, Akhenaton had become seriously disenchanted with the religion of his forefathers. The god Horus had lost all attraction for him; Osiris had lost his value...He wanted ONE god and found him in the Disk of the Sun. Aton, the Sun, was to be

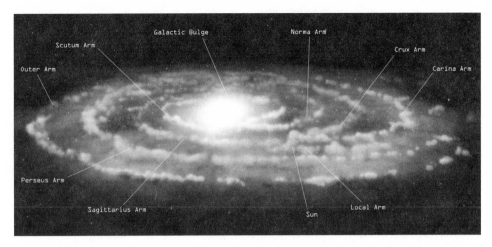

*View of the Milky Way showing the prominent arms
(NASA/CXC/M.Weiss)*

his god and, encouraged by his royal spouse, he embarked on
an adventure so daring, so "ungodly," that it made his newly
appointed priests quake with fear.... "He in whom Aton is satisfied" was the meaning of his name. The hieroglyphics of his
name [Akhenaton] can also be translated as "He in whom the
Solar Disk is satisfied."[103]

With this translation of the name Akhenaton, we are reminded
of the words recorded in Luke at the baptism of Jesus, when "a voice
came from heaven: Thou art my beloved Son in whom I am well
pleased" (Luke 3:22). With the incarnation of Christ in Jesus at the
baptism in the Jordan, it was a voice from the heavens that resounded,
the voice of the heavenly Father. In the case of Akhenaton, his name
brought to expression his "sonship" of the god Aton, the Disk of the
Sun. Who was Aton?

Here it is a matter of discernment, considering that the religion
of Aton was substituted by Akhenaton in the place of the religion
of Osiris (Christ)—noting that this attempt did not succeed at that
time. With Akhenaton's death in 1332 B.C.E. (= 2 x 666 years before
Christ),[104] the religion of Aton quickly disappeared, as his successor,
originally named Tutankaton ("living image of Aton") in his third
year as pharaoh changed his name to Tutankamun ("living image

of Amun"), expressing his rejection of the radical change brought by Akhenaton and reverting to the more traditional Egyptian religion.

As students of Egyptian history know, the life of Akhenaton was a dramatic event, concerning which the world is divided into "pro" and "contra" regarding this fascinating and enigmatic personality. As John Anthony West points out, "The drama of Akhenaton—next to the Great Pyramid—is the most controversial subject in Egyptian history."[105] The reason for dwelling upon Akhenaton at some length is Jeane Dixon's vision, on the one hand, and the synchronicity with the rhythm of 666 years on the other. Implicit in Dixon's vision is that the figure of Akhenaton holds a key to understanding the prophet of the Antichrist and, as the drama enacted some 3350 years ago shows, no doubt there will again be fierce "pro" and "contra" in relation to this figure of the prophet. There is no mistaking that Akhenaton was a highly evolved and charismatic figure, an initiate, like the pharaohs before him. However, he was not an initiate in the sense of Osiris—in the spirit of the instructions to the pharaoh for *death and resurrection in Osiris* given in the pyramid texts of Hermes. Rather, he was an initiate of Aton.

As mentioned, looking at the historical interventions of the Sun Demon Sorath, it is extremely difficult to discern—externally—what the principle elements in Sorath's agenda are. Perhaps the key is Steiner's statement: "The aim of the being who hoped to intervene in 666 was to make himself God."[106] In order to accomplish this aim, there has to be someone on Earth who can be a worthy vessel—in the sense of the words: "Thou art my beloved son in whom I am well pleased" (Luke 3:22)—through whom Sorath can achieve his ambition in the world of human beings. The more evolved this "beloved son" is, the greater the possibility for Sorath to achieve his aim. Thus, in the rhythm of 666 years we see a characteristic signature, that at these times there is someone on Earth who has great rulership potential:

1332 B.C.E. (1332 = 2 x 666): Akhenaton, pharaoh of Egypt's mighty kingdom

666 B.C.E. (666 = 1 x 666): Assurbanipal, king of the great Assyrian empire

The year 0 (0 = 0 x 666): Augustus, emperor of the vast Roman
  empire

666 (666 = 1 x 666): the "eminent teacher" of the Academy of
  Gondishapur—it is noteworthy that Mu'awiya, caliph of the
  mighty Muslim empire, was caliph in the year 666

1332 (1332 = 2 x 666): Philip the Fair, king of France, whose
  ambition was to be head of the empire

1998 (1998 = 3 x 666): the figure predicted to appear by Jeane
  Dixon as the prophet of the Antichrist

Judith von Halle's book *The Descent into the Layers of the Earth*
devotes much attention to Sorath.[107] It emerges from her description
that Sorath worked from the Sun (as the Sun Demon) until the coming of Christ or, more specifically, up to the descent of Christ into the
underworld associated with Holy Saturday (April 4, C.E. 33), which
ensued immediately following his Crucifixion and death at 3 p.m.
on Good Friday (April 3). Based on her visions of the life of Christ,
Judith von Halle describes that, with Christ's descent into the underworld, Sorath followed on the heels of Christ down into the depths
of the Earth and took up abode in the Earth's interior, primarily in
the ninth subearthly layer.[108] This explains why, in the account of
Sorath's emergence given in Revelation 13, John says, "And I saw
another beast that rose *out of the Earth*; it had two horns like a lamb
and it spoke like a dragon" (Revelation 13:11). Thus, there is a difference between the pre-Christian and post-Christian activity of Sorath;
prior to C.E. 33 he worked directly from the Sun, whereas since C.E. 33
he works from the interior of the Earth.

Given that the emergence of the prophet of the Antichrist and
the Antichrist himself is indicated to John by the Risen Christ in
Revelation 13, it is evident that the emergence of the two human
beings who are the bearers of the suprasensory entities known as
Sorath and Ahriman (Satan) is preordained in the divine plan. In the
case of Sorath it is a matter of a human being as the focus of the Sun
Demon's *inspiration*; in the case of Ahriman it is a human being who
is the vessel for the actual *incarnation* of Satan. The appearance of
these two human beings on the world stage is for a purpose, on behalf
of the evolution of humanity. It presents an opportunity for human

beings to make a great step forward in their evolution, provided that they pass through this event *together with the Etheric Christ*. In this respect, just as the Mystery of Golgotha was preordained in world history, so the current event of the enactment on the world stage of Revelation 13 is also preordained.

As to the deeper significance of the coming of the Antichrist—the incarnation of Satan/Ahriman—and how it may be turned to good, this is the subject matter of the final chapter of this book. Obviously, though, in order for this incarnation to be turned to good effect, it is important that humanity is not deceived into welcoming the Antichrist and his prophet as messiahs. And, of course, it is not just these two individuals themselves but also their entire entourage who will do everything possible to ensure that the population is deceived. These are the many individuals belonging to the inner circle of the associates of these two leaders. It is then the phenomenon of group conscious-ness, where individuals stop thinking for themselves and just follow the directives of the leaders, that is dangerous in this situation. This kind of group consciousness has to be avoided at all costs. However, it is not a matter of *rejecting* anyone. Far from it. We are one humanity, all offspring from the same divine source, and every human being is our spiritual brother or sister. Thus, an appropriate attitude is, while seeing clearly what is amiss, to pray for the higher essence of these leaders, to call upon their higher being. This can be exemplified in relation to Judas, for example, who was spiritually advanced but came under Satan's influence to the extent that he lost sight of the true significance of his beloved teacher and betrayed him for "thirty pieces of silver" (Matthew 26:14).

In order for the Mystery of Golgotha to be accomplished, there had to be a highly evolved human being, Judas Iscariot, to betray Christ in order for the Crucifixion to happen. The Crucifixion was the prerequisite for the Resurrection, which is the ultimate goal of human evolution. In a discussion of Judas, St. Augustine once argued that Judas was chosen by God so that he might precipitate the redemptive death of Christ, an idea that is supported by the recently discovered *Gospel of Judas*, which states that Judas, in his act of betrayal, was actually following the instructions of Jesus.[109] In the same way, the human being who is to be the prophet of the Antichrist and also the human being who will be the Antichrist (the vessel for the incarnated Ahriman) have each been chosen—and on some level they themselves have chosen—to play their role in the divine plan. Our task as human beings is to recognize these two human beings when they appear on the world stage; this recognition is possible through and together with the Etheric Christ. This is the necessary first step, and everything else follows from this through the inner guidance one receives from the Etheric Christ to guide one through the drama. Here, Jeane Dixon's words conclude our consideration of the great drama of the world at the present time:

> I see the youth flock to him and partake of his wisdom....
> With the world fully prepared for his coming, millions on our
> Earth will be brought into contact with him through our far-
> advanced communications network.... His field of labor will
> be the world.... He will lead many souls astray.... He gazed
> at the masses of worshipful humanity with a hypnotic look of
> wisdom and enticed them to follow him all the way to the end
> of the road.... I saw humanity arrive at the "valley of decision,"
> a fork in the road.... Here everyone individually was given the
> choice of either veering to the left...or going on, continuing to
> where the path became straight and narrow.... The uncountable
> masses followed him [to the left] in quiet adoration.... I looked
> ahead, and the vision dissolved into utter darkness and desola-
> tion that awaited them at the end of the road. Then I looked the
> other way and noticed small bands of faithful pilgrims wearily
> climbing their way across the obstacles that covered the narrow
> path. Tired and worn, but relying on their faith in the Son, they
> fought the last hurdle...that had prevented their close rela-
> tionship with the Lord for so long.... They were home, finally
> home. Satan and the grand deception...were now only a mere
> page in the annals of the long war between Christ and His
> adversary. With victory assured, once more the universe was
> in harmony with its Creator. God has revealed these things
> to come in order that those who believe His warning will pre-
> pare.... Each one of us can redirect our lives from material-
> istic, self-seeking pleasure and moral complacency to faithful

service to God, using the talents He gave us so each one of us may fulfill His purpose for us.[110]

With these words, Jeane Dixon brings to expression the same thing communicated through the Apocalypse Code: humanity's encounter with the Antichrist and his prophet is only one short episode in history, belonging to the "thirty-ninth" day in the wilderness that extends from 1988 to 2018. Just as humanity has passed through the first two temptations—belonging to the "thirty-seventh" day (1929–1958) and the "thirty-eighth" day (1958–1988)—so will humankind pass through and live beyond this third temptation on the "thirty-ninth" day, since there are still another 1,251 days of the 1,290 days of the Apocalypse Code to live through during which, as Christ said: "I am with you always, even unto the end of the Earth" (Matthew 28:20).

8. THE REDEMPTION OF LUCIFER

The name Lucifer applies to the tempter of humanity in the Garden of Eden, who is referred to in Genesis 3 as "the serpent." One of Rudolf Steiner's great contributions, discovered through his advanced faculty of clairvoyance, is the distinction between Lucifer (the serpent) and Ahriman/Satan (the dragon). The dragon is referred to in the Revelation, but here there is some confusion in relation to the identity of the dragon, who in the following passage is not clearly distinguished from the serpent:

> Now war arose in heaven, Michael and his Angels fighting against the dragon; and the dragon and his Angels fought, but they were defeated and there was no longer any place for them in heaven. And the great dragon was thrown down, that ancient serpent, who is called the Devil and Satan, the deceiver of the whole world—he was thrown down to the Earth, and his Angels were thrown down with him. (Revelation 12:7–9)

Here the terms *Devil* and *Satan* are used as if they apply to one and the same being. According to Steiner, however, *Devil* refers to Lucifer, whose name means the Light Bearer, and the term *Satan* to Ahriman, the Prince of Darkness in the ancient Persian tradition, going back to the great prophet Zarathustra. Even in the names Lucifer and Ahriman, a polarity of light and dark emerges here. Steiner's spiritual science gives an in-depth "theology" of the forces of good and evil which, as it is the concern of this book to bring clarity to this subject, will now be discussed briefly, before we proceed to the main theme of this chapter, which is the redemption of Lucifer.

In esoteric teaching there are four levels to the human being:

1. The physical body;
2. The life body (or etheric body) penetrates and sustains the physical body between conception and the moment of death, when it separates from the physical body, leaving behind the latter as a corpse;
3. The soul body (or astral body) surrounds and permeates the human being as an aura of colored light, and is the repository of thoughts, feelings and impulses of will, as well as passions and instincts;
4. The human "I" (also called the Self, or Ego) is a manifestation of the conscious spirit of the human being.

Corresponding to these four levels, which are of divine origin, there are four levels of attack on the part of evil, which is also fourfold and seeks to invert or corrupt the divine intention relating to the fourfold human being, as indicated in the following tabulation:

Levels of Evil	Level in the Human Being
Asuras	physical body / consciousness soul
Ahriman / Satan / Dragon	etheric body / intellectual soul
Lucifer / Devil / Serpent	astral body / sentient soul
Sorath / Sun Demon	"I"

At various stages in his life, Steiner gave much attention to clarifying how fourfold evil opposes the work of Christ, and that it is precisely through the work of Christ that the forces of evil are transformed and redeemed.[111] Thereby, human beings advance on the path of spiritual evolution—*by virtue of overcoming and transforming the forces of evil.* A first step, therefore, is to recognize evil when it is at work, which is one of the primary reasons for this book. A second step is to unite inwardly with Christ to receive assistance in overcoming and transforming the evil at work within oneself, which is the meaning of the words from the Lord's Prayer: "Deliver us from evil."

In terms of recognizing the four levels tabulated above, let us begin with the last line of the table and then consider the other lines. First, as is evident from the Academy of Gondishapur's influence in the period immediately preceding the year 666, Sorath works on the level of the "I." Second, in terms of the interventions of Lucifer, Ahriman, and the Asuras, these began at certain specific times in humanity's evolution: a) the intervention of Lucifer began in connection with the event known as the Fall and, in fact, actually brought about the Fall; b) the intervention of Ahriman/Satan took place later, in the time preceding the Biblical Flood and contributed towards bringing about the Flood; and c) the intervention of the Asuras is something new, which in 1909 Steiner prophesied would begin to manifest itself increasingly during the course of the twentieth century.[112] Indeed, it is evident that Steiner's prophecy concerning the intervention of the Asuras (who here and there exerted an influence already during the earlier part of the twentieth century) began in full force during the 1960s—in the wake of the great conjunction of all seven planets in Capricorn on February 5, 1962, the date in Jeane Dixon's vision of the birth of the human being destined to become the Antichrist.[113] To understand why this date relating to the incarnation of Ahriman is important in terms of the intervention of the Asuras requires some elucidation. First let us consider Steiner's words concerning the Asuras:

> These asuric powers are heralded today by the prevailing tendency to live wholly in the material world and to be oblivious of the reality of spiritual beings and spiritual worlds. True, the asuric powers corrupt the human being today [1909] in a way that is more theoretical than actual. Today they deceive the human being by various means into thinking that the "I" is a product of the physical world only; they imbue the human being with a kind of theoretical materialism. But as time goes on—and the premonitory signs of this are the dissolute, sensuous passions that are becoming increasingly prevalent on Earth—they will blind the human being's vision of the spiritual beings and spiritual powers. Human beings will know nothing nor desire to know anything of a spiritual world. More and more it will be taught not only that the highest moral ideals of humanity are merely sublimations of animal impulses...but also human beings will take this view in all earnestness and will order their lives in accordance with it.... Human beings will also live like animals, will sink into animal impulses, animal passions. And

in many things that need not be further characterized here, many things that in the great cities come to expression in orgies of dissolute sensuality, we can already perceive the lurid, hellish glare of the spirits we call the Asuras.[114]

These words reveal something of the background to the great revolution that began in the 1960s. "The Asuras are only now intervening...They are by far the most destructive, and mainly work in the sexual life, therefore in the physical body. The many sexual aberrations of the present age can be traced back to this strong influence."[115] Here it is important to note that Steiner is not speaking about sexuality in general, but about "sexual aberrations" (we need only think of the increasing problem of child pornography and prostitution, for example, to understand what he means).

It may seem to be a contradiction here that reference is made to the intervention of the Asuras in the physical body, whereas in the earlier tabulation the reference is to their intervention in the consciousness soul. Without going into the complexities regarding the intricate relationships between the different levels within the human being, briefly it can be said that the consciousness soul is that part of the human being's soul life that arises on account of the conscious experience of the "I" in the physical body, whereas the sentient soul and the intellectual soul arise in relation to the experience of the "I" in the astral and etheric bodies—as summarized in the above table.

Returning to the question of the intervention of the Asuras in the wake of the planetary configuration of February 5, 1962: Why is this significant? As indicated, the interventions of Lucifer, Ahriman, and the Asuras have occurred sequentially during the Earth's evolution: a) that of Lucifer initially on the level of the astral body, then later infiltrating into the sentient soul; b) that of Ahriman first on the level of the etheric body, then subsequently penetrating into the intellectual soul; and c) now that of the Asuras on the level of the physical body, simultaneously infiltrating the consciousness soul. It can be seen that a), b), and c) are levels within the human being. One can see that there is a stepwise infiltration. The interesting point is that Ahriman's infiltration came in the wake of Lucifer's intervention. "Ahriman makes his appearance as the karma of Lucifer.... Ahriman would have been unable to interfere in evolution...were it not for Lucifer."[116] By the same token, the Asuras are the karma of Ahriman. Their widespread intervention beginning in the 1960s was made possible by the commencement of Ahriman's approach into incarnation signified by the birth in 1962 of a human being destined to be the vessel for Ahriman's incarnation.

A careful study of the events of that time reveals that in order to pave the way for this incarnation the assassinations of both John F. Kennedy and his brother Bobby Kennedy were necessary. For, as Jeane Dixon points out, "The vibrations of the members of the Kennedy family are extremely powerful," and thus J. F. Kennedy and his brother represented a hindrance for the plans of Ahriman pertaining to his incarnation. With the birth on February 5, 1962, of a human vessel for this incarnation, it was not long before an opportunity presented itself to assassinate President John F. Kennedy—in Dallas on November 22, 1963. This was followed by the assassination of Bobby Kennedy on June 5, 1968, at the very spot in the Ambassador Hotel in Los Angeles where Jeane Dixon had foreseen that it would take place.[117] The point here is not to go into detail about the background to these assassinations—there are some meticulous studies that do this[118]—but to be aware that because of the "extremely powerful vibration of these members of the Kennedy family," combined with their enormously influential positions (as president and potential president of the United States), they would have led this country in a different direction than that intended by Satan/Ahriman, who had just begun his "earthly career" in 1962. Therefore, from Ahriman's perspective, they had to be eliminated. It goes without saying that there have also been many other occurrences—apart from these two assassinations—that took place as part of the process preparing the United States for Ahriman's incarnation, one of these being the events of September 11, 2001, which is referred to again briefly below and which is discussed in greater detail in chapter 9 of this book.

In contemplating the stepwise interventions of Lucifer, Ahriman, and the Asuras, it is important to grasp that each level of evil has its own intention, not necessarily aligned with that of the other levels. As mentioned in chapter 3, Rudolf Steiner pointed above all to the polarity between the luciferic (light) and ahrimanic (dark) forces of opposition, with Christ in between, who holds the balance between Lucifer and Ahriman. Lucifer seeks to lead human beings away from earthly reality through flights of fantasy, and so on. Thereby Lucifer tries to entice human souls into his kingdom, a false paradise removed from the Earth, with the goal ultimately that human beings remain there never to reincarnate upon the Earth again, thus separating them from Christ, who has united with the Earth, and not allowing them to fulfill their God-given mission on the Earth, a mission that is to be fulfilled together with Christ during the course of many, many incarnations. On the other hand Ahriman endeavors to bind human beings to the Earth, to enslave humanity under his sole direction as vassals in his dark kingdom in opposition to the rest of the universe. Hence Ahriman's striving is—through incarnating upon the Earth— to become world ruler. At that time in the early twentieth century the asuric intervention (1960s) had not yet entered in fully, and the sorathic intervention foreseen around 1998 also still lay in the future, which is why Rudolf Steiner did not give so much attention to Sorath and the Asuras. It was not yet time. But now it is, which is one of the reasons for going into this subject here in this book.

In her book *The Descent into the Layers of the Earth* Judith von Halle communicates that now is the time to know about all four levels of evil as well, of course, as "dedicating oneself to the Christ Mystery with one's whole thinking, feeling, and will."[119] She points out that not only does Sorath attack the "I" in the human being (she speaks about the *destruction* of the "I" by Sorath—and the only protection against this is the experience of Christ in one's "I" in the sense of St. Paul's words: "Not I, but Christ in me"), but also that Sorath utilizes the other three levels—the interventions of Lucifer, Ahriman, and the Asuras—to achieve his ends.

Returning to consider that the Asuras are the karma of Ahriman and that therefore their intervention in humanity's evolution on a widespread scale was timed to coincide more or less with the birth of a human being on February 5, 1962, destined to be the vessel of the incarnation of Ahriman, it is important to grasp the polarity: Ahriman—Asuras, just as Rudolf Steiner focused upon the polarity Lucifer—Ahriman. Ahriman's vision is aptly characterized thus: "Imagine a world of factories, clubs, sports, political meetings, utilitarian universities, utilitarian arts or recreations—in which you would hear not a single word of praise for the Holy Trinity."[120] To this list could be added: banks, computers, shopping malls, fast-food restaurants, etc. In other words, the world as a great smooth-running operation in which human beings function like cogs in a machine without ever giving a thought to Christ or the existence of the spiritual world in which our world is embedded. "The synagogue of Satan, Ahriman's congregation...names the ahrimanic cultural community...the essence of that culture being the...we-consciousness...of being the nuts and bolts of a machine."[121] (The "synagogue of Satan" is an expression used in Revelation 3:9, which aptly designates the community of human beings at the present time who have fallen under Ahriman's influence).

Against this background it emerges that the modern Western world has already taken on the appearance of an ahrimanic cultural community to a certain extent. A contrast to this smooth-running operation of an ahrimanic world is brought in by the Asuras (as the karma of Ahriman). The focus of the Asuras is on the physical body and their activity comes to expression on the one hand in sensuality, which binds the "I" to the physical body, and on the other hand in physical destruction, since—if they are unable to bind the "I" to the physical—then they seek to destroy the physical. In certain esoteric traditions the physical body is referred to as the temple of the spirit, i.e., it is the temple of the "I," which is a manifestation of the conscious spirit. The Asuras have no respect for this temple of the spirit and seek either to desecrate it through inciting the human being to acts of gross sensuality or to simply destroy it. The smoothly operating ahrimanic world is an invitation to the destructive force of the Asuras. The destruction of the World Trade Center on September 11, 2001, is an example of this, as is the whole phenomenon of terrorism. The act of blowing up, blowing to smithereens, including detonating oneself (as with the suicide bombers) is an asuric manifestation, showing total disregard for the physical body as the temple of the spirit.

A key to understanding the Asuras is contained in the words "sex and violence," which is how the "asuric spirits…prompt…the very core of the human being, the consciousness soul together with the "I," to unite with earthly materiality."[122] Thus, contemporary movie theaters—depending of course upon which movies are showing—are often teaching auditoriums for the Asuras to inculcate their message into human souls, with one film after another trying to out do previous films in terms of the level and number of acts of violence and sensuality. (This is not to condemn the medium of the cinema *per se*, but simply to draw attention to a tendency, as clearly there are also some very noble people, with lofty ideals and intentions, in the film industry.) The pernicious influence of the Asuras is the karma of modern ahrimanic culture, and in this sense it is world destiny that the phenomenon of terrorism has arisen in our time, the time of Ahriman's coming. The destruction wrought by terrorism and also the over-emphasis on sex and violence are aspects of the Asuric intervention that began in earnest in the 1960s. To understand the phenomena on a deeper level is already a step towards healing since, as every medical doctor knows, one has to first accurately diagnose the cause of illness, and then the next step is to find a remedy. And the remedy is Christ—he is the World Healer.

Now let us return to the main theme of this chapter, which is the redemption of Lucifer. As indicated in the text quoted above from Revelation 12, there is not only Satan (Ahriman) *but also his Angels.* The same applies to the other levels of evil. Thus, even if—as we shall see below—the process of Lucifer's redemption is underway, this does not mean that this process applies also to the Angels that serve Lucifer.

A central focus of this book is the three and a half years of The Beast, described in Revelation 13. This period lasts from the great solar eclipse of July 22, 2009, to the end of the Maya calendar at the winter solstice (December 21) in the year 2012.[123] In the language of traditional Christianity, The Beast is the incarnated Satan, also known as the Antichrist, and in Rudolf Steiner's terminology it is a matter of the "incarnation of Ahriman."[124] The Beast is aided and abetted by the prophet of The Beast, the human being connected with the rhythm of 666 (see chapter 7), who is a vessel or primary focus for the instreaming inspiration of Sorath connected with 1998 (3 x 666). Here it is a matter of considering the polarity Ahriman—Sorath. Rudolf Steiner, speaking in 1924, was looking ahead to 1998 at the end of the twentieth century: "[It] has already [been] decreed that at the end of this century Sorath will be on the loose again, so that the intention to sweep away anything spiritual will be deep-seated in large numbers of earthly souls.... That is why it is so important that all who are capable of doing so should strive for spirituality."[125] Here it is possible to see how the impulses of Sorath and Ahriman converge:

The Group by Rudolf Steiner

both have the "intention to sweep away anything spiritual." Yet their approaches are different, since they are working on different levels, as can be seen from the table on page 114. Ahriman's approach is more by way of the brute force of sheer power, financial and military, in order to gain world dominion—*full-spectrum dominance* is the modern term—whereas Sorath's way is more subtle, appealing to the "I" of the human being. In order to attain his long-term goal, at the present time Sorath is allying himself with the incarnation of Ahriman, intending to make use of what comes from this incarnation as something upon which he can build in future so as eventually himself to come to power and to make himself God.[126]

Now let us return to consider the polarity Lucifer–Ahriman, concerning which Rudolf Steiner said much more than he did about any of the other polarities that we have been considering. Steiner's most powerful and profound statement concerning Lucifer and Ahriman is summarized in his great sculptural creation known as "The Representative of Humanity," which on the one hand depicts Christ in the middle between Lucifer (above) and Ahriman (below), and on the other hand, alongside Christ, an additional portrayal showing Lucifer above Ahriman, with the two interlocking. Also known as *The Group*, it portrays the group of spiritual beings whose role is so decisive for the evolution of humanity. This majestic thirty-foot-high wooden sculpture, which Steiner worked on together with the English sculptor Edith Maryon in the years 1914 to 1921, portrays Christ as the vanquisher in the three temptations in the wilderness. Rudolf Steiner describes these events in his lecture series entitled *The Fifth Gospel*, and which are to be found—in the reverse order to which they actually occurred—in the gospels of Matthew and Luke, chapter 4.[127] In the temptation of the will to power ("All the kingdoms of the world I will give you, if you fall down and worship me"), Lucifer alone tempted Christ, but the temptation was overcome by Christ's words: "You shall worship the Lord your God, and him only shall you serve." Above Christ, where Christ's upward-stretched left arm holds the upside-down Lucifer at bay, Lucifer plunges down from the heights, upside-down, expressing the impact of Christ's words upon him when his temptation is overcome. Lucifer, who is full of pride, vainglory, and self-love, is cast down not only by the truth of the words of Christ indicating that he should serve God and God alone, but also because of being in close proximity to Christ. "Christ stands there as Love incarnate. Lucifer is not plunging down because Christ casts him down, but rather because he is in close proximity to Christ, and he cannot bear being close to the being who is Love incarnate."[128]

In the case of the temptation of plunging from the pinnacle of the temple, Steiner indicates that Lucifer *and* Ahriman together approached Christ to tempt him; it is this union of Lucifer and Ahriman that is depicted on the left side (from the viewer's perspective) of the wooden statue that reveals this second temptation—to cast oneself down from the pinnacle of the temple—Christ responded: "You shall not tempt the Lord your God."[129] With these words, Christ vanquished Lucifer and Ahriman in their joint attempt to assail him. For modern human beings this means that—as conscious, sovereign, and free beings—it is possible to refuse temptation, if one chooses to do so.[130]

The third temptation, that of turning stones to bread, is the ahrimanic temptation—Ahriman alone—and it is this temptation that is so significant for the present time, signifying humanity's encounter with Ahriman (as the Antichrist), just as two thousand years ago Christ encountered him in the wilderness and vanquished him. Christ's vanquishing of Ahriman shows Ahriman withdrawn into the cave of the earth, with Christ above, holding him in his place through the gesture of his downward-stretched right arm. The words of Christ, "Man shall not live by bread alone, but by every word that proceeds from the mouth of God," are that which holds the vanquished Ahriman in his rightful place, since these words express the truth, and Ahriman is held in check by the truth. The truth is that all existence owes its origin to that which proceeds from the Divine. The spiritual is primary, and material existence is secondary. It is this fundamental truth that Ahriman endeavors to conceal through materialism, leading human beings to behold only the material world and not to experience that the material realm is embedded in an all-embracing spiritual reality. Christ's reply goes straight to the heart of the matter, that the very existence of the human being depends upon the all-encompassing spiritual reality around. While this higher spiritual reality may not be seen by the majority of human beings of the present time, it is perceptible to those whose clairvoyant faculties are awakened. One of the remarkable aspects of the present moment, where so many institutions of the modern materialist West are failing, is that a clear picture is presented of the futility—and even deadly danger—of a civilization that attempts to live "by bread alone." No clairvoyance at all is necessary to grasp this, and this newfound realization is a first step toward a conscious seeking of a relationship to the restorative powers of Christ.

The wooden statue carved by Rudolf Steiner and Edith Maryon offers a powerful depiction as to how—together with Christ, through Christ within—it is possible to overcome the forces and temptations of Lucifer and Ahriman and hold them in their rightful place. However, as Steiner points out, whereas the first two temptations were *completely* vanquished by Christ, the third temptation—presented by Ahriman alone—was *not fully overcome*, since it is true that as long as we live upon the Earth, we do need bread, i.e., food, to live.[131] Thus, it is possible to speak of the redemption of Lucifer, but not—at least, not yet, at the present stage of humanity's evolution—of the redemption of Ahriman. This becomes clear when we contemplate the scene of the Crucifixion at the Mystery of Golgotha.

Christ was crucified between two criminals. One, the *repentant* criminal, was crucified to Christ's right, and the other, the *unrepentant* criminal, was crucified to his left. During the Crucifixion, the repentant criminal recognized that Christ was being crucified unjustly, was innocent, and was representing a higher, divine order of existence. On this account he spoke these words to Christ: "Jesus, remember me, when you come into your kingdom." And Jesus responded: "Today, you will be with me in paradise" (Luke 23:42–43). Meanwhile, the unrepentant criminal, while being crucified, taunted and cursed Jesus.

The two criminals on either side of Christ represent Lucifer and Ahriman, and the repentance of the good criminal points to the mystery of the redemption of Lucifer beginning at the Mystery of Golgotha. "The conversion took place within him when, looking at the Crucifixion on Golgotha, it pierced him with the insight that it was in fact he who should have experienced these sufferings. And now the other was bearing them in his place.... The inner conversion of Lucifer began."[132] Since it was Lucifer who through his intervention had brought about the Fall, and since the reason for Christ's sacrifice was to overcome the consequences of the Fall, Lucifer thus came to realize that, rightfully, he should have been the one to bear the sufferings, not Christ.

The good criminal's words to Jesus reflect the awakening of conscience in Lucifer in beholding the Crucifixion. A stream of inspiration proceeded from Lucifer to the good criminal, who responded accordingly and showed his repentance in his words to Christ. By the same token, the unrepentant criminal was receiving a stream of inspiration from Ahriman, and this criminal's attitude during the Crucifixion, expressed through his taunting and cursing, reflect the hateful attitude of Ahriman towards Christ. Therefore, whereas it is possible to speak about the redemption of Lucifer, it is premature to speak along these lines regarding Ahriman, since it is only where there is a willingness to be redeemed that redemption is possible, and the wall of hatred streaming from Ahriman towards Christ precludes this possibility—at least, for the time being. It is conceivable that a change could come about in Ahriman's attitude towards Christ at some future point in time.

The wooden statue, *The Group*, portrays Lucifer as tempter—as a lone tempter, and also as a tempter interlocked with Ahriman—and does not allude explicitly to the redemption of Lucifer. *The Group* was intended by Rudolf Steiner to be placed in the central position of the wooden building, the first Goetheanum, that he designed and built, with the help of many people from different countries during World War I. However, *The Group* (the central figure being "The Representative of Humanity," Christ) was still in Rudolf Steiner's atelier (he had not quite finished working on the statue), when on the evening of December 31, 1922, the first Goetheanum burned down. Thereby the statue was spared the fate of going up in flames together with the beautiful wooden building that was intended to house it.

Now, in considering the redemption of Lucifer, it emerges that this is actually a *central theme* in relation to the date 2012, as we shall see below. First, though, let us consider some statements regarding the redemption of Lucifer:

> It is a fact that when human beings looked into their inner being, when they sought the way to the world of the gods through the veil of their inner being, they entered—to use a collective name—the luciferic world. This too was the path upon which, in those olden times, human beings sought for wisdom...one being, who is the great teacher of all civilizations. The being who was the teacher of the holy rishis, of Zarathustra, of Hermes— the being whom we may designate as the Great Teacher...is designated, by means of an expression borrowed from the East, as the *totality of the bodhisattvas*. The Christian conception would designate it the *Holy Spirit*. The bodhisattva is a being who passes through all civilizations...as a part of that being who is the personified all-wisdom of our world. In this sense, then, we gaze upon the Wisdom element that in olden times was imparted to humankind from the luciferic worlds.[133]

After discussing the bodhisattva spiritual stream associated with Lucifer, and then the other spiritual stream connected with Christ, a union and cross-fertilization between these two streams is indicated:

In this way will come to pass the mutual fertilization of these two evolutionary streams of humanity. It has already begun; it began at the moment indicated in the story which tells us that the sacrificial blood of the Christ flowing from the Cross was received into the vessel of the Holy Grail and brought to the West from the East, where preparation for the understanding of the incarnation of Christ had been made in a very definite way by cultivating that which represents the light of Lucifer. In this way the union of these two streams in humanity will become more and more complete. Whatever humankind of the present time may say or do, the healing of the future humanity will be accomplished by the fact that within the union of the two streams, the mighty Christ being, guiding as he does the evolution of the universe and of humanity, is understood through the light received by the soul from within, out of the kingdom of Lucifer. Christ will give the substance, Lucifer the form, and from their union will arise impulses which shall permeate the spiritual evolution of humankind, and bring about what the future has in store for the healing and the blessing of the peoples.[134]

This is quoted at length because of its significance regarding the theme of the redemption of Lucifer. What is not addressed in the above words is that the participation of human beings is also essential in relation to the redemptive process, since the luciferic influence is *within* each human being. This influence inserted itself into the human astral body at the time of the Fall, which took place long ago in that period of the Earth's evolution known as Lemuria.[135] Through the luciferic influence, human beings acquired freedom, as discussed in detail in the last chapter of this book. Mention is made there also of the fact that with the coming of Christ, the Divine I AM consciousness came in seed form for humanity, as something that each human being can take into themselves. Through the I AM, a force begins to work in the human being—first on the level of the "I"—which then works down into the astral body as a redeeming impulse, gradually transforming the luciferic influence into something highly beneficial. "The time will come when the luciferic powers...will experience the power of Christ through human beings, and so will be redeemed.... It would have been impossible for us to progress in goodness, truth, and wisdom to the degree that we now can...[without having] to overcome these countervailing forces."[136]

It emerges from these indications that the work of overcoming and redeeming the forces of evil begins with the redemption of Lucifer, and that this is possible through the working of Christ within in the sense of St. Paul's words, "Not I, but Christ in me," which are also a protection against the influence of Sorath on the human "I." While the redemption of Lucifer on a cosmic level began with Christ's sacrifice on Golgotha, with the perspective that the working together of Christ and Lucifer will bring "the healing and the blessing of the peoples," there still remains the task for each individual human being to redeem the luciferic nature within themselves.

Perhaps the best way of grasping what this means is with reference to *The Group* statue. Indeed, it was precisely on this account that Rudolf Steiner created the wooden statue of *The Group* as a source of guidance and inspiration to human beings on their spiritual path. The luciferic nature within each human being is to be redeemed, and the ahrimanic nature within each human being is to be held in check—this is the deeper message of *The Group*. The far-reaching consequences of the inner work of redeeming one's own interior luciferic nature are brought out in the following passage:

> When one knows Christ, when one absorbs the wisdom that begets insight into who Christ truly is, then one redeems oneself and the luciferic beings through this knowledge of Christ.... These luciferic beings who have brought humanity freedom, also make it possible for one, *if one so wills*, to turn it to account in order to understand Christ. Then the luciferic spirits are cleansed and purified in the fire of Christianity and the wrong done to the Earth by them is changed into blessing.... Lucifer, resurrected in a new form, can unite with Christ as the good Spirit—this, as prophecy still, was told by Christ himself to those around him, when he said, "Ye shall be illumined by the

new Spirit, by the Holy Spirit!"... This "Holy Spirit" is none other than the Lucifer spirit, resurrected now in higher, purer glory—the spirit of independent understanding, wisdom inwoven.... The torch of the resurrected Lucifer, of the Lucifer now transformed into the good, blazons the way for Christ. Lucifer is the bearer of the Light—Christ is the Light! As the word itself denotes, Lucifer is the "Bearer of the Light."... Thus the Earth will more and more become the expression of its spirit, of the Christ spirit.[137]

Against this background, let us now consider the significance of the year 2012. As elaborated upon in this book, 2012 is a momentous date in humankind's evolution. On the one hand it has to do with the coming of the Antichrist, the incarnated Ahriman. On the other hand it has to do with the redemption of Lucifer. Humanity is called upon to awaken in two directions simultaneously: to recognize Ahriman and to keep him in check through the power of Christ within, and to allow the inner force of Christ to redeem and transform the luciferic to become the "Bearer of the Light" of the Holy Spirit. This is the deeper message at the present time of the wooden statue known as *The Group*. Having said this, it is necessary to clarify the expression "Holy Spirit" used here by Steiner.

The Holy Trinity—three aspects of the Godhead in one: Father, Son, and Holy Spirit—is at the heart of Christian theology. The Father is the Creator; the Son is the Logos, the Word, who enacted the creation and entered into the creation in order to redeem it; the Holy Spirit is the Enlightener, who brings spiritual awakening. These are the three Persons of the Holy Trinity. The clarification that is necessary here is that Rudolf Steiner—as far as I can tell—did not intend a straightforward identification of Lucifer with the third Person (*Hypostasis*) of the Trinity known as the Holy Spirit, and thus in the above citation the expression is always written "Holy Spirit" (in quotes). Rather, Steiner was identifying Lucifer with the Spirit that Christ would send, whom Christ "foretold that this Spirit would come to human beings after Him." This is the Spirit who in the Greek text of the Gospels is referred to as the *Paraclete*. While the *Paraclete* acts in the sense of the Holy Spirit, the *Paraclete*—contrary to what is taught by most modern theologians—is not identical with the Holy Spirit. "The *Paraclete* is not the Holy Spirit as the third *Hypostasis* of the Holy Trinity, but a revelation of the third *Hypostasis* such as was effected by the combined influences of Sophia and Lucifer."[138]

The Holy Spirit as the third Person (*Hypostasis*) of the Holy Trinity—being eternal—has always existed, whereas Lucifer is a created being, a being of the ranks of the spiritual (angelic) hierarchies.[139] Sophia, on the other hand, as the "Bride of the Lamb" (Revelation 21:9)—the Lamb being the name in Revelation for Christ, the Son, the second Person of the Holy Trinity, who is eternal—*is eternal.*[140] In order to understand the relationship between Lucifer and Sophia, it is helpful to consider the following account of the event of Pentecost:

> At the time of Pentecost, the twelve apostles represented a twelve-petalled flower in which the individual "petals" were arranged around a central point...Mary, the Mother of Jesus. In the Gnostic esoteric tradition, she is called the Virgin Sophia.... What is the nature of Mary Sophia and her role in bringing about the Pentecostal revelation?... Sophia manifests for human consciousness by bringing about the harmony of all spiritual hierarchies...She does not possess the force of *imagination*, the faculty for creating *imaginations*. She does not possess this faculty, because Lucifer robbed her of it.... When the Fall took place...Lucifer took for himself Sophia's imaginations.... At Pentecost, the barrier Lucifer had erected between Sophia and the realm of human consciousness was cleared...because of Lucifer's inner conversion at the Mystery of Golgotha.... At the hour of Pentecost Lucifer surrendered entirely to the Sophia impulse; he united with it and led it through his own being down to the life tableau of Christ where it reached human souls. In reality, the influence of Sophia united with that of Lucifer. It is the unified influence of these two beings that the Gospel of John calls the *Paraclete*, the Comforter.[141]

Something new came into existence at Pentecost: the *Paraclete*, the Comforter, promised by Christ, comprising the working together of the redeemed Lucifer with Divine Sophia. But what does this have to do with the year 2012?

In chapter 4—*Redeeming Lucifer, Rediscovering Itzamna*—it was pointed out that just as in Christian tradition Lucifer is the *morning star*, i.e., the planet Venus, Maya myth, religion, and astronomy identify Kukulkan with the planet Venus. Further, the Aztec Quetzalcoatl—at least, originally—was the same as the Maya Kukulkan. Also Rudolf Steiner spoke of "Lucifer, the Spirit of Venus."¹⁴² The Christian tradition shares the same image for Lucifer—that of the serpent—as in the Mesoamerican tradition, where both Quetzalcoatl and Kukulkan are represented as a plumed or feathered serpent. As already mentioned in chapter 4, the devotion of the Mayans to the serpent was so strong that they practiced the *polcan* operation on new born babies, which consisted of placing the head in a tight frame and thus forcing the head to take on certain serpent-like features, such as a flattened forehead and slanting eyes (*pol* = head; *can* = serpent).¹⁴³

In *La serpiente emplumada, eje de culturas* [*The Plumed Serpent: Axis of Cultures*] and in other works, José Díaz-Bolio (1906–1998) refers to the cult of the serpent underlying Maya culture. Díaz-Bolio was an unorthodox anthropologist from Yucatán, Mexico, who maintained that certain features of Maya civilization developed out of the reverence of the Maya for the *Ahau-Can* ("Supreme Serpent"). The *Ahau-Can* (*Crotalus durissus*) rattlesnake exists in Central and South America, and Díaz-Bolio presented the theory that the Maya calendar is based on certain biological features of this rattlesnake. For example, he noted the finding that the *Ahau-Can* rattlesnake grows new fangs every twenty days, and that, coincidentally, the twenty-day Uinal glyph from the Maya calendar shows two rattlesnake fangs, one on each side. Prior to this discovery, no one knew the reason for the twenty-day period as the basis for the Maya *Tzolkin* calendar. Also the central part of the dorsal skin of the *Ahau-Can* rattlers comprises a pattern of interlocking squares, the so-called *Canamayte*, whereby each side of the squares is formed by thirteen scales, and, the number thirteen appears by counting the number of labial (lip) scales on the *Ahau-Can*. In this way José Díaz-Bolio found a bio-mathematical basis for the 13 x 20 days of the Maya 260-day *Tzolkin* sacred calendar.

The ancient Maya were sophisticated astronomers, as demonstrated by the *Dresden Codex*, an ancient Maya book of the eleventh or twelfth century of the Yucatec Maya in Chichén Itzá, containing agricultural timing predictions and information on rainy seasons, floods, illness and medicine, and also showing a tabulation of a complete 584-day Venus cycle. The *Dresden Codex* and other archeological evidence show that the Maya assiduously observed Venus and also worshiped Kukulkan, the god of Venus, as their primary deity. The planet's synodic period (the time between successive conjunctions with the Sun) is 584 days, during which it sweeps out a five-pointed star (pentagram) on its orbital path both as morning and evening star, where the five points of the star are formed by the conjunctions of Venus with the Sun.[144] The inescapable conclusion here is that the Maya were followers of the god of Venus (i.e., Lucifer, to use Christian terminology). In other words, the Maya Kukulkan is identical with Lucifer of Christian tradition.

By implication, the same applies to the Aztecs, if Quetzalcoatl is identified with Kukulkan, which is usually taken for granted. However, given the far-reaching differences between the Maya and the Aztec cultures, a simple identification of Quetzalcoatl with Kukulkan is not so straightforward, even though the same image—that of a plumed or feathered serpent—applies to both and is indeed the meaning of both words: Kukulkan and Quetzalcoatl. In addition to the Aztecs and the Maya, other Mesoamerican civilizations that worshiped the plumed or feathered serpent include the Olmec, the Mixtec, and the Toltec, and there can be no doubt that originally it was a matter of worship of one and the same being: Lucifer, the god of Venus. Originally, therefore, it is possible to speak of an identity between Quetzalcoatl and Kukulkan. In the course of time, however, a radical divergence took place.

To understand the relationship between Kukulkan and the later Quetzalcoatl, it is helpful to borrow a concept from Jungian psychology: the *shadow*, lurking in the subconscious, which is understood to be the dark side of the human being, a repository of the human being's repressed weaknesses, shortcomings, and instincts. This shadow nature, when considered collectively, is denoted in the French language by the word *egregore*. As an example, it is possible to consider the Nazi movement in Germany as an expression of the *egregore* of the German people. If we consider the German people at the time of Goethe and Beethoven, in the early nineteenth century, it is apparent that there were a remarkable number of outstanding philosophers, scientists, composers, musicians, poets, and such. By contrast, the rise of the Nazi movement was a manifestation of the dark side of the German psyche—an *egregore*—that arose and took possession of the German people. Hitler became the voice of that *egregore*, symbolized by the "blonde beast" with its ferocious will to power. "Human beings would have been turned into a kind of 'centaur,' consisting of head and limbs (intellect and will), but without heart—in other words, a clever beast. Devotion to the Sacred Heart of Jesus had the task of rekindling the heart. Thereby the light, warmth, and life streaming from the heart of Jesus was to counteract the will to power and the intellect serving this will."[145]

The devastating practices connected with the sacrifice of the human heart described in chapters 3 and 4 are depicted there as inversions, and this is a good way of describing the *egregore*, the shadow side of the collective psyche. The *egregore* expresses the negative, the very opposite, of what is positive in the collective psyche. This relationship aptly summarizes the contrast between the Maya and the Aztec cultures. From a general perspective (and of course it is always dangerous to generalize, as there are always exceptions to the rule), the Aztec culture appears as the *egregore* of the Maya culture. The classical Maya culture was highly creative, innovative, and peace-loving. These qualities, which are characteristic of Lucifer's influence as god of the planet Venus, later became completely inverted in the bloodthirsty Aztec culture described in chapters 3 and 4. This leads to the conclusion that, at some point in Aztec history, the worship of Kukulkan-Lucifer became the worship of the *egregore,* or the dark side of Lucifer[146] under the name "Huitzilopochtli" (rather than Quetzalcoatl), as discussed in chapter 3.

As mentioned in chapter 4 of this book, one of the most popular authors on the subject of 2012, Daniel Pinchbeck, has cast it as "the return of Quetzalcoatl."[147] Of course, Pinchbeck is not thinking of the bloodthirsty Quetzalcoatl *egregore* that was worshiped under the name "Huitzilopochtli" in later Aztec culture. Rather, he has in mind the original wise and benevolent Quetzalcoatl—the Maya Kukulkan. Pinchbeck's ideas are symptomatic of a whole movement, the New Age movement. Many of the culturally creative people in this movement conceive of a paradisiacal culture arising in the wake of the winter solstice of the year 2012. Is this widespread view simply wishful thinking, or is there something real behind it?

From a Christian perspective, Lucifer is associated with the Fall and the expulsion of humanity from paradise. At that time Lucifer created his own realm, the luciferic sphere, also known as the "belt of lies,"[148] surrounding the Earth. It is this "belt of lies" or "sphere of mirages" into which the human being is brought into contact through the working of the unredeemed Lucifer. In the description above of Pentecost, the redeemed Lucifer, by surrendering to Sophia (Divine Wisdom), facilitated the instreaming of Sophia's blessing at Pentecost, whereby this Sophianic grace, because it was united with the working of the redeemed Lucifer, signified an overcoming of the Fall and, correspondingly, an experience of the breath of paradise. This paradisiacal quality is the hallmark of the *Paraclete*, the Comforter, which could be the gift of the cosmic event of the galactic alignment in 2012, just as there was a galactic alignment at the original event of Pentecost.[149]

In chapter 1, a Maya depiction (interpreted by some to relate to the Galactic Center) is presented, as drawn by Linda Schele. It is from the central panel of the Temple of the Cross at Palenque in Chiapas, a vertical, up-ended ("Moses style") serpent crowned by a bird. Perhaps this bird is a representation of the quetzal, a strikingly colored long-tailed bird native to Central America. Bird (*quetzal*) + serpent = *Quetzal + coatl;* since the serpent is transformed from a creeping to an up-ended position, it is redeemed and crowned by the bird as an image of higher consciousness. The etymology of the word *quetzal* is from Nahuatl *quetzalli*, "large brilliant tail feather," from the Nahuatl root *quetz*, meaning "stand up," referring to the upstanding plume of feathers.

Let us call to mind again that the galactic alignment at the winter solstice 2012 signifies that the Sun at 5° Sagittarius will be at the intersection (5° Sagittarius) of the Milky Way with the sidereal zodiac in the area between the tip of the Archer's arrow and the sting at the tail of the Scorpion and that in this area the Galactic Center is located at 2° Sagittarius.[150] As the Milky Way (and also the zodiac) is seen as a broad band of stars, the whole area around 5° Sagittarius is a band of intersection between the two great defining circles—the zodiac and the Milky Way—of the starry heavens. Without going into too much detail here, briefly it may be said that these two circles are the outer manifestation of higher planes of existence in which our existence (as humanity on Earth) is embedded.

The Milky Way is the outer visible manifestation of the galactic plane of existence that corresponds to the divine world, and the zodiac outwardly represents to our visual senses the boundary of our cosmos that corresponds to the spiritual world. The places of intersection of these two circles in the early degrees of Sagittarius (and also on the opposite side of the zodiac in the early degrees of Gemini) signify "gateways" leading from the spiritual world to the divine world, also where impulses from the divine world can flow into the spiritual world and thus into our cosmos. These regions of intersection (early degrees of Gemini and Sagittarius) are therefore areas of high pressure or high tension. No wonder that divine revelation on the one hand and crisis on the other hand is often the signature of the passage of the Sun, Moon, or planets across these areas. We need only consider that at the event of Pentecost the Sun was located at 2½° Gemini.[151] Here the Holy Spirit, pictured as tongues of flame above the heads of the disciples, flowed in from the galactic plane, the divine world, as an archetypal revelation of the Divine.

By contrast, on August 1, 1914, when Saturn was at 4° Gemini, World War I broke out. This was a historical crisis of the first magnitude, when the consciousness of world leaders was clouded, rather than illumined by the light of the Holy Spirit. Destructive forces were unleashed at that moment in time. And when Saturn reached the opposite gateway, at 2½° Sagittarius, on Friday, October 25, 1929, there took place the Wall Street "Black Friday" slump, opening the greatest stock market crash of the twentieth century, which continued until Tuesday, October 29 (Saturn at 3° Sagittarius), during which time an estimated fifty billion dollars were lost through the drop in share prices. In the heavens Saturn was crossing the gateway to the divine world, having reached conjunction with the Galactic Center (2° Sagittarius) on October 17, just eight days before the "Black Friday" crash.

Thus, it may be seen that such galactic alignments are extremely potent, either in a positive sense (Pentecost) or in a negative sense, precipitating crisis. It is important to remember, also, that it is not just the winter solstice in the year 2012 but every winter solstice in the "2012 window" from 1980 to 2016 that constitutes a galactic alignment. What makes the year 2012 particularly significant within this window, returning to our theme of Venus and the influence of Lucifer (redeemed or unredeemed), is that on June 6, 2012, there is a transit of Venus across the face of the Sun, which is a great astronomical event.[152] Considering the significance of Venus for the Maya people, perhaps 2012 really does hold something of the promise of the "return of Kukulkan"? If so, the question is: Will this "return"—in the sense of the redeemed Lucifer—be a Pentecostal manifestation of the *Paraclete*, or Comforter? Or will it be an intervention of the unredeemed luciferic influence, the *egregore*? The answer to this question depends upon humanity.

What can be said is that the whole of humankind is currently undergoing a great trial, and the image presented by the wooden statue of *The Group*, referred to earlier, summarizes this trial, particularly if we focus upon "The Representative of Humanity" (Christ) in the middle, with Lucifer above and Ahriman below. This image is of the unredeemed Lucifer, the one who, as described earlier, seeks to entice human beings, through wild flights of fantasy and other means, into his "sphere of mirages" (the false paradise). Christ—Love incarnate—within the human being brings about the transformation of the luciferic nature within human beings, giving rise to the possibility of the redeemed Lucifer to bestow blessing, together with Sophia, as the *Paraclete* or Comforter. This is the deeper meaning of the words of the Risen Christ to John on the island of Patmos: "I will give you the morning star" (Revelation 2:28). Here, with these words, Christ is promising the true Spirit of Venus, the morning star, to humanity (the Romans called Venus, as Morning Star, Lucifer). This is one aspect of 2012.

The other aspect and a primary focus in this book is the ahrimanic temptation, in terms of the image presented by *The Group* coming from below in contrast to Lucifer's presence above. Again, it is Christ who holds Ahriman in check, and thus for humanity of the present time undergoing the ahrimanic temptation, it is Christ within who enables us to vanquish Ahriman.

In summary, the New Age began in 1899 with the onset of Christ's Second Coming in the aura of the Earth (becoming a reality in human consciousness in 1933). Since then, the work of Christ in the etheric realm has been underway. On account of this activity of Christ, the gradual redemption of the luciferic nature of human beings is also underway, and it is partly this which has given rise to the New Age movement. This redemptive work is only at its beginning; and so, while it is not possible to say that the year 2012 signifies historically a culminating point in the process of Lucifer's redemption, neverthe-less—with the Venus transit and the galactic alignment and, most important, the end of the three and a half years of the Antichrist—it would appear that there is a possibility of a Pentecostal revelation beginning then. Right now, however, the return of Christ in the ethe-ric is being countered by the temptation of Ahriman coming upon the whole of humankind, and the actual incarnation of Ahriman in the flesh represents the culmination of this temptation.

If it were only Lucifer and Ahriman at work, humanity would grad-ually divide into two groups: on the one hand the spiritually oriented New Agers and on the other hand the rest of humankind embroiled in present-day ahrimanic culture. With Christ in the middle, however, the ahrimanic temptation can be overcome, and the New Age will find its fulfillment in the Pentecostal revelation of the *Paraclete*, the Comforter, cosmically preordained to begin in 2012—to which date the Maya, through their devotion to Kukulkan-Lucifer, were attuned. I believe this is why so much spiritual hope and expectation is focused upon the year 2012.

This excursus on the redemption of Lucifer would not be complete, however, without also referring to Sophia, even if only briefly, as the Divine Feminine is a vast theme in itself. First, though, let us return to consider Venus in the context of the revelation to John on the island of Patmos over nineteen hundred years ago: "I will give you the morning star" (paraphrase from Revelation 2:28). The one who is speaking to

John is Christ, referred to in Revelation as the Lamb, since he says: "He who conquers and who keeps my works unto the end, I will give him power...even as I myself have received power from my Father; and I will give him the morning star" (Revelation 2: 26–28). These words that were addressed to John over nineteen hundred years ago are now, in this time of Christ's Second Coming, addressed to all human beings, hence the paraphrase: "I will give you the morning star," whereby it is implicit in these words that there is a conditional clause: "If you conquer and if you keep my works unto the end."

As I have described elsewhere, the planet Venus (referred to in Revelation as the "morning star") describes in its orbit around the Sun the sphere or globe of the next stage of evolution, spoken of in Revelation as the Heavenly Jerusalem.[153] In saying, "I will give you the morning star," the Risen One is pointing to the future abode of humanity after the present Earth evolution will have come to an end. And in the references to the Heavenly Jerusalem in the last two chapters of Revelation it is indicated that the Bride of the Lamb, Divine Sophia, plays a central role in the arising of the Heavenly Jerusalem:

> Come, I will show you the Bride, the wife of the Lamb. And in the Spirit he [an Angel] carried me away to a great, high mountain, and showed me the holy city Jerusalem coming down out of heaven from God, having the glory of God. (Revelation 21:9–10)

The descent of Divine Sophia, the Bride of the Lamb, is proclaimed by the Russian seer, Daniel Andreev (1906–1959) in his magnum opus *The Rose of the World,*[154] and it is also foretold in Revelation, where it is indicated in these words from Revelation quoted above that Sophia is indeed the very heart of the Heavenly Jerusalem. Therefore it is not solely Lucifer but also Sophia who holds a key to understanding the orbit of Venus around the Sun, since Sophia's realm, together with the Lamb, is that of the Heavenly Jerusalem, the realm that will be located within the orbit of Venus around the Sun, just as the present stage of evolution is located on the Earth orbiting around the Sun. Sophia's inspiration enters from the future, as it were, since she is already there, at the center of the Heavenly Jerusalem. Her inspiration, among other things, is to draw forth each human being's *creativity*. For, by becoming creative, we draw nearer to the Creator. For this reason Sophia was called in the Middle Ages the Patron (or Patroness) of the arts. In light of the foregoing, the year 2012 can be seen just as much in relation to Sophia as to Lucifer (redeemed or unredeemed) and on this account, I would like to close this chapter with these words by Daniel Andreev: "By warning about the coming Antichrist, and pointing him out and unmasking him when he appears, by cultivating unshakeable faith within human hearts and a grasp of the meta-historical perspectives and global spiritual prospects within human minds, it will inure generations and generations against the temptations of the future spawn of darkness." In other words, we help Sophia bring to birth the new culture of love and wisdom, which Andreev calls "The Rose of the World."

> [Sophia's] birth in one of the *zatomis* will be mirrored not only by the Rose of the World. Feminine power and its role in contemporary life is increasing everywhere. It is that circumstance above all that is giving rise to worldwide peace movements, an abhorrence of bloodshed, disillusion over coercive methods of change, an increase in woman's role in society proper, an ever-growing tenderness and concern for children, and a burning hunger for beauty and love. We are entering an age when the female soul will become ever purer and broader, when an ever greater number of women will become profound inspirers, sensitive mothers, wise counselors and far-sighted leaders. It will be an age when the feminine in humanity will manifest itself with unprecedented strength, striking a perfect balance with masculine impulses. See, you who have eyes. [155]

These words of Daniel Andreev, the great prophet of the coming Age of Sophia, offer inspiration regarding the future Sophianic culture that he called "The Rose of the World." (In the above quote, *zatomis* refers to a heavenly realm within the Earth's aura.) Andreev refers to Sophia as *Zventa-Sventana*, meaning "the Holiest of the Holy."

> A mysterious event is taking place in the meta-history of contemporary times: new divine-creative energy is emanating into our cosmos. Since ancient times the loftiest hearts and most subtle minds have anticipated this event that is now

taking place. The first link in the chain of events—events so important that they can only be compared to the incarnation of the Logos—occurred at the turn of the nineteenth century. This was an emanation of the energy of the Virgin Mother, an emanation that was not amorphous, as it had been before in human history [at Pentecost, when there was an emanation of Sophia into the Virgin Mary], but incomparably intensified by the personal aspect it assumed. A great God-born monad descended from the heights of the universe into our cosmos.[156]

The words of the great Russian seer, Daniel Andreev, are prophetic words. As I have indicated elsewhere,[157] he points to the descent of Sophia and the resulting Sophianic world culture, the Rose of the World, in a most inspiring way:

> She is to be born in a body of enlightened ether... There She is, our hope and joy, Light and Divine Beauty! For Her birth will be mirrored in our history as something that our grandchildren and great-grandchildren will witness: the founding of the Rose of the World, its spread throughout the world, and...the assumption by the Rose of the World of supreme authority over the entire Earth.[158]

Could it be that the year 2012—with the Venus transit and the galactic alignment—will see a decisive impulse toward the arising of the Rose of the World? In light of the research presented in this book, especially in chapters 9 and 10, this question is answered in the affirmative.

9. THE ROSE OF THE WORLD

"Rose of the World" (*Rosa Mira* in Russian) is the name that Daniel Andreev gave to the future global community of humanity, which is destined to arise through the influence of Divine Sophia in creating a new culture—initially in Russia and the Slavic countries, and then worldwide. Andreev, as well as others (notably Rudolf Steiner, who referred to this future culture as the "sixth cultural epoch"), have predicted a future community based on love. The designation in the book of Revelation is *Philadelphia,* meaning "brotherly and sisterly love." The coming Philadelphian community, according to the Apocalypse Code, is destined to arise during the Age of Aquarius, which lasts 2,160 years, from 2375 to 4535. This period of 2,160 years is the length of a zodiacal age, the time it takes for the vernal point to regress through thirty degrees (one zodiacal sign) at a rate of one degree every seventy-two years.[159]

This may seem like a far distant future, and one could ask: What does this have to do with the present? Considering that it is one of the strategies of Satan/Ahriman to preempt the future, *the current drive toward global dominion can be seen as an ahrimanic preempting of the Rose of the World.* Whether the peoples of the Earth like it or not, the world is to be forced into a New World Order. Before we look more closely at Andreev's penetrating vision, let us first consider who he was and under what circumstances he wrote his masterpiece entitled *The Rose of the World.*

Andreev, as a poet and very sensitive soul, had the misfortune to live in Russia during the time of Stalin. Poets, especially mystically inclined poets such as Andreev, were persecuted. Atheism was the official state doctrine, and the state was invested with unlimited powers to eradicate anything considered "spiritual." Andreev and his wife were arrested by Stalin's secret police in 1947, along with many of their relatives and friends. Andreev was sentenced to twenty-five years of prison and his wife to twenty-five years of labor camp. They were "fortunate" in so far as the death penalty in the Soviet Union had been temporarily suspended at that time. With his arrest, all of Andreev's writings were confiscated and destroyed.

Daniel Andreev, 1958

While in prison, his mystical experiences continued unabated and attained a new level of intensity. During the hours when his fellow prisoners were asleep, Andreev's spiritual guide allowed him to behold not only the spiritual realms but also demonic ones. Miraculously, he found opportunities to write down his spiritual experiences; even more miraculously, somehow his manuscript was spared during routine prison searches. Thus, his magnum opus, *The Rose of the World*, came into being. After Stalin's death, Andreev's prison sentence was reduced from twenty-five to ten years, and he was released in 1957. By this time, however, his health was so impaired that he lived only a short while after his release, until March 30, 1959. He had completed his manuscript and entrusted it to his wife. It was not until 1991, with the demise of the Soviet communist regime in Russia, that the full text of *The Rose of the World* could be published. It is estimated that, since then, more than a million Russians have since read the book. In 1997, it was published in English by Lindisfarne Books.[160]

Central to the book is Andreev's vision of the descent of Holy Sophia, *Zventa Sventana*, the Divine Wisdom of existence, from celestial heights as the bearer of a new culture to the Earth. The divinely ordained future Sophianic global community based on wisdom and love is currently being preempted by Ahriman's push for global dominion under his rule as the Antichrist. Andreev referred to this as the "deadliest of all threats":

> The strongest [state] will conquer the globe, even at the cost of turning one-third of the world's surface into a moonscape. The cycle of wars will come to an end, but only to be replaced by the greatest of evils: a single dictatorship over the surviving two-thirds of the world. At first it will perhaps be an oligarchy. But, as often happens, a single Leader will emerge. The threat of global dictatorship—this is the deadliest of all threats hanging over humanity...a dictatorship compared to which all previous tyrannies will seem like child's play.... Something not everyone takes into consideration...is a mystical fear, originating during the age of the Roman empire, of the future unification of the world. It is the indefatigable concern that in a single universal state lies a pitfall that will inevitably lead to an absolute dictatorship and the rule of the "prince of darkness.".... Such a tyranny would be all the more absolute because even the last tragic means of casting it off would be closed—its overthrow from without by war. With every nation under one rule, there would be no one to war against. Global unity—the dream of so many generations, the cause of so many sacrifices—would then reveal its demonic side: *the impossibility of escape* if the servants of the dark forces were to seize control of the world government. [161]

While seeing the danger of the world rule of the Antichrist very clearly, Andreev does not draw attention here to the prophecy of Revelation 13, which indicates that the "prince of darkness" is indeed destined to rule the world, but only for three and a half years. The Apocalypse Code reveals that this time is almost upon us—perhaps even the three and a half years from July 22, 2009, to December 21, 2012; or, if not, then some other three-and-a-half-year period prior to the end of the cosmic day (1988–2018) of the third temptation of humanity. Though more specific, this time indication is essentially the same as Rudolf Steiner's 1917 prophecy of the incarnation of Ahriman shortly after 2000, which Steiner spoke of as inevitable. [162] The question arises: How will this three-and-a-half-year period end?

Biblical prophecy is clear that the Antichrist sets up his world government with Jerusalem as his capitol. "When, therefore, you see the abomination of desolation, which was spoken of through Daniel the prophet, standing in the holy place" (Matthew 24:15). The corresponding passage in the Gospel of Luke reads, "When you see Jerusalem surrounded by armies, then know that its desolation has come near" (Luke 21:20). Taking these passages together and looking at the context in which these words were spoken, the expression "abomination"—Daniel refers to the "abomination that makes desolate" (Daniel 12:11)—is clearly Christ's reference to the Antichrist, indicating that he will set up his rule in Jerusalem. Jeane Dixon, too, saw in her vision the Antichrist "center his work around the city of Jerusalem."[163] This is precisely the interpretation of Vladimir Solovyov in his Antichrist story referred to earlier. Solovyov also describes the demise of the Antichrist during the fourth year of his rule. Let us recall that Solovyov's work was completed in the year 1900, long before the (re)formation of Israel in 1948, and yet he clearly envisioned the future State of Israel:

His [the Antichrist's] residence at this time had been changed from Rome to Jerusalem. Palestine was then an autonomous State inhabited and governed principally by Jews.... When he moved to Jerusalem, secretly spreading the report in Hebrew circles that his principal problem was to establish the world-wide dominion of Israel, the Hebrews recognized him as the Messiah, and their enthusiastic devotion to him knew no bounds. But suddenly they rose in rebellion.... The Hebrews, deeming the Emperor entirely Jewish by race, discovered by chance that he was not even circumcised. That very day Jerusalem, and the following day all Palestine, was in revolt. The boundless and fervent devotion to the Savior of Israel, to the promised Messiah, was changed into equally boundless and fervent hatred of the wily deceiver and brazen imposter.... The Hebrews went forth to meet him [and his army] with small hope of success. But hardly had the vanguard of both armies come together, when an earthquake of unprecedented violence occurred...and swallowed up the Emperor himself and his numberless forces.[164]

A great earthquake in Jerusalem is also forecast in Revelation: "And at that hour there was a great earthquake, and a tenth of the city fell" (Revelation 11:13). Whatever, ultimately, may be the cause of the Antichrist's end—and it has to be admitted that there is an almost journalistic quality to Solovyov's account—it is clear that the Biblical prophecy sets a clear limit of three and a half years upon his rule. Thus, somehow or other, by human or divine intervention, the Antichrist's reign will be abruptly curtailed. The key question is *when* this may be, and that is the central question with which this book is occupied—looking to December 21, 2012, as a possible candi*date* for this event. And, moreover, the political significance of the conflict centered in Jerusalem *at the present time* is also highly relevant to our theme, meriting paying close attention to all developments connected with the State of Israel and it's relationship to the United States and other key players in the world scenario that is now shaping up.

With regard to the date December 21, 2012, the skeptical reader may shrug this off simply by saying, "Why should I regard the Apocalypse Code as valid?" However, it is not just the Apocalypse Code that leads us to consider the end of the Maya Long Count calendar as a prophetic heralding of the end of the three-and-a-half-year reign of the Antichrist, but also reading the images of Revelation which clearly indicates to us where we stand in the unfolding of world history. What do we mean by "reading the images of Revelation"? It is here, in relation to this question, that Daniel Andreev's work proves very helpful.

The Rose of the World is offered as a pioneering work of what Andreev terms *meta-history*, which he defines as "the sum of processes—as yet outside the field of vision, interest, and methodology of science—that take place on planes of being existing in other time streams and other dimensions and are sometimes discernible through the process we perceive as history."[165] Andreev here is framing his own rare and powerful visionary experience of history, which clearly echoes the sort of experience captured in Revelation, as a new form of historical knowledge, one which will become more widespread with the approach of the Rose of the World:

[In the past] the astonishing insights of Revelation remained hidden from people's eyes by a blanket of allegories and innuendoes; its code of images allowed for every imaginable interpretation. Thus, a genuine framework for understanding historical processes did not take shape. Historical knowledge was as yet scarce and limited in scope...and the mystical mind was not yet ready to grasp the internal logic of meta-history.... But the appearance of the Rose of the World has been preceded by the scientific era [and]...by yet another era: one of radical social changes and upheavals, of revolutions, and of world wars. Both kinds of phenomena have loosened humanity's psychological crust, which had remained for so many centuries unbroken. In that soil, plowed up by the iron teeth of historical catastrophes, the seeds of meta-historical revelation will fall. And the entire planetary cosmos will reveal itself to people's spiritual sight as a constantly evolving system of variegated worlds, a system speeding toward a blindingly brilliant goal, spiritualized and transformed from century to century and from day to day.... The goal of the Rose of the World is to become a receptor, fosterer, and interpreter of that knowledge. [166]

This conveys something of the spirit in which this book is written. It is an attempt to translate the meta-historical meaning of Revelation into a comprehensive grasp of the time in which we are living. Let us recall that the book of Revelation was revealed more than nineteen hundred years ago to John by the Risen Christ as a series of mighty images relating to the future of the world. What was at that time future (for John) is now—at least in part—in the past.

One person whose power of clairvoyance was such as to allow him to read the images of Revelation and relate them to specific historical events was Rudolf Steiner. In his lecture series, *The Fall of the Spirits of Darkness,* he gives a very precise historical indication as to when the so-called war in heaven took place, which is the subject of Revelation 12.

Now war arose in heaven, Michael and his Angels fighting against the dragon; and the dragon and his Angels fought, but they were defeated and there was no longer any place for them in heaven. And the great dragon was thrown down, that ancient serpent, who is called the Devil and Satan, the deceiver of the whole world—he was thrown down to the Earth, and his Angels were thrown down with him. (Revelation 12:7–9)

According to Steiner, the war in heaven took place between 1841 and 1879:

> The second half of the nineteenth century was an extremely important period.... This, of course, is not discovered by look-ing merely at the events that happened in the physical world, but only by studying these events in connection with what was going on in the spiritual world. The year 1841 was, in truth, the critical year in respect of the onset of the age of materialism, for at that time a very definite battle began in the spiritual worlds—a battle waged by certain Spirits, Spirits of Darkness as we may call them.... In the spiritual worlds they fought out this battle until the autumn of 1879.... These Spirits of Darkness were defeated in the war they waged against the Spirits of Light dur-ing this period. In the year 1879, on a smaller scale, an event came to pass of the kind that has several times come to pass in the course of evolution, and has always been pictured symboli-cally as the victory of Michael, or St. George, over the Dragon. In the year 1879, too, the Dragon was overcome in a certain realm.... In 1879, therefore, they [the Spirits of Darkness] were cast out of the spiritual world into the world of human beings.... Their aim is to achieve here, with the help of human beings, what they were unable to achieve with the help of the Spirits in yonder world. Their aim is to bring ruin to that part of the good plan for world evolution. [167]

The publication of the *Communist Manifesto* in 1848; of Charles Darwin's *Origin of the Species* in 1859; the births of Lenin (1870), Stalin (1879), Hitler (1889), and Mao Tse-Tung (1893): these are just some of the books and names that come to mind in relation to the activity of Dark Spirits working through human beings to interfere with and even to bring to naught the true goal and purpose of human evolution. The exact dating given by Rudolf Steiner of the period from 1841 to 1879 in connection with the war in heaven is an example of translating from the realm of meta-history to that of earthly history, which is the goal, also, of this book. Steiner's indication shows us that Revelation contains a precise account—clothed in magnificent, mythical images—of human history since the first century C.E. and extending into the distant future, seen from the meta-historical (archetypal) level. Since the war in heaven (1841–1879) is described in Revelation 12, it follows that events in chapter 13 follow that period chronologically.

In terms of reading the images from Revelation, it is a matter of "scenes," rather like in a stage play, unfolding one after the other. Periodically there takes place a change of scene, and a major change of scene generally occurs at the *end* of a chapter in Revelation. The tremendous forces of hindrance that were unleashed into the world through Lenin and Stalin in Russia (and subsequently the whole Soviet Union), through Hitler in Germany (engulfing virtually the whole of Europe), and through Mao in China came to an end, for the main part, with the collapse of Soviet Communism in 1991.[168] The end of the communist era in 1991 announced that one scene was coming to an end and that a new scene was in preparation. The new scene on the world stage then opened just ten years later, on September 11, 2001, announcing the transition from Revelation 12 to chapter 13.

How do the events of September 11, 2001 on the historical level "fulfill" the opening scene of Revelation 13 on the meta-historical level? Let us go back to the words describing the opening scene of the chapter: "And I saw a beast rising out of the sea with ten horns and seven heads.... One of its heads seemed to have a mortal wound" (Revelation 13:1–3). The "mortal wound" beheld by John a little over nineteen hundred years ago can be seen as the "wound" inflicted through the destruction of the twin towers of the World Trade Center, the computer-laden "head" of world trade. Thus, this dramatic event on September 11, 2001, announced to the world the "beast" arising, Satan/Ahriman on his way into incarnation, with one of his heads wounded. The ensuing War on Terror, intended to keep humanity in a perpetual state of fear, is exactly what creates the atmosphere needed by The Beast for his incarnation as the Antichrist.[169] The events since September 11, 2001—the war in Afghanistan, the Iraq

war, the torture prisons, the draconian security measures under-
mining the freedom of the individual, etc. (a long list of many other
things could be added here)—all support the meta-historical perspective that we have entered the chapter in world history of the coming
of The Beast and his prophet, as elaborated upon in this book.

In terms of meta-history, given that we have entered Revelation 13,
what is our hope for the future (*hope* being a key word here)? To
answer this question, it is helpful to look back to Revelation 12:

> And a great sign appeared in heaven, a woman clothed with the
> Sun, with the Moon under her feet, and on her head a crown of
> twelve stars. She was with child and she cried out in her pangs
> of birth, in anguish for her delivery. And another sign appeared
> in heaven. Behold, a great red dragon, with seven heads and ten
> horns, and seven diadems upon his heads. His tail swept down
> a third of the stars of heaven, and cast them down to the earth.
> And the dragon stood before the woman who was about to bear
> a child, that he might devour her child when she brought it
> forth. She brought forth a male child, one who is to rule all the
> nations. (Revelation 12:1–5)

John's great vision of a heavenly woman is a vision of Divine Sophia
in celestial heights. Later in Revelation she is referred to as the *Bride
of the Lamb*, indicating that she is the divine feminine counterpart of
the Lamb, the name in Revelation for Christ.

The vision of chapter 12 revealed to John that at some point in
evolution Divine Sophia would commence her descent from celestial
heights in order to participate in the unfolding of evolution. Thanks
to Daniel Andreev, the approximate time of the beginning of Sophia's
descent is indicated. "The first link in the chain of events—events
so important that they can only be compared to the incarnation of
the Logos—occurred at the turn of the nineteenth century."[170] With
the words "incarnation of the Logos" he means the incarnation of
Christ, which also took place over long aeons of time, during which
Christ manifested himself in different forms to different cultures on
his path of descent from celestial heights. What Andreev is pointing
to is that the incarnation of Sophia is an event comparable to the
incarnation of Christ, and that Sophia's incarnation began "at the

turn of the nineteenth century." From a meta-historical perspective, just as Christ's incarnation was a long process, so the incarnation of Sophia is also something that takes place over a long period of time. However, before examining the incarnation of Sophia in detail, the first question is: Who is Sophia, and what does her incarnation signify for humanity and for the Earth?

When the Old Testament was translated into Greek the Hebrew word *Hokmah* (pronounced "chokmah" with a gutteral "ch") was translated as *Sophia*. In the English translation of the Bible this is translated as *wisdom*. In the book of Proverbs, one finds words that Sophia speaks through King Solomon, who was widely regarded as the wisest human being of antiquity. People came from all over the ancient world to seek out King Solomon, including the fabled Queen of Sheba. Solomon was a human being who had a special relationship with Sophia, Divine Wisdom. All of the so-called Old Testament Wisdom Books that are attributed to Solomon speak of Sophia. [171]

If we read Proverbs, we see words that Sophia speaks in the first person. This answers one of the questions which is often raised with regard to Sophia: Is Divine Wisdom simply an attribute of God? We speak of God's power, God's wisdom, and God's love, for example. But it is clear if you read the Wisdom Books in the Old Testament that it is a matter not simply of an attribute of God but of an actual being, because she speaks in the first person. She says, for example: "I was present at the beginning of creation…participating at the side of the Lord in the work of creation" (Proverbs 8:22, 30). This is a statement that tells us something about Sophia. It is a matter of an actual being, whose nature is wisdom, who participated in the work of creation. It is clear also from the words spoken that Sophia is a feminine being—a great, divine feminine being. This raises many interesting questions of a philosophical and theological nature about the nature of the Godhead. These questions were asked by some thinkers in the ancient world, for example, the Jewish philosopher Philo of Alexandria (ca. 15 B.C.E. to ca. C.E. 45), but then with the rise of Christianity the theme of Sophia more and more receded into the background. The main reason for this was that early in the history of Christianity Sophia was identified with Christ in the sense that all biblical references to Sophia

Sophia, the All-Wisdom of God
(seventeenth-century icon of the Moscow School)

(wisdom) were considered to mean Christ's wisdom. With this, at one stroke Sophia disappeared from human consciousness, at least in the Christian world of the West.

Christianity in the West, because it developed increasingly as a patriarchal religion, by and large lost the Divine Feminine—although there was (and still is) devotion to the Virgin Mary, which is the remnant within Christianity of the once widespread devotion to the Divine Feminine in antiquity. On the other hand, however, in the Russian Orthodox Church there lives a devotion to Sophia. It is not immediately apparent how this came about. One can see from the various Sophia icons belonging to the Russian tradition that all of them show Sophia as a majestic divine feminine being who is raying out wisdom. Above her is Christ, so she is clearly not the same as Christ. To her right is the Virgin Mary, so she is clearly not the same as the Virgin Mary. To her left is John the Baptist. This is something—the Sophia icon tradition—that has lived in the history of the Russian Church. In fact there are two cathedrals named after Sophia: the cathedral of Divine Sophia in Kiev in the Ukraine, which was founded in the eleventh century, and the cathedral of Holy Sophia in Novgorod, northwest of Moscow, also dating from the eleventh century. The Novgorod Sophia cathedral was regarded for centuries as the spiritual center of Russia. Moreover, there are also numerous Sophia churches in Russia. The Russian people simply took this as a matter of fact, this devotion to Sophia, without really questioning it or asking: Who is Sophia? And there is even (going back to the seventeenth century) a church liturgy dedicated to Sophia in the old Slavic language (Church Slavonic). All this shows that in the Russian tradition there has lived a devotion to Sophia. Moreover, this continues in our time.

We referred earlier to the great Russian philosopher Vladimir Solovyov, who was born in 1853, and who studied philosophy in the West. His mission was to help the Russian people in the development of philosophy. Already as a child, in the tenth year of his life, when he was attending a church service in Moscow, he had a vision of Sophia who appeared to him as a radiant divine feminine being wrapped in azure light. On this account, a sense of Sophia was living in him. It was a living presence, not just something that he had merely seen from the icons. He knew that Sophia is a real being. In his philosophical quest he was searching for the deeper meaning: Who is Sophia, and what is the relationship of Sophia to the Trinity—the Father, the Son, and the Holy Spirit, who are imbued with masculine qualities?

His search led him to London. He studied in the Library of the British Museum, and there one day he had a second experience of Sophia. This time he saw only her face. She said to him: "Go to Egypt." And that is what he did. He took the train across Europe, down through Italy, and then took the ferry from Brindisi across to Egypt and stayed at a hotel in Cairo. There were some Russian émigrés staying there. One night he received the inner message to go into the desert. He was dressed wearing a long coat, a tall silk hat, and black gloves when he set off into the desert—a very strange sight. Some Bedouin nomads captured him, uncertain whether to kill him outright or to hold him for ransom. Fortunately for him, because of his appearance they thought he was the devil, and so they released him.

That night it was approaching dawn when he had the third and most momentous experience of Divine Sophia, who appeared to him in her full glory and showered him with love. "Today my Queen appeared to me in azure; my heart was beating in sweet ecstasy," he wrote.[172] From that point, for the rest of his life, he was devoted to Sophia to help bring an understanding of Sophia to the Russian people. He is regarded as the founder of Sophiology—the theology of Sophia.

For Sophiology, Sophia is at the pinnacle of creation. Thus all creation has a relationship to Sophia, because all of creation has come into existence by way of the Divine Wisdom that Sophia embodies. She is the plan of creation and also participates in the work of creation. In Proverbs 9 there is a reference to Sophia's temple having seven pillars. This gives us some idea about the nature of Sophia. To use an analogy: an architect, before he sets to work building a house, will draw an architectural plan and work from that. One could think, by way of analogy, of the Creator as the great architect and Sophia as the plan. She embodies the plan of creation. The seven pillars in Sophia's temple indicate the seven stages of the unfolding of creation, which is referred to as the "seven days of creation."

Along with the Russian Sophiologists, Rudolf Steiner has greatly enriched our knowledge of the divine plan in relation to the being of Sophia. Steiner's central teaching is about the unfolding of creation through seven stages or "days," going far beyond anything that anybody has ever taught before concerning the stages or "days" of creation. Through the teaching of Rudolf Steiner, an unveiling of the being of Sophia has taken place. In fact, Rudolf Steiner called his life's work *Anthroposophia*—*anthropos*, from the Greek, meaning "human being," and *sophia* is the Greek for *wisdom*. *Anthroposophia* is a new revelation of Divine Sophia in and through the human being. In Anthroposophy there is an understanding of Sophia as a divine feminine being.

In Revelation, it is clear that the one who is called the "Lamb" is Christ. That is also the name that John the Baptist gave to Christ, as indicated in John's words: "Behold the Lamb of God" (John 1:29). In Revelation reference is made to the "Bride of the Lamb"; this is Sophia. There is a deep and profound relationship between Christ and Sophia. The final two chapters of Revelation refer to the working together of the Lamb and his Bride—the *hieros gamos* ("sacred marriage") of the Lamb and his Bride. The image is given of Sophia the Bride descending from above and coming down as the bearer of the new heaven, coming down and uniting with the Lamb, who through his sacrifice brings about the spiritualization and transformation of the Earth into the new Earth. Through this sacred marriage takes place the creation of a new heaven and a new Earth, as described in the last two chapters of Revelation (21–22).

Already in chapter 12, Sophia is mentioned as a majestic cosmic being. She is depicted as the "woman clothed with the Sun, with the Moon under her feet, and on her head a crown of twelve stars" (Revelation 12:1). The image on page 154 is a representation of Divine Sophia based on a sketch by Rudolf Steiner, drawn directly from the description of Sophia in Revelation 12. He presented this sketch as the fifth of the seven Apocalyptic Seals.

In the image of the fifth Apocalyptic Seal, Sophia is bringing to birth a child, and she is attacked by a great red dragon with seven heads. This expresses something from meta-history to us in

The Fifth Apocalyptic Seal by Clara Rettich
(based on a design by Rudolf Steiner)

a remarkable way. Rudolf Steiner spoke of the next age, the Age of Aquarius, as the age when Russians and other Slavic peoples would come into their true mission, aided by Sophia. That Sophia lives so strongly among the Slavic peoples, in the Russian Orthodox Church, is not something coming from the past, but instead has to do with the future mission of Russia and of the Slavic peoples. The coming Age of Aquarius will bring forth a new culture that will develop first in Russia and other Slavic countries and will then spread around the world to become a global culture—the Rose of the World (to use Andreev's expression for the global Sophia culture of the future, destined to arise during the Age of Aquarius).

If we consider this picture of the future, we can then begin to understand what took place through Vladimir Lenin, who was the leader of the Bolshevik Revolution, and who was instrumental in putting Communism into practice, to which Karl Marx had given birth on a theoretical level. Soviet Communism (Marxist-Leninist) took over not only in Russia but also in *all* the Slavic countries. Soviet Communism represented the opposite of the coming Sophia culture. What Solovyov and many other Russians—notably Daniel Andreev— were working for was to prepare Russia for the future culture of Sophia, the Rose of the World, but they were bitterly opposed by the atheistic Soviet regime.

In the vision that John beheld on the island of Patmos, he saw that Sophia would be attacked by a great red dragon. The Bolsheviks' name for themselves—the *Reds*—points to the image from John's vision.[173] Bolshevism was literally an attack by demonic forces—the dragon—who worked through Lenin, and then through Stalin, after the way had been prepared by Karl Marx's *Communist Manifesto* published in 1848, shortly after the start of the "war in heaven" in 1841. It is noteworthy, too, that Stalin was born in 1879, the year when the war in heaven was concluded by the casting down of the Spirits of Darkness upon the Earth. The way the dark forces work is that they see what the true image for the future is, and then they attempt to substitute a caricature or an inversion of it. This substitute is often able to take hold, because it has *some* element of truth in it, and it resonates on an inner level with the human being's sense for the true spiritual impulse of the future.

The future age of Sophia will be an age of the flourishing of community, brotherhood and sisterhood, called in Revelation "Philadelphia." The Greek word *delphos* means the womb, and *adelphi* means "springing from the same womb." *Philadelphia* expresses the love that exists between brothers and sisters coming from the same womb. In a more extended sociological sense, Philadelphia is the community of brotherly and sisterly love, which is destined to come to birth as the Rose of the World in the Aquarian Age. The longing for community, as something belonging to the spiritual future of humanity, was the point of entrance for the seduction that lay at the root of Soviet Communism.

Communism is supposedly based on community, and it was this element of apparent truth that deceived the Russian people. As the world then witnessed, Soviet Communism turned out to be a dictatorship of an élite, who led their extravagant lifestyles at the expense of millions of people whom they subjected to their will. The great tragedy that overcame Russia and the Slavic peoples was the preempting by dark forces of the future that is to arise in the coming Age of Aquarius. The visions presented in Revelation are true. They offer a picturing of the future, part of which now already lies in the past. However, we have to learn to read the images correctly, and this is what we mean by "reading the images of the Apocalypse."

The great cosmic vision of Sophia at the opening of Revelation 12 announces the beginning of her descent as the bearer of the Rose of the World, especially into the region where the Philadelphian epoch will begin after C.E. 2375. The attack upon Sophia by the great red dragon in chapter 12 took place in the twentieth century in the shape of Soviet Communism, which took hold in precisely that region of the Earth— encompassing the Slavic countries—where the Rose of the World is initially destined to arise. Lenin's political and economic program (prepared beforehand on a theoretical level by Marx) was executed with an unprecedented brutality by Stalin, preempting the initial phase of the Rose of the World in Russia and the Slavic countries. The Apocalyptic image of the tail of the red dragon sweeping down "a third of the stars of heaven" (Revelation 12:4) is an uncannily accurate image, since Communism—including China, Cuba, North Vietnam, and North Korea together with Russia and the Slavic countries—enslaved almost one-third of the world's population. Soviet Communism was clearly a preempting of the initial phase of the Rose of the World, using the word "preempting" here in the sense of dark forces taking hold of something that is divinely ordained to unfold in the future and bringing it in forcefully into the present, before humanity is ready. It was precisely this tactic that Sorath (whose number is 666) attempted in the seventh century C.E. through the Academy of Gondishapur, as discussed in chapter 7.

With the event of September 11, 2001, and the unfolding of Revelation 13, another level of preempting is apparent. This time it is a matter of preempting the *global form* of the Rose of the World.

The global community of the Rose of the World is destined to arise in the Aquarian Age through the love and interest that people will increasingly experience for the culture and religion of *other people*. In this connection Daniel Andreev speaks of *interreligion* as the driving force behind the arising of the Rose of the World. Since the world's great religions and spiritual traditions have arisen through the teachings and revelations of their founders and prophets, and since Sophia, Divine Wisdom, has worked inspiringly through these religious founders and prophets, the coming of Sophia will draw together all the different religious and spiritual streams into one all-embracing whole—united in herself, her own being. This is the image of the rose, where each of the petals represents a religion or spiritual tradition.

> The Rose of the World...will be an *interreligion* or *pan-religion*, in that it will be a teaching that views all religions that appeared earlier as reflections of different layers of spiritual reality, different sets of variomaterial facts, and different segments of our planetary cosmos.... If the older religions are petals, then the Rose of the World will be a flower: with roots, stem, head, and the commonwealth of its petals.... One can compare the Rose of the World to an upturned flower, the roots of which are in heaven and the petals here, among humanity, on Earth. Its stem is revelation, through which flow the spiritual juices that feed and strengthen its petals, our fragrant chorus of religions. Besides the petals, it has a heart: its own teachings. It's teaching is not a random blend of the highest beliefs of various theosophies of the past. In addition to a new perspective on our religious legacy, the Rose of the World will establish a new perspective on nature, history, the destiny of human cultures and their tasks, on creative work, love, the paths of cosmic ascent, and the gradual enlightenment of *Shadanakar* [meaning humanity and the Earth together with its various subtle bodies or levels of existence].[174]

By driving a wedge between Islam and the West, the attacks on September 11, 2001, have led to an *inversion* of the Rose of the World. However, if we accept the validity of Jeane Dixon's vision of the coming of the Antichrist, he will *usurp* the uniting aspect of the Rose of the World into his own person: "Like Christ, the Antichrist will center his work at the city of Jerusalem. I get the distinct feeling that the religions of the world will somehow merge with the philosophies of the East. I see the youth flock to him and partake of his wisdom."[175] As well as seeing him as "a military figure beyond anything the world has ever previously seen" she also sees that the Antichrist "will establish and lead a strange and fundamentally anti-human 'religion' of atheism and anti-religion."[176] This is clearly both an inversion and a usurping of the Rose of the World based on divine love and Wisdom and on interreligion. However, the most striking aspect of the usurping of the Rose of the World—in its phase as a global community—is the *global reign* of the Antichrist, ruler of the New World Order[177] established by force rather than by love and mutual interest of the peoples of the Earth for one another and their cultures and religions. Revelation 13, therefore, is about the preempting of the Rose of the World in its global phase through The Beast (Antichrist) and the prophet of The Beast, whereas chapter 12 is about the preempting of the Rose of the World in its initial phase—that of the arising of the Sophia culture in Russia and the Slavic countries—through the great red dragon, the Apocalyptic image for Communism.

Reading the images of the Apocalypse, after the red dragon of Communism (chapter 12) comes The Beast of chapter 13—Satan/Ahriman/Mammon—who is the being underlying the manipulation of money (Mammon), the wielding of the brute force of military power (Ahriman), and the enslavement to the dark forces of the instinctual life (Satan).[178] The twentieth century was a time of preparation for his full emergence upon the world stage, and then this beast arose at the beginning of the twenty-first century.[179] The World Trade Center represented one of his "heads"—world trade being a means of ensnaring all the peoples of the Earth in the web of the world's financial system. This "head" received a mortal wound when the twin towers were destroyed. A short time thereafter, the prophet of The Beast comes to the rescue. The prophet appears as a "lamb" (meek and gentle in appearance), and yet he "exercises all the authority of The Beast." In other words, he has the full support of The Beast and acts in the capacity of a fulfiller of the impulses of The Beast. Veiled by his "lamb mask," he causes humanity "to worship The Beast whose mortal wound was healed" (Revelation 13:11–12). The healing of the mortal wound means that world trade under the banner of the New World Order proceeds. Globalization is the order of the day. It is "business as usual." In this sense, the mortal wound is healed, and it does not matter that the World Trade Center was physically destroyed, because the cause of the globalization of world trade that it represented continues unabated.

Against this background, it is evident that the historical enactment of chapter 13 is the drama of the twenty-first century, just as the playing out historically of chapter 12 was the overriding drama of the twentieth century. The importance of focusing upon the Rose of the World as the true archetype for the future of humanity and the Earth becomes clear in light of an Apocalyptic reading of the events of our time.

During John's lifetime, of course, everything related to Soviet Communism lay far in the future. For us now it lies in the past. During the time of Soviet Communism the vision of the true future of Russia was kept alive in at least one person, Daniel Andreev, who has been called the "Russian Dante." Andreev's *The Rose of the World* continues the stream of Russian spirituality devoted to Divine Sophia that emerged with Vladimir Solovyov. It is a difficult book to read, because Daniel Andreev was faithful to everything that was said to him by his spiritual guides, which was related in a language which is not known on Earth. Despite employing expressions such as *Shadanakar*, *Bayushmi*, and *Zatomis* to describe his spiritual experiences, Adreev's work presents an extraordinary revelation. [180]

Like Solovyov, who not only was devoted to Sophia but also wrote his short story about the Antichrist, Andreev's great Sophianic work also gave some attention to the coming of the Antichrist. Andreev's name for Satan/Ahriman is Gagtungr, and he is clear that the Antichrist is an incarnation of Gagtungr in a human vessel, whom he describes as a "human puppet" of Gagtungr:

> After the incarnation of the Planetary Logos [Christ], humanity became the decisive battleground, and an idea began to form in the demonic mind to create—slowly, if need be—a

human puppet who would be capable of achieving absolute tyranny, of turning the population of the Earth into a
satanohumankind. But once again the demonic lack of creativity made itself felt. Unable to come up with anything
original, all the demonic forces could do was resort to the
law of opposites and devise a blueprint to create a distorted
mirror image of the efforts of Providence. The Anticosmos
was counterposed to the Cosmos, the principle of form to
the Logos, satanohumankind to theohumankind, and the
Antichrist to Christ...Gagtungr had no alternative but to use
a human monad...in the person of one of the Roman emperors...guided from incarnation to incarnation, overcoming its
[the emperor's] resistance, and over time causing an almost
total extinguishment of its will to Light.... [This] demonic
human puppet...assumed the outward guise of an active
champion of global theocracy...[referred to in literary form
in] "The Legend of the Grand Inquisitor" in Dostoevsky's *The
Brothers Karamazov*. The one who is to become the Antichrist
in the not too distant future [these words were written in the
late 1950s] was, one could say, captured by Dostoevsky at one
of the most crucial stages of its previous existence. It is true
that he is not a widely known historical figure. His name is
known now only to medievalists as the name of one of the
rather notable figures of the Spanish Inquisition. It was about
that time that Gagtungr was forced to admit the failure of his
overall scheme to turn historical Catholicism into his lackey
and the impossibility of unifying the whole world on the basis
of a Roman cosmopolitan hierocracy. Absolute tyranny was
impossible without the unification of humanity, and a host
of prior conditions for unification of any kind was still lacking.... As Jesus Christ foresaw [and revealed to John], the
course of events has led to the imminence of the decisive battle [the battle with the Antichrist], a battle made inevitable by
the ancient hunger for power of the demonic powers and by
their pursuit of universal tyranny. [181]

Clearly there is much in this excerpt that demands further explo-
ration: in particular that Andreev offers critical information for recognizing the individual who will provide the vehicle for Ahriman's

incarnation. Given the errors in other parts of *The Rose of the World*, obviously the accuracy of the information has first to be ascertained. Andreev's remark about "the unification of humanity" is prophetic in the sense of pointing to the current time and the "New World Order," i.e., a global ruling power. For Andreev there was no doubt that the battle with the Antichrist is fought by Christ, through his Second Coming, from the etheric realm:

> The Second Coming is to occur simultaneously at a multitude of points on [Earth] ... so that every single being will have seen and heard Him. In other words, the Planetary Logos is to attain the inconceivable power to materialize simultaneously in as many places as there will then be consciousness to perceive Him ... so that all peoples and nations on Earth will see "the Son of Man coming on the clouds of heaven."[182]

Through my own research I have been able to confirm Daniel Andreev's indications concerning the imminent (or, for clairvoyant perception, already ongoing) manifestation of Christ in an ethereal raiment and of the coming of the Antichrist "in the not-too-distant future." Also, I have found, as I shall describe below in more detail, confirmation of Daniel Andreev's basic thesis about the future. Concerning this, we are approaching an event comparable to the incarnation of Christ two thousand years ago—the incarnation of Divine Sophia. It will have an enormous impact on the whole of the planet. Let us contemplate this coming event with the help of star wisdom (*Astro-Sophia,* or Astrosophy). Through the wisdom of the stars, it is possible to penetrate to an understanding of the approaching incarnation of Sophia, which culminates during the coming Age of Aquarius. The stages of incarnation of Sophia are the same as those of the incarnation of Christ, the Logos. Therefore, let us follow the stages of the incarnation of the Logos, starting with the *Central Sun* at the heart of our galaxy as the place of origin of both Christ and Sophia, who each follow the same path of incarnation.[183] In the case of Christ, his descent from the *Central Sun* began long ago and took place in stages. An important stage was the entrance of Christ into our local part of the galaxy.[184]

About eight thousand years ago, Christ descended from the local part of our galaxy, the Orion Arm, to unite with our Sun, and this event was witnessed by the great Persian prophet Zarathustra, who proclaimed Christ as *Ahura Mazda* ("Aura of the Sun"). After entering our solar system and uniting with the Sun about 6000 B.C.E., some six thousand years elapsed before Christ then descended into the human being Jesus of Nazareth at the moment of the baptism in the River Jordan about two thousand years ago. This is the moment that is addressed in the words: "This is my beloved Son whom today I have begotten" (Luke 3:22). This is how it is expressed in the ancient manuscripts. In later manuscripts it was changed to, "This is my beloved Son, in whom I am well pleased." With this later translation the significance of the moment of the incarnation was obscured. However, in the ancient manuscripts of Luke, one can read, "This is my beloved Son whom today I have begotten." This moment of baptism in the Jordan signified the incarnation of the Logos into the human being Jesus of Nazareth. It denoted the beginning of a divine mission which lasted for three and a half years. I was able to exactly date most of the major events in the life of Christ in my book *Chronicle of the Living Christ*. This mission was to bring the impulse of divine love from the *Central Sun* (Plato's *Supra-Celestial Sun*) to the Earth for humanity and the future evolution of the Earth.

There was some knowledge of this—the cosmic origin of Christ, his solar nature—in early Christianity, where Christ was referred to as the *Spirit of the Sun*. There was a knowledge that Christ came as a cosmic being from a higher world. Similarly, speaking of Sophia as the "woman clothed with the Sun," she is also an emissary from the *Central Sun* as the bearer of the divine feminine aspect of the Godhead. In the case of Christ and Sophia, we can speak of *God-born* beings coming directly from the heart of God at the center of our galaxy. God-born beings have to be distinguished from all other beings, who are created beings. Angels and all beings of the celestial hierarchies, and also human beings and all other beings are created. However, Christ and Sophia are God-born beings. This means that they are *essentially and substantially* part of the Godhead, originating from the Divine Heart at the center of our galaxy. (There is a manifestation of the Divine Heart or *Central Sun* at the center of every galaxy, whereby the Godhead is mystically present throughout the universe.) When Christ spoke the words: "I and the Father are one" (John 10:30), what did he mean by this? To understand the cosmic being of Christ, one has to grasp that the essence of his being extends all the way to the *Central Sun*, and thus he could speak these words in their full and profound sense. The same applies to Sophia, the Bride of the Lamb, who is the divine feminine counterpart of Christ.

Let us now endeavor to follow the stages of Sophia's incarnation. In the year 1300 Dante had his vision, subsequently described in *The Divine Comedy*, in which he saw the snow-white rose—the celestial image of Divine Sophia united with the throne of God in the *Empyrean*, the highest divine realm.[185] When Dante had this vision, Sophia was still united with the *Central Sun*. She was at that time still dwelling in this highest sphere, the *Empyrean*, the divine realm united with the throne of God. Through the star wisdom of Astro-Sophia it emerges that since approximately 1775, Divine Sophia has united with the local part of our galaxy, the Orion Arm, and is now working especially through the twelve constellations of the zodiac, representing the central axis—for our solar system—within the Orion Arm. This is revealed in the image of Sophia "crowned by twelve stars." Sophia is "crowned" with the twelve zodiacal constellations and at the present time works as a source of inspiration for humanity from the level of the zodiac.[186]

Daniel Andreev's indication regarding the descent of Sophia, referred to earlier, points to "the turn of the nineteenth century," i.e., around 1800, so the date 1775 found through astrosophical research is close to this. This point in time of Sophia's entrance into the local part of our galaxy coincides with the founding of the United States of America in 1776. There is a very deep connection here between these two events, which it is not possible to go into now because it is too complex. However, it can be said that there is a relationship between the Declaration of Independence in 1776 and the descent of Sophia to unite with our cosmos. Since 1775 Sophia has been working from the level of the zodiac.

Sophia's "biography" may be read by following the reflection of her wisdom as it appeared in the works of a select group of late nineteenth and early twentieth century authors: H. P. Blavatsky's Theosophy— *Theo-Sophia*, the wisdom of God; Russian *Sophiology*—the theology of Sophia; and Rudolf Steiner's *Anthroposophy* (Anthropo-Sophia), the wisdom of Sophia manifested in and through the human being. These three spiritual streams are important ones (other spiritual streams could be named here as well) connected with Divine Sophia; their historical appearance expresses the opening words of Revelation 12 about "the woman clothed with the Sun, with the Moon under her feet, and on her head a crown of twelve stars." What distinguishes Anthroposophy is that, over and above it being an expression of Sophia's wisdom in our time, it is also an expression of the *whole series* of images presented in chapter 12 of Revelation. John not only beholds Sophia, the heavenly woman, but also sees that she gives birth to a child. What or who does this image of the child represent? Against the background of Anthroposophy it is clear that this image stands for the *reappearance of Christ*. It was not simply *alongside* his transmission of the wisdom of Anthropo-Sophia, but precisely *through and by means of* this wisdom that Rudolf Steiner made his proclamation of the *return of Christ in the etheric realm*.[187] It is this event which is the greatest event of our time and which is the true meaning of the New Age. Rudolf Steiner was the prophet of this event. He even stated that: "Anthroposophy has the mission of proclaiming Christ in His etheric form."[188] Rudolf Steiner thus—at least, in part—brought to expression historically the meta-historical image of *Sophia giving birth to a child* that is the predominant image in the first part of Revelation 12.

In the second part of chapter 12 comes the description of the war in heaven led by the Archangel Michael, which we referred to above. Here, too, Rudolf Steiner lived through on Earth the meta-historical reality of the impulse of the Archangel Michael, and he communicated more concerning the Archangel Michael than anyone else in the entire history of the Earth.[189] Towards the end of his life, in 1924, Steiner founded an esoteric school. Called the *Michael School*— also known as the *First Class of the School of Spiritual Science*—it embodies an extensive path of spiritual training, under the aegis of the Archangel Michael.[190] In this sense, Rudolf Steiner's life's work not only fulfills the first image from Revelation 12, that of the heavenly woman (*Sophia*), but also the image of the heavenly woman giving birth to a child (Christ—more specifically, the proclamation of the *return of Christ in the etheric realm* through and by way of Sophia's new revelation of Divine Wisdom in our time). Steiner's life and work—particularly through the founding of a Michael School on Earth—also clearly fulfill the Apocalyptic image of the *Archangel Michael*, the leader of the heavenly hosts in the war in heaven. Finally, by prophesying the impending incarnation of Satan/Ahriman, i.e., by pointing to the coming historical manifestation of the meta-historical scenario portrayed in chapter 13, Rudolf Steiner brought to expression even further the series of images presented in Revelation. Thus, the spiritual stream of Anthroposophy founded by Rudolf Steiner can be distinguished from the other spiritual streams devoted to Sophia that have arisen in or since the nineteenth century.

These spiritual streams have arisen directly in the wake of the approach of Sophia, who around 1775 came from the *Central Sun* into our local cosmos, the Orion Arm of the Milky Way Galaxy. The coming of Sophia was revealed to John on the island of Patmos over nineteen hundred years ago when the Ascended Christ showed him the unfolding of the future of human evolution. In the middle of this unfolding, in this series of visions that he received and wrote down in Revelation, in chapter 12 he suddenly beheld Sophia appearing. John was seeing into the future. He was seeing a certain moment in time. He saw that Divine Sophia was going to appear on the world stage.

We are presented in Revelation 12 with a blueprint of the incarnation of Sophia. Sophia first appeared on the world stage around 1775, simultaneous with her coming into our cosmos.[191] She is now emanating from the realm of the zodiac, symbolized in Revelation by the "twelve stars" around her head. In John's vision—expressed by his vision of the woman "clothed with the Sun"—Sophia then comes into our solar system and connects with the Sun, as Christ did some eight thousand years ago at the time of Zarathustra. According to astrosophical research, this uniting of Sophia with the Sun will occur around the year 2375, an interval of six hundred years after her entrance into our local cosmos (Orion Arm) with its central band of stars—the twelve constellations of the zodiac.[192] Then Sophia will come into our solar system and unite with our Sun, becoming the "woman clothed with the Sun."

This landmark in Sophia's biography is marked by a significant astronomical event. Presently the vernal point is at 5 degrees in the sign of Pisces. Due to the precession of the equinoxes, it moves back through the zodiac at a rate of one degree every seventy-two years. We can thus calculate the exact date when the vernal point will enter into the sign of Aquarius signifying the beginning of the Age of Aquarius. This will be in the year 2375. This is the date that I have arrived at, based on an exact definition of the zodiac as presented in my PhD thesis.193 This date is also confirmed by a publication called the *American Sidereal Ephemeris*.[194]

Already now preparation for the incarnation of Sophia on the Sun is taking place. This is one of the great events in the history of our solar system. The entrance of Sophia into our solar system will signify a profound shift in the evolution of the Earth and humanity, when this being of sublime majesty, beauty, celestial power, grace, divine light, and love will unite with the Sun at the start of the Age of Aquarius. Even now, during the last part of the Age of Pisces, Sophia's influence is streaming in from the world of the fixed stars. Her heavenly influence is beginning to be received by our solar system, giving rise to a new culture here on the Earth, the Sophia culture known as the Rose of the World. The more that human beings experience this inflow of Sophia, the more there will arise a new sense for life here on Earth. Daniel Andreev speaks of this:

> A mysterious event is taking place in contemporary times: new divine creative energy is emanating into our cosmos. Since ancient times, the loftiest hearts and minds have anticipated this event that is now taking place. This is an event so important that it can only be compared to the incarnation of the Logos nineteen hundred years ago. Vladimir Solovyov was given a glimpse of her when on a starry night in the Egyptian desert he experienced a stunning breach of his consciousness and saw the great

feminine being with his own eyes. We call her *Zventa Sventana*, the Holiest of the Holy, she who is the brightest and all good, the experience of the feminine hypostasis of the Trinity. The long-awaited day approaches when she will descend. There she will be born in a body of enlightened ether. A host of the loftiest souls will descend with her. There she is, our hope and joy, light and divine beauty. With her coming, there will be the founding of the Rose of the World.[195]

Daniel Andreev also points to the forces of opposition against the Rose of the World. The greatest opposition is presented by the incarnation of the Antichrist. The culture that will arise through the coming of the Antichrist is the opposite of that which is to come into the world through the coming of Sophia and the founding of the Rose of the World. In connection with the incarnation of the Antichrist, clearly there are great challenges to be faced, challenges for the whole of humankind. In meeting these challenges, we can especially find strength by focusing upon the Rose of the World and gaining an idea of the coming great culture of Sophia. The Rose of the World offers a true focus and aspiration, a beacon of light shining at the end of the tunnel, through which we are able to navigate our path, at the same time clearly beholding the usurping and inverting of the Rose of the World that is taking place here on the Earth at the present time.

When Andreev speaks of an incarnation of *Zventa Sventana*, the Holiest of the Holy (i.e., Sophia), he makes it clear that this is not an incarnation into a physical human being, as was the case with the incarnation of Christ in the physical human being Jesus of Nazareth. Rather, it will be an incarnation of Sophia in an "ethereal body." This ethereal body, according to Andreev, is already being prepared, and it is a body of life forces, a radiant body. This, then, is the fourth stage of incarnation of this great being, who will work here on the Earth in her radiant ethereal body and will bring about a far-reaching transformation giving rise to the culture of the Rose of the World, which Rudolf Steiner calls the *sixth cultural epoch*, the future Slavic culture. Everything that Rudolf Steiner describes about this future culture is elaborated upon by Daniel Andreev in his book *The Rose of the World*.

To summarize the stages of Sophia's incarnation, which are important to hold in consciousness: The first stage was around 1775, coming from the *Central Sun* at the heart of the galaxy into our cosmos and uniting with the Orion Arm, represented by the central band of stars, the twelve constellations of the zodiac, the "twelve stars." Six hundred years later, in 2375, the Age of Aquarius begins and Sophia will then unite with the Sun, when she will appear as "the woman clothed with the Sun." A further six hundred years later, in 2975, Sophia will start to work increasingly from the Sun down to the level of the Moon, to stream in her inspiring life energy through the phases of the Moon. Then the third aspect of Divine Sophia beheld in John's great vision—"with the Moon beneath her feet"—will become a reality. Sophia's incarnation means that she is coming ever closer toward the Earth. And then a further six hundred years later, in 3575, the incarnation of Sophia in an ethereal form, in a life body within the Earth's aura, will take place, in the realm surrounding and penetrating the Earth—what is called the "world of the elements." The year 3575 is the date indicated by Rudolf Steiner for the beginning of the *sixth cultural epoch*. This is what Daniel Andreev is referring to with the birth of the Rose of the World as a new world culture inspired by Divine Sophia. Thus, with the help of the star wisdom of Astro-Sophia (Astrosophy), it is possible to come to a precise understanding of the incarnation of Divine Sophia bringing the future culture known as the Rose of the World, underlying the sixth cultural epoch, which will last for 2,160 years, from 3575 to 5735. This is our *true hope* for the future, and correspondingly we may focus our attention upon the descent of Sophia from celestial heights not only as our hope, but also as our joy and our source of comfort for the future.

10. The Mystery of Love

Many readers of this book may ask, "What is the point of it all? Why do we have to encounter the Antichrist and his prophet? Surely this cannot be part of God's plan for humanity?" These are valid and understandable questions; in this final chapter an attempt will be made to set the coming of the Antichrist—the incarnation of Ahriman—in context.

In chapter 8 an overview of the different negative influences at work upon humanity's spiritual evolution is given. There attention is drawn to the triad represented by the three crosses on Golgotha—Christ in the middle, represented by Jesus; and Lucifer and Satan/Ahriman on either side, represented by the repentant and unrepentant criminals. Further, in chapter 8 the significance of Rudolf Steiner's sculpture *The Group* ("The Representative of Humanity") is discussed, as a powerful aid in coming to a sense for the work of this triad upon and within the human being. Contemplation of *The Group* awakens the sense of balance that has to be striven for—on the one hand not to be elevated away from the Earth through ungrounded spiritual practices or an overactive fantasy life, which is the luciferic temptation, and on the other hand not to become overly preoccupied with the physical-material level of existence, which is the ahrimanic tendency. By becoming aware of these two tendencies—one "upward" and one "downward" (metaphorically speaking)—one becomes aware of the Christ power of divine love, which holds the balance. "The true nature and essence of the human being is essentially the effort to hold the balance between the powers of Lucifer and Ahriman; the Christ impulse helps contemporary humanity to establish this equilibrium."[196] The "Representative of Humanity" represents *all* human beings and is *the* central figure in *The Group*. Christ went through the three temptations in the wilderness and *overcame them on our behalf*. It is of vital significance for us to consciously grasp this and, at the same time, to align ourselves with Christ in the continual finding of the balance between the two extremes. For Christ *is* the balance—this is the Mystery of Love.

Among the many extraordinary things that Steiner spoke of regarding this triad, there is one indication in particular that is highly relevant to our theme, which we have not taken into consideration so far, and that is his overview concerning the *historical working upon the Earth* of this triad. He points not only to the approaching *incarnation of Ahriman* shortly after the year 2000, but also to the *incarnation of Lucifer* that took place in the far-distant past: "Just as there was the incarnation which culminated in Golgotha, the incarnation of Christ in the man Jesus of Nazareth, there was an actual incarnation of Lucifer in far-off Asia, in the third millennium B.C.E.... what can only be described as an earthly incarnation of Lucifer in a man of flesh and blood."[197] Elsewhere he spoke of this as an incarnation in China, and described the circumstances surrounding the upbringing of the human being who served as the vessel for this incarnation of Lucifer:

A child of a distinguished Asiatic family of the time was allowed to grow up in the precincts of the mystery ceremonies. Circumstances were such that this child was actually permitted to take part in the ceremonies, undoubtedly because the priests conducting the rights in the mysteries received the inspiration to allow such a child to participate. And when the [human] being incarnate in that child reached the age of about forty—approximately that age—something very remarkable came to light. It became evident—and there is no doubt at all that the priests of the mysteries had foreseen the event prophetically—it became evident that this man who had been allowed to grow up in the precincts of one of the mystery centers in the east of Asia, began suddenly, at the age of about forty, to grasp through the faculty of human intellect itself what had formerly entered the mysteries through revelation alone. He was the first to make use of the organs of human intellect, but still in association with the mysteries...In this man Lucifer himself was incarnated—no more and no less than that! It is a significant, momentous fact that... at the beginning of the third millennium B.C.E. there was a Chinese incarnation of Lucifer.[198]

Thanks to the research of Richard Dickens, the identity of the Chinese incarnation of Lucifer is now known.[199] It is Huang-Ti, the Yellow Emperor, who lived around 2800 B.C.E.[200] Research shows that Chinese civilization owes much to this great ruler, who is said to have started the silk clothing industry and cultivated mulberry (for silkworms) and hemp. Ancient scribes took care to write accounts— of course written long after, but based on legends that were handed down—of the Yellow Emperor. One of the ministers at Huang-Ti's court, Ts'ang Chieh, was credited with the invention of the Chinese characters for writing.

Among the many accomplishments ascribed to the Yellow Emperor were his designing of clothes, his manufacturing of boats, his building of palaces, and his instruction of his court official Ling Lun in the art of making musical instruments.[201] The famous *Yellow Emperor's Canon of Internal Medicine*, considered the definitive source of traditional Chinese medicine, is in dialogue form comprising questions and answers between Huang-Ti and six of his ministers.[202] He is also considered the author of the oldest books on love, the Chinese *Handbooks of Sex*.[203] Moreover, ancient Chinese writings indicate that the Yellow Emperor was responsible for the invention of warfare. Victorious in a series of battles, he was recognized as the "Son of Heaven" by the conquered tribal chieftains, whom he united under his rule, thus becoming the first emperor of China. In short, Huang-Ti, the Yellow Emperor, is regarded as the originator of the Chinese culture.

Legend has it that he was conceived mysteriously when his mother was struck by lightning. She is said to have given birth to Huang-Ti on Xuanyuan Hill in the northwest of present-day Xinzheng County, Henan province, in the region of the Yellow River valley, the rich agricultural region that was the cradle of Chinese civilization. It is said that the boy was a genius, and already in early childhood he was an eloquent speaker, which must be how it came about that he was allowed to participate in the ceremonies cultivated by priests at a nearby mystery center. It is recounted that as a young man he observed the movements of the Sun, Moon, and stars, and paid attention to the properties of metals and gems; also that he mastered the art of prophecy from celestial and terrestrial signs, and ascertained how to use fire, water, wood, and other elements in the optimal way. It is reported that there was an auspicious omen of the Earth's energy that took place in his presence, and on account of this he was called the "yellow god." Tradition relates that he had twenty-five children, fourteen of them sons. It is said that when he was enthroned as emperor, a mysterious and auspicious bird, a phoenix, presented itself at his palace, which was located in the Kunlun mountains, perhaps in the area of the watershed between the catchment basins of China's two longest rivers, the Yangtze River and the Huang He (Yellow River), although he frequently changed his residence.[204]

It is interesting to consider the relationship between Huang-Ti (third millennium B.C.E.) and Lao Tzu (sixth century B.C.E.), who is generally considered to be the founder of Taoism.[205] Lao Tzu is the author of the "Taoist Bible," the *Tao Te Ching.* Alongside Confucianism, Taoism is the most important religion stemming from ancient China, although some followers maintain that Taoism is more a way of life than a religion. However, there can be no doubt that the thoughts and ideas written down in the *Tao Te Ching* are an expression of the Chinese spiritual-cultural tradition extending back to the Yellow Emperor, with the principle idea being the belief in a harmony existing between heaven and Earth expressed by the natural flow of nature called the Tao or "the Way." Given the continuity of tradition between Huang-Ti and Lao Tzu, Huang-Ti is widely regarded as the original founder of Taoism and Lao Tzu as a renovator of this religious stream, having inherited the legacy of the Yellow Emperor.

With regard to the incarnation of Lucifer in the Yellow Emperor, there are various signs that he was not a mere mortal. In fact, he was revered as a god—the "Dipper god"—because at the time of his birth his mother went out and felt in resonance with a huge bright lightning flashing around the constellation of the Big Dipper.[206] To this day Chinese from countries around the world gather once a year around March 3 on a special festival day in the Chinese lunar calendar at the birth place of the Yellow Emperor in Xinzheng County to offer sacrifices and worship the first ancestor of the Chinese people—Xinzheng being regarded as the birthplace of the Chinese people and Huang-Ti as the father of this people. As mentioned above, during his life Huang-Ti was recognized as the "Son of Heaven," a designation that indicates his godlike nature. This became a generic term for the rulers of China, and only much later—with the founding of the Qin dynasty in 221 B.C.E.—was the word "emperor" substituted in its place. Thus, like Huang-Ti, each Chinese emperor after him was acknowledged as the "Son of Heaven"—and as the only legitimate ruler, his authority extended to "all under heaven." Moreover, the Chinese character for Huang means "god-king" and the Chinese character for Ti means "sage-king." The name Huang-Ti therefore conveyed the god-like and wise status of the first emperor of China. And, as reported in the official China Daily newspaper in April 2002, a 5,000-year-old meteorite unearthed near a mausoleum for the Yellow Emperor in the Shaanxi province county of Huangling may lie behind the cataclysmic shattering of the land that historical records say killed Huang-Ti. Will it also be some cataclysmic event that will end the life of the Antichrist, the incarnated Ahriman?

At any rate, the legend concerning Huang-Ti states that immediately preceding his birth—precipitating his birth—remarkable celestial phenomena took place, and there occurred "a radiance from the great star Chi and [from] the Dipper constellation (*Ursa Major*)."[207] One can only conjecture which star the great star Chi was. However, since in China the star Regulus in the constellation of Leo is popularly referred to as the "star of the Yellow Emperor,"[208] Chi is almost certainly identical to Regulus.[209] At the time of Huang-Ti's birth, the summer solstice was in the vicinity of Regulus, and the conjunction of the summer solstice point with this royal star was exact around 2300 B.C.E. In Chinese astronomy Regulus is officially called *Xuan Yuan shí sì*, where Syuan Yuan (*Xuan Yuan*) is identified with a particular stellar region (asterism) in the constellation of Leo that includes the star Regulus, known in Chinese astronomy as the "fourteenth star" (*shí sì*), i.e., Regulus is the *fourteenth star* in the Syuan Yuan constellation. Traditionally Regulus is a star associated with royalty, its Latin name meaning "Little King," so the association of the first emperor of China with this star fits well.

There is another deeper sense to this correspondence between the constellation of Leo and the first emperor of China. If we follow the precession of the equinoxes back through history, we return to the time preceding the great flood that marked the end of civilization on the continent of Atlantis. The great deluge which destroyed Atlantis, that was located in the region of the Atlantic Ocean, occurred around the time of the transition from the Age of Leo to the Age of Cancer, around 8400 B.C.E. The last culture on the Atlantean continent flourished during the Age of Leo (10,586–8426 B.C.E.) and was called the *ancient Mongolian* civilization, and Chinese civilization represents a continuation of the ancient Mongolian civilization, implying that there is a relationship between China and the constellation of Leo.[210] Atlantis was the time of the flourishing of the primal Tao religion: "When an Atlantean spoke about the Great Spirit, the Atlantean expressed it by the word … Tao."[211] Elsewhere, we read the following description of the primal Tao experience, which flourished on ancient Atlantis:

> The Tao gives expression to the highest to which a large part of humanity looked up to and revered for thousands of years. It is something which was considered as a distant goal of the world and of humanity, the highest element which the human being carried as a germ within, which would one day develop into a fully opened blossom from the innermost depths of human nature. Tao signifies both a deeply hidden basis of the soul and at the same time an exalted future. Not only the name Tao, but the very thought of Tao filled those who had insight into it with awestruck reverence. The Tao religion is based on the principle of development, and it proclaims: That by which I am surrounded today is but a stage which has to be overcome. I must clearly see that this development in which I am involved has a goal, that I am going to work toward an exalted goal and that within me there lives a power which spurs me on to come to the great goal of Tao. If I can feel this great force within me and if I can feel that all creatures are aiming toward this great goal, then this force becomes the guiding force rushing toward me in the wind, sounding out of the stones, flashing in the lightning, rumbling in the thunder, sending its light to me from the Sun.

In the plant it is revealed as the force of growth, in the animal as feeling and perception. It is the force which will continually create form after form for every exalted aim, through which I know myself to be at one with the whole of nature, which flows out from me and into me with every breath I take, the symbol for the highest evolving spirit which I experience as life itself. I feel this force as Tao.[212]

This passage has been quoted at length in order to convey the essence of the Great Spirit of the Tao that Atlantean human beings experienced resounding through nature, expressed by the sequence of sounds T-A-O. It was this experience of the Great Spirit that was undergone by human beings during ancient Atlantis. This is significant for a number of reasons, one of them being (as described in chapter 3) that it was an ahrimanic being named Taotl who instituted the black-magic practice of human sacrifice in Mexico, and Taotl was an opponent ("caricatured counterpart") of the Great Spirit. In other words, Taotl was an ahrimanic distortion of the Great Spirit. Here we come back full circle to the Mexican mysteries, and below we shall elucidate the manifold connections here. Before doing so, however, let us continue our study of Huang-Ti, the Yellow Emperor, who was the human vessel for the incarnation of Lucifer in China during the early part of the third millennium B.C.E. Just as Taotl was an ahrimanic distortion of the Great Spirit active to the West of Atlantis, in Mexico, Huang-Ti carried over in a luciferic way the Tao impulse from Atlantis to the East, incarnating this impulse in China.

According to legend, Huang-Ti constructed twelve gigantic mirrors and used them to "follow the Moon," to keep track of it through its various phases.[213] Here again, we find a striking image of intention to connect the Earth with the cosmos, albeit in a luciferic way, i.e., to bring about a relationship with the Moon as an *externally mirrored reality* rather than as an awakening to the *inner reality of the lunar sphere* through spiritual development.[214] Huang-Ti is said to have lived for one hundred years and some sources indicate that he then returned to his home star, "ascended the heavens, and became the ruler of the Great Infinite, again turning into the star Syuan Yuan [Regulus]."[215]

As the founder of Taoism in China, the Yellow Emperor carried over much from the Atlantean mysteries of the Tao. However, he did this in a luciferic way. An analogy with the mirrors utilized by Huang-Ti can help us to understand this. "It was Lucifer himself, in a human body, who was the first to grasp through the power of the intellect what formerly could be imparted to humanity only through revelation."[216] The word "intellect" here is of key significance. For the intellect is like a mirror. It mirrors reality, but is not that reality itself. When people look at themselves in a mirror, what they see is *not* themselves but only a mirrored image of themselves. And so it is with the intellect. The intellect offers a mirror of reality, but it is only a mirror. Thus, one of the most far-reaching impacts of Lucifer's incarnation in ancient China, which started with him but is now the experience of almost everyone on Earth who can think, is that the intellect has become substituted in place of the reality of experience. What was a living experience of the Great Spirit for Atlanteans, became mirrored in a distorted way through being transmitted by way of the power of the intellect in ancient China. The Taoism that was introduced into China by the Yellow Emperor was extraordinarily profound, a carrying over of the content of the Atlantean mysteries, but it was distorted—in comparison with the original pure experience of the Tao that was accessible to human beings during the Atlantean period. This is in no way to undervalue the profound wisdom of Chinese Taoism. It is simply to draw attention to the transition that took place from Atlantis (living experience of the Great Spirit resounding in the Tao) to the form of Taoism—a luciferic wisdom—transmitted through Chinese culture in the wake of Lucifer's incarnation there.

Nevertheless, "luciferic wisdom was of the utmost benefit to humankind during that epoch of evolution. The whole of Gnostic thought at the time of the Mystery of Golgotha, an impressive wisdom shedding profound light on cosmic realities—this whole Gnostic knowledge was inspired by the impulse derived from luciferic forces."[217] In grasping this, it becomes evident that Lucifer's incarnation was of great benefit to humankind! And the same applies (at least potentially) to Ahriman's impending incarnation.

Now it is essential for the favorable effect of what Ahriman will bring to humanity—he will bring beneficial gifts too, just as Lucifer did—that we take the right attitude. The all-important thing is that we do not sleep through Ahriman's arrival and fail to perceive it. When the incarnation of Ahriman takes place in the western world a birth will be registered, John William Smith (although that will not be the name of course), and people will look upon the child as a solid citizen like any other, sleeping through in reality what has taken place.... In the ahrimanic age it is all-important that people should know that they have here to do only externally with John William Smith, that inwardly Ahriman is present, and that they must not deceive themselves through sleepy illusion about what has happened.... Ahriman will walk the Earth, bringing with him an extraordinary increase of power to earthly human reason.... Human beings must value rightly and make a right use of what enters the world through Ahriman. Humanity will only be able to do this if it is able to adjust in the right way now to what Ahriman is already sending to the Earth in order to control financial affairs upon Earth without being noticed. This must not happen. Ahriman must not control financial affairs and economics on the Earth without being noticed. We must thoroughly familiarize ourselves with his particular qualities and recognize what he does. We must be able to oppose him with full consciousness.[218]

In order to better understand the benefits of Ahriman's incarnation, let us consider the following figure, which indicates the triad of incarnations: that of Lucifer in Huang-Ti in China around 2800 B.C.E.; that of Christ in Jesus in Palestine in the period C.E. 29–33; and that of Ahriman "in the western world" possibly in the three-and-a-half-year period 2009 to 2012 (or perhaps in the three-and-a-half-year period 2012 to 2016, if the end of the Maya calendar signifies the *start*, and not the end, of the reign of the Antichrist).

Contemplating these three incarnations of higher beings, we behold again the mystery of *The Group* discussed in chapter 8. It is only when we contemplate the three key players—Christ, Lucifer, and Ahriman—in their interrelationship, that we can crack the code

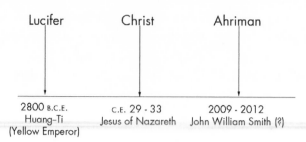

of historical evolution comprising the interventions of three spiritual beings in humankind's development here on Earth. For this reason considerable attention is given here to Lucifer's incarnation in Huang-Ti, as it helps us to understand and relate to Ahriman's incarnation in a human personality in our time. In a deeper sense, however, this is only possible by continually holding in consciousness the central incarnation, that of Christ in Jesus of Nazareth. For it is this incarnation alone that enables us to turn the other two incarnations to something of inestimable value.

On a personal level, the central focus of my life centers around the incarnation of Christ and a continuous ongoing endeavor to see the events of Christ's life as cosmic archetypes that periodically return. It took many years of research to discover the actual chronology of Christ's life, from which then the correspondences of the Christ events with the stars could be determined.[219] The discovery of the Apocalypse Code, discussed in chapter 2 and in appendix 2, is a nugget of gold that came to light through this ongoing astrosophical research. Also, the *Christian Star Calendar*, that has appeared yearly since 1991, offers monthly commentaries of the day by day changing stellar configurations in relation to the Christ events, intended as a help to attuning to the presence of Christ in the Earth's etheric aura in our time.[220]

Finding an inner relationship with the incarnation of Christ in Jesus is the most important thing in order to turn Ahriman's incarnation to good. Before turning our attention to Ahriman's gift to humanity, let us first consider the good that has come from Lucifer's incarnation. The gift of the intellect—abstract thinking—has enabled human beings to become free; otherwise we would still be inextricably interwoven with the forces of nature and, although we would be experiencing nature as a living being of which we are a part, we would not be free. This was the step from primal Taoism on Atlantis to the historical Taoism of ancient China. Within the Chinese Taoist tradition itself, Taoist masters who attained enlightenment broke through the veil of the intellect and came to know the "real Tao," as indicated in the opening phrase of the *Tao Te Ching*, "The Tao which can be spoken about is not the absolute Tao." The good that has come about through the abstract nature of the intellect is that we are free, able to cognize that we are separate from nature, and thus we are able *through our own volition* to find our way back to the reality of the experience of the world around us. On a deeper level this is the continual quest of all human beings.

On the other hand, the extraordinary cultural achievements of humankind over the last five thousand years are largely thanks to the development of the intellect. Moreover, it is this very intellect that allows us to turn to Christ *in freedom* and to begin to seek—through him—to find reality again. This was the endeavor of the Gnostics, referred to earlier, and it has been the endeavor of theology down through the centuries. It is now, in our time, through the Second Coming of Christ, that a fulfillment of all that humanity has striven for is possible for everyone, not just for the few who attain or have attained enlightenment. Further, it is precisely through the intellect—taken to a new level of cognition—that this step is possible. This is the *new Taoism*, expressed by Rudolf Steiner in his *Intuitive Thinking as a Spiritual Path*: "The universe appears to us in two opposite parts: *I* and *world*.... Only when we have made the *world content* into our *thought content* do we rediscover the connection from which we have sundered ourselves.... We can find nature outside us only if we first know her *within* us.... In thinking, we are given the element that unites our particular individuality with the whole of the cosmos.... Life within reality, filled with thought content, is at the same time life in God." [221]

What is alluded to here in a philosophical way is expressed more explicitly in terms of spiritual awakening in the following words concerning the development from thinking to spiritual beholding (clairvoyance):

If a pearl is lying in the roadway and a chicken finds it, the chicken does not especially value the pearl. Most men and women today are chickens in this respect. They do not value the pearl that lies there in full view before them. What they value is something quite different. They value their mental pictures, but no one could *think* abstractly, could have thoughts and ideas, if he or she were not clairvoyant. For in our ordinary thinking the *pearl of clairvoyance* is from the start contained. These thoughts and ideas arise in the soul through exactly the same process as that which gives rise to its highest powers. And it is immensely important to learn to understand that clairvoyance *begins* in something common and everyday. We only have to recognize the suprasensory nature of our concepts and ideas. We must realize that these come to us from the suprasensory worlds; only then can we look at the matter rightly. When I tell you about the highest spiritual hierarchies, about Seraphim, Cherubim, and Thrones, right down to Archangels and Angels, these are beings who speak to the human soul from higher spiritual worlds. It is from those worlds that concepts and ideas come into the human soul, not from the world of the senses.... O, human being, make bold to claim thy concepts and ideas as the beginning of thy clairvoyance![222]

Against this background, and also in relation to what has been expressed already in chapter 8 on the redemption of Lucifer, it can be understood that the incarnation of Lucifer in the Yellow Emperor was very much part of the divine plan for the evolution of humanity and that this incarnation brought something of great benefit to humankind. However, without the incarnation of Christ, the incarnation of Lucifer would have led humanity to brilliant achievements through luciferic wisdom but human civilization would have been devoid of love.[223] Just as wisdom was the gift of Lucifer, Christ's gift was divine love. When wisdom is placed in the service of divine love, Lucifer is redeemed, as described in chapter 8 of this book. Yet what is the prospect for Ahriman, and what is the gift that he is bringing to humanity through his incarnation?

We must not simply steer clear of Ahriman, but conquer Ahriman's forces for the progressive culture of humanity. For into our culture these forces must be received.... The task of humanity is to receive Ahriman together with his strong forces—all those forces of intellect, for instance, that are pre-eminently forces of intellect, but that can also assume a form that is more akin to feeling—those forces that have been applied, for instance, to the problem of how a state is established. Think of the numbers of people who have wrestled with this problem, some more theoretically, some more practically. The most intense efforts have been made to solve this problem. Such forces must be wrested into the good service of humanity, and must not be made ahrimanic by resolutions to have nothing to do with Ahriman, or refusals to be concerned with what, in social problems, for instance, is alleged to proceed from Ahriman. That would lead to nothing.[224]

This gives us an idea as to what is required in order to turn Ahriman's forces to good. It is a matter of wresting something from Ahriman. In order to understand what is meant by this, let us consider again that it was the intellect that, originally, was the gift of Lucifer. This gift led to the acquisition of freedom but at the same time to an estrangement from reality—through the "mirroring principle" of the intellect described above. Ahriman's influence is able to penetrate human thinking in the wake of this luciferic principle. In other words, as it was expressed earlier in this book, Ahriman is the *karma* of Lucifer. The influence of Ahriman upon humanity began to make itself felt especially from around the fifteenth century onward with the rise of modern science. "Modern science gives us an external illusion of the universe.... We must rise from [this] illusory character to true reality."[225] This external illusion, concerning both the world around us and our relationship to the world, has developed primarily since the fifteenth century, from which time the human thinking capacity has received a powerful boost through this ahrimanic influence. Wherever human thought has led unwittingly in the direction of materialistic scientific thinking (Charles Darwin's book *The Origin of the Species* published in 1859 is a classic example) humankind has come more and more under Ahriman's influence. With the initial estrangement from reality that came through Lucifer's gift of the capacity to think intellectually, human thinking was nevertheless still preoccupied with spirituality. For example, Huang-Ti's thinking was filled with the content of the Atlantean mysteries of the Tao, which he carried over into intellectual thought. Now, however, since Ahriman has begun to influence human thought life, a further degree of estrangement from reality is taking place, in that the intellect is presently, by and large, not concerned with spirituality or the inner life, but more with the scientific thought processes relating to the outer world or with thoughts of an egotistical nature. In this sense, Ahriman is the *karma* of Lucifer. It is vitally important that we recognize the illusory nature of most of our scientific conceptions; at the same time, we need these conceptions as a starting point in our quest for reality. And it is here that the "Tao point" in our thinking has to be found.[226] What is this?

The brightest point in ordinary consciousness is where we take initiative in thinking—in other words, where we freely choose to think about something. This is the "Tao point" from which, if we meditate upon that which we have chosen to think about, light streams upward, connecting with the realm of spirit (superconsciousness), and at the same time downward into the realm of the subconscious. The important thing is that our conscious "I" is actively engaged, then our thinking activity—if it is directed with pure aims—is freed from Ahriman's (and also Lucifer's) influence. Our intellect is always pushing further, wanting to acquire more and more knowledge, more and more concepts, and in order to find the "Tao point" we have to deliberately decide to interrupt the normal flow of intellectual activity. Where the intellect grasps something and an understanding lights up, *this* is the point of departure for meditation and contemplation, to plumb the depths of that which has been grasped. In this way we break through to another level of thought. And it is this other deeper level of thinking that leads eventually to seeing clairvoyantly, the prerequisite for which is that our thinking is permeated morally, i.e., that it is placed in the service of the Good.

There is one central thought that enables us to find the "Tao point" in our consciousness right away, and that is when we concentrate upon the thought I AM in the right way. The pure I AM is an expression of our "I"—itself an expression of our spirit—and by focusing upon the I AM we find ourselves as spirit beings. However, there is the pure way of experiencing I AM and there is the old luciferic way and the modern ahrimanic way. What characterizes the latter two is a quality of self-assertion. An example of luciferic self-assertion would be the thought, "I am an enlightened being" or "I am a god," and an example of ahrimanic self-assertion would be, "I am the wealthiest person in town." The pure I AM experience, however, is not characterized by self-assertion but by gratitude—thankfulness toward God for the gift of creation, including one's self or "I," which is an eternal gift. In this case the I AM is experienced as something originating in the heights of heaven, which shines in us and through us. This experience of the pure I AM is heightened further, if we offer ourselves up to Christ in love and devotion in the sense of St. Paul's words, "It is no longer I who live, but Christ who lives in me" (Galatians 2:20), which can be abbreviated simply to, "I in Christ— Christ in me." Then, through this new level of experience of I AM, we come into connection with the *Central Sun*, the ultimate source from which our entire existence has originated.[227] The "Tao point" in consciousness is the rediscovery of the Great Spirit within—or, through Christ, of the *Central Sun* within—which has *also* brought into existence the entire world without. This is the *new Taoism* in our time, a Tao experience at a different level from that which Atlantean human beings experienced.

Against this background we are now in a position to understand the experience of the Tao from Atlantis and the caricatures and distortions that have arisen over time, including the Mexican mysteries discussed in chapter 3. We have to distinguish between the I AM experience bestowed on humanity by Christ through his descent from the *Central Sun* and his sacrifice on Golgotha, which is the Mystery of Love, and the I AM experience of human beings prior to Christ's incarnation. The pre-Christian pure experience of the I AM was that of the Great Spirit and, simultaneously, the experience of the essence of the external world summarized in the word Tao— with the sense that the echoing of the Tao in surrounding nature was united with the Great Spirit. In ancient times what or who was the Great Spirit?

Human beings could look up to the Sun and perceive the Spirits of Form through a sea of mist.... This cooperative activity of the seven Spirits of Form was called by the Atlanteans the Great Spirit who revealed itself to human beings in ancient Atlantis.[228]

The Spirits of Form are Sun beings, whose abode is the Sun. In the Bible they are called the Elohim. "Then the Elohim said: Let us make the human being in our image, after our likeness" (Genesis 1:26). The word *Elohim* is usually translated from the Hebrew simply as *God*. It is the Elohim, working from our Sun, in service of the *Central Sun*, who bestowed the rudiments of the "I" upon human beings. The Elohim (Spirits of Form) are powerful beings—their Latin name *Potestates* means "Powers"—who have participated in the creation of human beings, along with hosts of other spiritual beings during long aeons of time.[229] There are many more Spirits of Form than the seven referred to collectively as the Great Spirit. However, these seven are of key significance to humanity as the bestowers of the "I." One of the seven left the Sun and united with the Moon in order to work from there—this is the one who is called in the Bible *Yahweh Elohim* or simply *Yahweh*.[230] This meant that there were then six Elohim working directly from the Sun and one Elohim, *Yahweh*, working from the Moon. The human sense of the "I" on Atlantis was connected with the Sun by day and with the Moon by night. And the third cosmic body that was of overriding significance for the Atlanteans was the Earth, which received what was streaming down from the Sun and Moon. The response of the Earth to the instreaming influences from the Sun and from the Moon—collectively experienced as the Great Spirit, the source of the "I"—was felt in the sequence of sounds T-A-O. The Atlanteans experienced how the Great Spirit bestowed on them divinity, the "I," and how the world around them echoed the Great Spirit in the Tao; also, that the Tao and the Great Spirit were a unity. From our vantage point, looking back, we can understand that this sense of unity—this Tao experience—reflects the fact that the Earth is born out of the cosmos, and so the creative forces at work in the cosmos, streaming from the Sun and also from the Moon, are the same forces that created the Earth and are echoed by the Earth in the sequence of sounds T-A-O.

The new Tao experience that is possible through Christ is that one's "I"—in and through Christ as the Divine I AM—is united with the ultimate source of existence, the *Central Sun*, and that all that exists derives ultimately from the *Central Sun*. Thus, the sense of unity between the human "I" and the surrounding world, which in earlier times—through the Great Spirit—included the Moon, the Sun, the planets, and the visible starry heavens, is extended through the Divine I AM to include the entire Milky Way Galaxy centered in the *Central Sun*.

As mentioned already, the Tao from ancient Atlantis was brought over in a luciferic way to China by Huang-Ti, the Yellow Emperor. The Tao also came to America, as is evident from the spirituality of indigenous people, the Native American Indians, who also refer to the Great Spirit and describe their "Tao experience" of the Earth as their mother:

> A few more moons, a few more winters, and not one of the descendants of the mighty hosts that once moved over this broad land or lived in happy homes, protected by the Great Spirit, will remain to mourn over the graves of a people once more powerful and hopeful than yours. But why should I mourn at the untimely fate of my people? Tribe follows tribe, and nation follows nation, like the waves of the sea. It is the order of nature, and regret is useless. Your time of decay may be distant, but it will surely come, for even the white man, whose God walked and talked with him as friend to friend, cannot be exempt from the common destiny. We may be brothers after all. We will see.... Every part of this Earth is sacred to my people. Every shining pine needle, every sandy shore, every mist in the dark woods, every clearing and humming insect is holy in the memory and experience of my people. The sap which courses through the trees carries the memories of the red man.... The rivers are our brothers, they quench our thirst.... The air is precious to the red man for all things share the same breath, The Beast, the tree, the man, they all share the same breath...The Earth is our mother (Chief Seattle).²³¹ The Great Spirit is in all things: he is in the air we breathe. The Great Spirit is our father, but the Earth

is our mother. She nourishes us; that which we put into the ground she returns to us.[232]

Even though the word Tao is not used to describe the core experience of the Native American Indians, it is clearly along the same lines as that which was described earlier as the Tao experience on ancient Atlantis.

In chapter 3 reference is made to the Mexican mysteries—this is the name given by Rudolf Steiner in his 1916 lectures describing the battle between the great white magician Huitzilopochtli and the black magician who was inspired by Taotl:

> When the Atlantean spoke of the Great Spirit, he expressed it in a word that sounded something like the word Tao, which is still preserved in China. An ahrimanic, caricatured counterpart appeared in the West as opponent of the Great Spirit Tao.... This spirit was called by a name that sounded something like Taotl. Taotl was thus an ahrimanic distortion of the Great Spirit.... A great many were initiated into the mysteries of Taotl but the initiation was of a completely ahrimanic character.[233]

In chapter 3 it is described how Huitzilopochtli overcame the black-magic initiate-leader of the Taotl mysteries in the year C.E. 33, at the same time as the Mystery of Golgotha. However, it is also described how these dark mysteries reemerged in metamorphosed form in the fifteenth century under the black magician Tlacaellel. Against the background of the Great Spirit—understood as the seven Elohim, the bestowers of the "I" upon human beings in preparation for the coming of Christ as the bearer of the Divine I AM—it is evident that the Taotl mysteries, opposing the Great Spirit Tao, were directed against the human "I." Since the whole meaning of humankind's evolution on the Earth is to develop the "I" and to spiritualize the "I" through uniting with Christ, it can be seen that these dark mysteries were opposed to the evolution of humanity and the Earth. Therefore they *had* to be overcome—first by Huizilopochtli in C.E. 33, and then by the coming of the Spanish in 1519 and, more important, by the appearance of the Virgin of Guadalupe on Tepeyac Hill in 1531. What is described in chapter 3 in relation to the Mexican mysteries is that the true Mexican mysteries were represented by Tezcatlipoca, "That was the name given to the being who, though he belonged to a much lower hierarchy, was partly connected through his qualities with Yahweh."[234] Not only was there ahrimanic opposition (the god Taotl) to Tezcatlipoca, but there was also luciferic opposition (the god Quetzalcoatl), "a spirit who could disseminate malignant diseases through certain magical forces, afflicting those whom he wished to injure in order to separate them from the relatively good god, Tezcatlipoca."[235]

The white magician Huitzilopochtli came to help restore the true Mexican mysteries centered on Tezcatlipoca, by overcoming the leader of the Taotl mysteries. In so doing he restored the Tezcatlipoca mysteries, and Quetzalcoatl, the luciferic opponent of Tezcatlipoca also withdrew—and, as described in chapter 8, there began a process of redeeming Lucifer at the time of the Mystery of Golgotha. Huitzilopochtli later became elevated to the status of a god, the Sun god, indicating a relationship (on a lesser level) with the six Sun Elohim, just as Tezcatlipoca, according to Steiner, had a relationship (on a lesser level) with Yahweh, the Elohim who works from the Moon. It can be seen here that through the deed of Huitzilopochtli there was an endeavor to restore the impulse of the Great Spirit in a good sense, in line with the working of the Elohim, but on a lesser level than had been the case in Atlantis—and this was in accordance with the whole stream of those ancient mysteries concerned with the development of the human "I" in pre-Christian times.

As depicted in chapter 3, the dark mysteries under Tlacaellel returned to the Mexico of the Aztec empire, this time disguised *outwardly* under the banner of the gods Huitzilopochtli and Tezcatlipoca—thus a complete inversion! In secret, another being altogether was the instigator of the reinstated ancient Mexican mysteries of blood sacrifice. Under Tlacaellel's reform, Quetzalcoatl officially played only a relatively minor role, the idea being put forward that Quetzalcoatl was opposed to human sacrifice—unlike the inverted Huitzilopochtli and Tezcatlipoca—and thus Quetzalcoatl appeared after Tlacaellel's religious reform in a beneficial light, rather than as the opponent of Tezcatlipoca, as in the former Mexican mysteries. The opposition

between Tezcatlipoca and Quetzalcoatl in the old Mexican mysteries mirrors the conflict between Yahweh and Lucifer depicted in the
Old Testament. Both Lucifer and Quetzalcoatl are symbolized by the
image of the serpent, the difference being, however, that Quetzalcoatl's
image is not simply the serpent, but the plumed or feathered serpent.
Possibly, something of the redemption of Lucifer (discussed in chapter
8) begins to show itself here, with the serpent elevated to a new level
by way of being merged with the sacred Quetzal bird.

However, in Steiner's exposition concerning the Mexican mysteries, he indicates that the Quetzalcoatl mysteries developed over millennia in secret in an *ahrimanic* form.[236] This may be understood in the
sense of a twofold process taking place in relation to the redemption
of Lucifer: on the one hand, Lucifer is undergoing a transformation,
becoming a servant of the forces of Light—in particular, through an
alliance with Sophia—and on the other hand there is a casting off or
falling away of unredeemed luciferic elements, becoming ahrimanic in
the process. This ahrimanic Quetzalcoatl is an example of an *egregore*,
a kind of shadowy double of the original Quetzalcoatl. And there is
no doubt that this *egregore* of Quetzalcoatl, like the Canaan Moloch,
did demand the blood of human sacrifice.[237] Just as the earlier Taotl
mysteries of blood sacrifice were overcome by Huiztilopochtli, and the
true Mexican mysteries, those of Tezcatlipoca, were established, so the
later black-magic mysteries under Tlacaellel—secretly they were the
mysteries of the ahrimanic Quetzalcoatl *egregore*—were overcome by
the Spanish conquistadores under the banner of Christ, and the cult
of the Virgin of Guadalupe was established by the miraculous appearance of the Virgin in 1531. It is remarkable in this connection to contemplate the passage in Genesis 3:15 of the woman treading the serpent
under foot, which can be interpreted here in relation to the Virgin
of Guadalupe treading under foot the stone serpent representing the
ahrimanic Quetzalcoatl *egregore* with its demand for blood sacrifice.

The ambitions of the Aztec empire were thus thwarted, just as the
dark Mexican mysteries were overcome almost exactly fifteen centuries earlier. In light of the theme of the coming of the Antichrist,
both the endeavor of the black magician initiate of the ahrimanic
Taotl Mexican mysteries and that of Aztec empire mastermind

Tlacaellel as an initiate of the ahrimanic Quetzalcoatl *egregore* can be seen as forerunners of the endeavor of the Antichrist, whose ambition is to establish a world empire under the inspiration and leadership of Ahriman *himself*. It is for this reason, to draw attention to the historical antecedents of Ahriman's interventions on the American continent, that these earlier ahrimanic mysteries on this continent have been explored in this book. The way in which these earlier interventions were overcome is also instructive. Clearly, as with the previous interventions, the current plan of Ahriman to establish a world empire—a new world order—can only be countered with the help of divine intervention. In this current situation, we can turn to Christ in his Second Coming and to Sophia descending from heavenly heights. We are also called upon to become active ourselves. And here we return to the question: How to turn the incarnation of Ahriman to good?

In order to turn to good Ahriman's strong forces—those accessible, for example, on the level of the intellect—we have to find the "Tao point" in our own consciousness. In the Hindu tradition this is identified with the so-called *third eye* in the middle region of the brow, a little above our two physical eyes. In the ancient Hindu tradition the word OM is the *bija mantram* ("seed mantra") for developing the power of the third eye, which is the faculty of clairvoyance. The divine word OM or AUM of the ancient Hindu tradition[238] corresponds precisely to the I AM of human beings in the post-Christian era, when the latter is spoken in the right way. I AM is a metamorphosis of AUM. What AUM signifies macrocosmically is conveyed microcosmically by I AM.[239] AUM (or OM) connects us with the Divine Word or Logos stemming from the *Central Sun*. However, as described in appendix 1, the Logos came from the *Central Sun* and incarnated upon the Earth. Since then, I AM is the modern *bija mantram* for awakening the third eye—I AM being the true name of Christ, who appeared in his pre-incarnatory form to Moses and at that time announced himself with the words: *Ehyeh asher Ehyeh* ("I AM the I AM"). By meditating or concentrating upon the I AM in the pure way described above, not in a self-assertive way, one awakens to one's own "I" or spirit being. This experience can be carried over into all thinking activity, so that the

"I" is then always engaged in one's thought activity. If undertaken in a selfless, non-egotistical way—for example, by applying one's thinking activity to finding solutions to problems on behalf of others—a remarkable new power of thinking can open up.

The point is that Ahriman's influence usually extends into our thinking in such a way as to encourage thinking either in a materialistic direction or in an egotistical way. The force underlying this can be wrested from Ahriman if we consciously direct our thinking in a spiritual direction and in a non-egotistical way. The I AM consciousness is decisive here, in being able to consciously take hold of Ahriman's force and turn it to good. In endeavoring to accomplish this, we are helped by the forces of Good, in particular by the Archangel Michael, who is the regent of cosmic thought. The image of Michael treading the dragon under foot is a very real one, as it applies directly in the forum of our consciousness whenever we engage in conscious thinking activity as outlined above. One great example of someone who accomplished the wresting of Ahriman's forces and turning them to good in a remarkable way is Rudolf Steiner. It was through this accomplishment in the forum of his thinking consciousness that Rudolf Steiner developed to full blossom his powers of clairvoyance— a clairvoyance simultaneously informed by his thinking activity, so that he was able to clothe his clairvoyant perceptions in the language of thought (*spiritual science* as he called it). Rudolf Steiner is a radiant example for all humanity of what is possible when Ahriman's forces are wrested into service of the Good.

Chapter 8 drew attention to Rudolf Steiner's sculpture *The Group*, also known as "The Representative of Humanity." Of all of Steiner's remarkable artistic creations in the building of the first Goetheanum, only *The Group* survived the flames that destroyed the building in the inferno that took place on the night of December 31, 1922. Fortunately, however, there are sketches and photos that inform us of what was there in the first Goetheanum. Looking from the great auditorium into the stage area intended for eurythmy performances and presentations of the four mystery plays written by Steiner, the location intended for *The Group* was at the back in the center of the stage.[240] Looking up to the ceiling of the cupola above the stage,[241] one was able to see

Rudolf Steiner's painting Christ between Lucifer and Ahriman
(for the small cupola of the first Goetheanum)

Steiner's extraordinary painting of *The Group*—in a different composition, however, than his sculpture of the same theme.

What does this image reveal? Again, as with the sculpture of *The Group*, we see Christ in the center, Lucifer above him to his left and Ahriman below him, in a cave within the Earth, to his right, and we see also the scene of the Crucifixion. First it has to be clarified that this painting was Rudolf Steiner's *design* for the great composition that was then painted on the small cupola of the first Goetheanum. Photographs were made of the cupola painting, and Steiner gave a lecture about the first Goetheanum using slides to illustrate his presentation. This is what he said about the composition on that occasion:

> Here you see the figure of Ahriman lying in a cave. Above him is "The Representative of Humanity," whom one can think of as Christ. From my spiritual beholding I have depicted him as the Christ figure. Rays of lightning proceed from his right hand, which surround Ahriman like winding snakes. The upward extended arm and hand go to Lucifer, who is painted in reddish yellow.... The face is yellow-red. The luciferic is that which in the human being strives up above his head in a state of exaltation, that which thereby estranges us from our true humanity, making us unworldly, so that we lose the ground beneath our feet.[242] Ahriman is in the cave, his head surrounded by the rays of lightning proceeding from Christ's hand.... The composition on the cupola shows Christ painted between Lucifer and Ahriman. Beneath, later (as it is not yet finished), the thirty-foot-high wooden sculpture, *The Group*, will stand: in the middle "The Representative of Humanity," Christ, his right arm extended down, the left arm above, so that this gesture portrays incarnated Love.[243]

This gesture, according to Judith von Halle, is precisely the gesture of Christ at the Ascension:

> In the early morning darkness on Ascension Day, Christ and the disciples left the house of the Last Supper.... He radiated all the love that can ever possibly be given on Earth. They climbed the Mount of Olives together.... He then became brighter than the Sun.... He was himself the Sun. Before it became impossible to make him out in this extremely bright sun-like radiance, he gave the Earth his blessing by raising his left arm as though he was letting the power of the cosmos flow into him and out into the Earth through his right arm, which pointed down to the ground.... It was an indescribable stream of cosmic love which sent the whole superhuman love of Christ out from its home in the stars to the Earth by flowing out of the cosmos through the left hand into the heart, and streaming out of the heart through the right hand

to the Earth. So it appeared as though the resurrected Son of God was binding—by raising his left hand to the heavens and holding his right hand down to the Earth—the macrocosmos and the microcosmos together through an eternal divine bond of unqualified devotion and self-sacrificing love. (The wooden statue "The Representative of Humanity" by Rudolf Steiner and Edith Maryon manifests this.)[244]

The reason for going into this in some detail is that Steiner himself obviously lived the inner reality of the image of *The Group* ("The Representative of Humanity"), and thus it does hold an important key in terms of communicating to us how we can meet the incarnation of Ahriman. Steiner's choice of the expression "The Representative of Humanity" shows that every human being is represented here by Christ, and thus the image is meant for each one of us personally. In inwardly identifying ourselves with this powerful image, we need to connect with the heavens above ("Our Father, who art in heaven") in love and devotion, and we need to feel the strength of our love for the Earth and to allow this love to flow through us to the Earth. In this way we allow Christ—as at the Ascension and as depicted in the image of "The Representative of Humanity"—to stream his love into and through us, and thereby Ahriman is held in check, holding in consciousness that, "Christ's descent into the abyss of the Earth [after the Crucifixion] put Ahriman into chains.... Christ does not carry any weapons in order to battle against Ahriman; it is the love of this radiant child of God that lays the powers of Ahriman in chains."[245] Awakening to the I AM presence in our consciousness connects us with the heights of heaven and allows the divine creative force of love to stream through us, to stream even all the way down through our feet into the Earth, and Ahriman is bound by the light-filled radiance of divine love—as depicted in the image painted by Steiner reproduced above.

There is another aspect concerning this image to which German author Hans-Joachim Aderhold draws attention. Describing the painting, he says:

> We see here Christ (yellow) in a rose-violet aura standing upon the Earth (brown). Within the Earth Ahriman (black) is bound.

This bondage is to be seen in connection with the scene of the Crucifixion (also brown) on the right side of the image. Above the scene of the Crucifixion there is a dark aura (also black). At the top left of the image, from the source of divine love (also red-violet) a yellow-white (Comforter) Light is streaming down upon the Earth and penetrates Ahriman with the force of dissolution. Simultaneously, ascending from the heart of Christ appears the *redeemed* Lucifer (red) amidst the radiant yellow of divine power imprinting itself upon the whole. [246]

What Hans-Joachim Aderhold draws attention to here is that the representation of Lucifer in this painting by Steiner can be seen in relation to the *redeemed* Lucifer. Since it is a matter of the redemption of the luciferic element within each individual, this representation of Lucifer can be seen either as presenting a temptation, as in the wooden sculpture of *The Group*, or as an aspect of the Comforter—the redeemed Lucifer working together with Divine Sophia, as discussed in chapter 8. At that time—Steiner executed this design in 1914—it was prior to the onset in 1933 of Christ's Second Coming in the human sphere and was thus too early to address the vast theme of Lucifer's redemption. Yet in the painting of this design (page 193), Steiner evidently felt it appropriate to portray this mystery artistically, leaving it for future generations to grasp the deeper significance of this portrayal of Lucifer in his work of art. At the present time, however, the situation is different from then, after more than seventy-five years of Christ's activity in the etheric realm, whereby the redemption of the luciferic influence within individual human beings is now underway. In chapter 8 attention is drawn to the year 2012 as a significant moment in time in relation to this process of Lucifer's redemption, and in this context the painting by Steiner takes on a new and inspiring dimension—beholding the redeemed Lucifer *working together with Christ* in the great conflict with Ahriman.

There is still a further aspect to the harnessing of Ahriman's force in order to turn it to good. Let us again consider the triad of incarnations of spiritual beings historically. The incarnation of Lucifer around 2800 B.C.E. in ancient China, in the far East, brought a great wisdom to humanity—the wisdom of the Tao, carried over from

Atlantis, albeit focused through the lens of the intellect. This wisdom, in metamorphosed form, has been of tremendous benefit to humanity—for example, it gave rise to gnosis, spiritual cognition, that was invaluable in comprehending the coming of Christ. Then came the incarnation of Christ in Jesus in the period C.E. 29 to 33—the incarnation of divine love, coming from the ultimate source, the *Central Sun*, to bestow the true I AM upon human beings and to begin the work of the transformation of the Earth into the "new Earth" (Revelation 21:1)—also, on account of Lucifer's conversion at the time of the Mystery of Golgotha, to begin the work through human beings of the redemption of Lucifer. Now, however, it is the time of the incarnation of Ahriman, whose endeavor can be summarized in one word: *power*.

So far we have discussed wresting the force of Ahriman from him in the realm of our thinking consciousness through finding the "Tao point" of the I AM. This was Steiner's focus, which he brought to expression above all in his philosophical work *The Philosophy of Freedom*, which was published in 1894 and which can be regarded as a key book for the *new Taoism* that is now opening up for humankind. It is also a matter, however, of harnessing Ahriman's force on the level of the will, and this aspect was the focus of attention of the anonymous author who wrote the book *Meditations on the Tarot*. In this work a series of twenty-two spiritual exercises are described in relation to the cards (Major Arcana) of the Tarot deck.[247] The first three spiritual exercises are the most important, called *mysticism, gnosis,* and *sacred magic*. Mysticism is the most important of the three. It is the exercise, or continual endeavor—primarily of the heart—to unite with divine love, with Christ, who is the guide of human beings on the spiritual path and who—as the Master—supervises the initiation that one undergoes on this path. Gnosis is the exercise of the conscious mind to unite with Divine Wisdom. Sacred magic is the exercise of the will to align with divine will. Gnosis, mysticism and sacred magic could be characterized as the endeavor to think, feel, and will as Christ did (and continues to do). As already referred to, gnosis is a gift of Lucifer's incarnation, and it is attained by placing Lucifer's wisdom in the service of Christ. Similarly, sacred magic (white magic) is a gift that can be acquired through harnessing Ahriman's impulse of power and placing it in the service of Christ. The spiritual formula for this is, "Not my will, but thy will be done" (Luke 22:42). For the true strength of the human being lies in fulfilling the divine will, which is the power to "move mountains" (Matthew 17:20). However, as the author of *Meditations on the Tarot* points out, sacred magic is dependent upon mysticism and gnosis. In other words, a prerequisite for the guidance of the will to accomplish sacred works in service of divine power is the union on a heart level (mysticism) with the Divine and a true spiritual knowing (gnosis) regarding what is to be done. Through mysticism and gnosis, sacred magic can then be accomplished, signifying the highest fulfillment of the human being on the Earth in the alignment of human will with divine will. This is *true power*. This possibility of true power is opening up to all humankind now through Ahriman's incarnation *if it can be harnessed in the right way*, as outlined above. The deed of the great white magician Huitzilopochtli, which signified the end of the black-magic Taotl mysteries in ancient Mexico in C.E. 33 can be viewed in this light, as *sacred magic*, as an expression of *true power*. It is to such deeds that we are called again now, in our time, in relation to the coming of the Antichrist. Over and against the mighty external power of the world empire of the Antichrist, which is not true power, since it is not aligned with the Divine, we can set the divine power of white magical will aligned with Christ who is the real regent of the world, he who is "King of kings, and Lord of lords" (Revelation 19:16).

Steiner spoke of three incarnations of suprasensory beings: Lucifer, Christ, and Ahriman. Against the background of the incarnation of Divine Sophia as the bearer of the Rose of the World, described in chapter 9, a new perspective is opened up: that of four incarnations of suprasensory beings, whereby the fourth—that of Sophia—is not like the other three, which were/are incarnations into a physical body, since her's is an incarnation into an etheric body.

The activity of Sophia in an ethereal raiment as the inspiration underlying the sixth cultural epoch, the Rose of the World, will extend over a period of 2,160 years.[248] As described in the previous chapter, the Rose of the World will initially flourish in Russia and the Slavic countries and will then become global. The Rose of the World

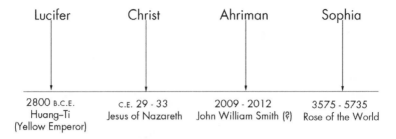

Lucifer	Christ	Ahriman	Sophia
2800 B.C.E. Huang-Ti (Yellow Emperor)	C.E. 29 - 33 Jesus of Nazareth	2009 - 2012 John William Smith (?)	3575 - 5735 Rose of the World

is the true global community of the future, based on love and wisdom, of which the world empire of the Antichrist, based on fear and coercive power, is a preemptive counterfeit caricature. In fact, just as the coming of Christ was the heavenly response to the Fall brought about by Lucifer, so the coming of Sophia is the answer of the heavens to the second Fall which Ahriman is now seeking to bring about. As discussed in chapter 8, the intervention of Lucifer was in the astral body and that of Ahriman is in the etheric body. At the time of the first Fall the luciferic influence inserted itself into the human astral body as the principle of *desire*. Now, with the second Fall, the intervention of Ahriman is penetrating into the human etheric body as the principle of *mechanization*.

The first Fall was part of the divine plan. Humanity at that time was nurtured within the womb of the Divine Mother in the Garden of Eden. Lucifer was allowed to intervene in order to insert desire into human beings, in the astral body, as a motivating force to encourage human beings to leave the paradise of the Garden of Eden and to begin to incarnate upon the Earth. Without Lucifer's intervention there would have been no cause for human beings to forsake paradise. However, there were consequences to this step. The human soul/spirit ("Eve/Adam" in Genesis), by embarking upon the series of incarnations on the Earth in a physical body, suffered three major consequences. These, as referred to in chapter 3 of Genesis, were toil, suffering, and death. The divine plan foresaw these consequences, and it was envisaged that later Christ would incarnate upon the Earth to overcome toil, suffering, and death. And this came to pass. First, though, through the series of incarnations upon the Earth in a physical body, human beings learned to know freedom—by virtue of being separated from the creative spiritual powers who brought forth the human being and with whom humanity was still united in the Garden of Eden. Freedom was the great gift brought about by Lucifer's intervention at the first Fall. However, it came at the expense of experiencing 1) toil, the toil of work upon the Earth in order to acquire the food that one needs to live in a physical body on the Earth; 2) suffering, the suffering of illnesses that one undergoes on the Earth, the suffering caused by the lack of fulfillment of earthly desires, the suffering of childbirth, etc.; and 3) death, the inevitable end of every human life on Earth in a physical body. In paradise there was/is no toil, no suffering, and no death. These were new experiences that human beings underwent, and continue to undergo, since the Fall.

Christ's coming signified the overcoming of these three "primal curses" as they are known.[249] He overcame toil through his teaching: "Come to me all who labor and are heavy laden...for my yoke is easy and my burden is light" (Matthew 12:28–30). This does not mean, of course, that Christ's teaching signifies the end of toil, but that whoever unites with Christ finds that toil is transformed and that one's life burdens become lightened. Second, Christ overcame suffering through his activity as a healer. Not only was he a teacher, but he was also a healer, and he healed human beings everywhere that he went. For example, the suffering of the paralyzed man who had lain on his pallet at the Pool of Bethesda for thirty-eight years was removed instantly when he was healed by Christ, who said to him: "Rise, take up your pallet, and walk" (John 5:8). Third, through the Resurrection Christ overcame death, saying: "Behold, I am alive for evermore, and I have the keys of death and Hades" (Revelation 1:18). With these words he indicated that death had no power over him anymore, and that he had power over Hades—we can think, in particular, of his having bound Ahriman in the underworld (Hades) on his path of descent following the Crucifixion. In the sense of Christ as "The Representative of Humanity," every human being can participate—at least to a certain extent—in Christ's triumph over the consequences of the Fall, his overcoming of toil, suffering, and death. In this sense, Christ's incarnation can be seen as the antidote to—and the overcoming by way of transformation of—Lucifer's intervention at the time of the Fall.

Similarly, Sophia's incarnation, bringing the Rose of the World, may be seen as the world-historic event that will signify the antidote to and transformation of Ahriman's incarnation in our time, bringing with it the second Fall. What is meant by this term? The first Fall was brought about by Lucifer's intervention in the human astral body, implanting desire into the astral body. The fundamental significance of the insertion of desire into the astral body was cognized by Gautama Buddha, who taught that desire is the root of all evil, which at that time (sixth/fifth centuries B.C.E.) it was. On the basis of this cognition, Buddha elaborated a spiritual path to eradicate desire and return to paradise (*nirvana*). In our time, a second Fall is being brought about by the insertion of Ahriman's influence into the human etheric body by way of technology. There is now sufficient evidence demonstrating the negative influences upon the human life-support system through over-exposure to electricity, to electromagnetic radiation, and to radioactivity—to name just three "effects of technology" to which modern human beings are exposed. We have to remember that there has never been a technological age like our own before in the history of the Earth, so what is currently being unleashed upon humanity by way of technology is unprecedented. There are, of course, enormous benefits to the right application of technology. However, these are at a cost, and the cost is the penetration of the etheric body with pernicious influences that have a detrimental effect upon human well-being. The word I am choosing here to characterize these effects is *mechanization*, which may not be the best choice, but it does convey something of the whole gamut of the mechanistic overlay of technological influences now working upon every human being. Everyone in modern society is exposed to these influences. Even if one chooses to live in a remote area and to have nothing to do with electricity or other modern conveniences, one cannot escape the electromagnetic waves transmitted through the atmosphere. For example, every time a satellite passes overhead, it is transmitting electromagnetic radiation, which has an impact to a greater or lesser extent upon the etheric (life) aura of everything on its path. Never before have human beings been exposed to all these technological influences at work upon the etheric body, and the overall mechanizing effect is taking its toll. For instance, it is recognizable in the dramatic increase of illnesses affecting the human being's immune system.

The role of the computer in this process of mechanization is enormous. Apart from anything else, as every computer programmer will acknowledge, the computer forces one as a programmer to think like a machine. There are those who early on in the computer era recognized the significance of the computer as a vessel for Ahriman's incarnation.[250] More and more, through a kind of symbiosis between humanity and the computer, the computer is invading human soul life. One example of this is the addiction to surfing the Internet; another is the addiction to computer games. The most Apocalyptic prospect, however, is the introduction of computers *into* the human being by way of computer chips. The computer is then—in a metamorphosed form—inside the human being and works directly and immediately upon the mechanization process from within, instead of from outside the human being. Remarkably this, too, was foreseen by John, as described in Revelation 13: "It [The Beast, whose number is 666] causes all...to be marked on the right hand or forehead, so that no one can buy or sell unless he has the mark [of The Beast]." At the time when John received this revelation, no one could envisage what was meant by these words concerning the mark of The Beast. Now, though, it is transparently clear that they refer to the computer chip, which—in the worst-case scenario—would replace all credit cards, etc., so that a chip the size of a grain of rice implanted under the skin, say, on the right hand, could be read directly by a scanner at the check-out desk of any store.[251] Moreover, by virtue of the implanted computer chip it would be possible to keep track of the whereabouts of everyone. Those who propagate the benefits of the computer chip do not pause to consider the incredible dehumanizing effect of having a computer—in this case a miniature computer terminal—inside one's organism.

The mechanization principle at work on the etheric body through the influence of Ahriman is the exact opposite of that which Christ in his Second Coming is bringing, which is the inflow of new life forces for humanity and the Earth. Access to this inflow is opened up along the path of moral development, which in turn is the prerequisite for sacred magic. The counterpart to *mechanization*, which is the consequence of Ahriman's amoral influence on the etheric (life) body, is known as the *moral ether*, which is the result of Christ's moral influence upon the life body. "Moral ether comes into being when the Christ impulse permeates human volition and activities... allowing the moral element to access nature in a way that has value for nature. The purpose of moral ether is to become an organ for the constructive influence of goodness in nature.... By means of actions that express a morally awakened will, and with flashes of moral ether, human beings will penetrate natural events."[252] This is a clear expression of sacred magic directed toward the world of nature. On the other hand, the mechanizing influence of Ahriman has the effect of removing us from nature, as is evident when we see little children playing with their computers instead of, as used to be the case, playing outside in nature.

The vast impact of this second Fall cannot be overestimated. Christ in his Second Coming is the bearer of the counter-impulse to the second Fall, but it is in the freedom of each individual to turn to the Etheric Christ or not. Because of this freedom of choice, it is likely that the second Fall will impact most of humanity and also—through the deeds of humankind—the Earth. It will be the task of the Rose of the World to heal the devastating effects upon human beings and upon the Earth of the consequences of the second Fall (see figure on page 197). The influence of Ahriman can be summarized in the words *abstraction* and *mechanization*. Abstraction denotes his influence upon human consciousness, taking hold of the human intellect and leading it further and further away from the Divine, which is the true reality of our existence. Christ's return in the etheric, if we take in the impulse proceeding from the Etheric Christ, is to lead our consciousness back into connection with the heart, with love, and thus away from abstraction back to that which is truly real. And the Etheric Christ counters mechanization through his moral influence upon the etheric body, leading to the activation of the moral ether as the bearer of goodness streaming out from the human being. It is upon this foundation—heart-oriented thinking on the one hand, and goodness of will on the other hand—that Sophia is able to bring the Rose of the World into being as the great future culture of love and wisdom.

An important moment in time—cosmically speaking—for the coming about of an impulse leading in the direction of the arising of the Rose of the World is indicated by two astronomical events in 2012. One is the transit of Venus across the face of the Sun on June 6, 2012. This is a rare astronomical event, which is important on account of the relationship between Sophia and Venus, also on account of the connection between Lucifer and Venus, holding in consciousness that the *Paraclete*, the Comforter, is a designation for the working together of the redeemed Lucifer and Sophia, as discussed in chapter 8. Then there is also the alignment of the Sun at the winter solstice (December 21) with the galactic equator, coinciding with the end of the Maya calendar. I am convinced that the date of December 21, 2012, as the end of the Maya Long Count calendar is not arbitrary, and that the deeper meaning of this date as a pivotal moment in humankind's spiritual evolution cannot be grasped without recourse to the meta-historical perspective offered by the book of Revelation. Clearly much more could be said about this, and this book cannot do more than give the reader a stimulus to explore further the various themes that are touched upon here. It is obvious, too, that I have relied heavenly on Rudolf Steiner, whom I regard as a reliable and accurate researcher, whose meta-historical and prophetic perspectives are far-reaching and breathtaking in scope. From his vantage point over ninety years ago he prophesied the incarnation of Ahriman in the flesh for our time—the event more popularly referred to as the "coming of the Antichrist." He also predicted "the fall of The Beast and his associate, the false prophet."[253] In 1990, based on a completely different astrosophical approach than the one used in this book, I came to the period between 2004 and 2016 as the time when this fall is going to take place.[254] Here in this book, a sharper focus is given by the date December 21, 2012. Whether this will really and truly signify the time of the prophesied fall of The Beast and the false prophet cannot be said with certainty, since one has to reckon with freedom. The great solar eclipse on July 22, 2009, appears to be the cosmically appointed moment in time in the life of the individual (according to Jeane Dixon, he was born on a very special day,[255] February 5, 1962) when, at the age of almost forty-seven and one-half, the incarnation of Satan/Ahriman will take place into this human vessel, signifying the start of a three-and-a-half-year period leading up to the end of the Maya calendar. Ahriman is surveying the situation from his vantage point, and will decide to incarnate then—or not, if things are not yet far enough advanced, as far as he is concerned, for him to achieve his goal of becoming the ruler of the world. It is also conceivable that he will wait until the end date of the Maya calendar in order to incarnate. The three-and-a-half-year period from the end of the year 2012 until halfway through the year 2016 also still falls within the "2012 window" of the galactic alignment, as discussed in chapter 2, and it coincides with the end of the period 2004 to 2016 mentioned.

Either way, it is clear that the prophesied event of the fall of The Beast and his associate, the false prophet, opens the way for humanity to embark upon a new course—hopefully in the direction of the Rose of the World. As I have described elsewhere, a new six-hundred-year cultural rhythm is due to begin in the year 2014, and this coincides with the prophesied date of the coming of a great leader of humanity, the Kalki Avatar.[256] Kalki is awaited in Hinduism as the coming Avatar—after Rama, Krishna, and Balarama (the brother of Krishna), who are regarded as the seventh, eighth, and ninth Avatars. In the Hindu tradition Kalki (also Kalkin or Kalaki) is the name of the tenth and final Avatar of Vishnu, the Maintainer, the second Person of the Hindu *Trimurti*, corresponding to the Son in the Holy Trinity. The prophecy quoted below indicates that Kalki will come at the end of *Kali Yuga*. The name *Kalki* denotes the "Annihilator of Ignorance." He is said to be the ruler of the realm of Shambhala. As Kalki, Vishnu will descend to annihilate ignorance and restore the golden age of virtue, *Satya Yuga*. It is imagined that he will come on a white horse, wielding a flaming sword with which to destroy wickedness and restore righteousness to the Earth. His is a two-edged sword—for the good, and against evil. He is the same as the Maitreya Buddha (*Maitreya*, "bearer of goodness"), the successor of Gautama Buddha, who is awaited in the Buddhist tradition.[257]

The source for this prophecy is the *S'rîmad Bhâgavatam* (also known as the *Bhâgavata Purâna*), which is one of the most important sacred books of India. It is arranged in twelve so-called cantos, and comprises 335 chapters with a total of about 18,000 verses. It stresses the prime importance of the *maintaining* aspect of God personified by the transcendental form of *Vishnu.* According to tradition, the writer of this work was Vyâsadeva (Vyâsa), also known as Bâdarâyana. He is said to have compiled the Vedas and also the great epic poem entitled the *Mahâbhârata,* of which the *Bhagavad Gîtâ* is the most important part. Vyâsa also wrote the *Purânas,* as well as the *Brahma-sûtra.*

Given that the date forecast for the emergence of the Kalki Avatar as the bearer of a new and mighty impulse for the evolution of the Earth and humanity is July 27, 2014 (see below), this dovetails closely with the date of the end of the Maya calendar. On this account, bearing in mind the elucidation in chapter 6 concerning the dating of *Kali Yuga* in relation to the Maya calendar, where the transition (from a "modified Hindu perspective") of the *Kali Yuga* to the New Age of *Satya Yuga* is equated with December 21, 2012, it seems fitting to close with the prophecy concerning the coming of the Kalki Avatar. For the Kalki Avatar, like Christ, is a bearer of the Mystery of Love.

> When the Supreme Lord has appeared on Earth as Kalki, the maintainer of religion, *Satya Yuga* will begin, and human society will bring forth progeny in the mode of goodness.... When the Moon, the Sun, and Brhaspati (Jupiter) are together in the constellation Karkata (Cancer), and all three enter simultaneously into the lunar mansion Pushya—at that exact moment the age of *Satya,* or *Krita,* will begin. (*S'rîmad Bhâgavatam* 12.2.22, 24)

Thus, when the Sun, Moon, and Jupiter are in conjunction in the Hindu lunar *nakshatra* Pushya (4°–17° Cancer), the emergence of the Kalki Avatar, the "bearer of goodness," is expected. It is in this lunar mansion that Praesepe, Jupiter's place of exaltation, is to be found. Evidently the Hindus attributed something special to Jupiter's location in this part of the zodiac: a special impulse of the Good comes to expression here.

The prophesied conjunction of the Sun, Moon, and Jupiter in Pushya will take place on July 27, 2014, possibly signifying the emergence of the Kalki Avatar to inaugurate a new spiritual era after the historical three and a half years of the Antichrist, when something of the impulse of goodness, connected with the work of the Kalki Avatar, might be expected to begin to stream in. For the Kalki Avatar is the teacher of morality (goodness). The Kalki Avatar's possible emergence in 2014 should manifest in a new spiritual impulse along the lines discussed in this chapter, strengthening moral consciousness and deeds of sacred magic. For the Kalki Avatar, also known as the "maintainer of religion," works in particular with white magic. His coming in 2014 fits well with the thesis developed in chapter 6 that, although according to Rudolf Steiner the *Kali Yuga* ended and the New Age began in 1899, there is now a transition period until the end of the Maya calendar, so that the full flowering of the New Age, *Satya Yuga*, will only begin at the winter solstice of the year 2012. The coming of the Kalki Avatar in 2014 could thus be seen as fulfilling the inauguration of this New Age. Thus, let us consider the following words by way of attunement to the work of the Kalki Avatar in our time as the transmitter of the power of goodness that our modern world so desperately needs:

> By the time the age of *Kali* ends...religious principles will be ruined...so-called religion will be mostly atheistic...the occupations of men will be stealing, lying and needless violence, and all the social classes will be reduced to the lowest level.... Family ties will extend no further than the immediate bonds of marriage...homes will be devoid of piety, and all human beings will have become like asses. At that time, the Supreme personality of the Godhead will appear on the Earth. Acting with the power of pure spiritual goodness, he will rescue eternal religion.... Lord Kalki will appear in...the great soul of *Vishnuyasha*[258].... When the Supreme Lord has appeared on Earth as Kalki, the maintainer of religion, *Satya Yuga* will begin, and human society will bring forth progeny in the mode of goodness. (*S'rîmad Bhâgavatam* 12; 2; 16–23)

AFTERWORD

Given the monumental significance for humanity of the event of Ahriman's incarnation, only certain dimensions of this event have been touched upon here. Among the themes worthy of attention and further research are the following:

1) Rudolf Steiner said the following on October 28, 1917 (Collected Works [CW], vol. 177): "It is interesting that the excellent statement was made in 1910 [by Francis Delaisi, *La Démocratie et les Financiers*, 1910]: '...*that big capital has succeeded in creating out of democracy the most wonderful, the most effective, the most flexible instrument for the exploitation of the population as a whole. We usually imagine that the men of finance are opposed to democracy*—the author in question says in his book—*but this is fundamentally mistaken. On the contrary, they lead it and consciously promote it. For it is this*—meaning democracy—*that provides the screen behind which they conceal their method of exploitation, and they find in it the best means of self-defence against any popular resentment that may arise.*' This shows how someone who has woken up sees that the main thing is not to make loud speeches proclaiming democracy; the main thing is to see clearly the reality of the situation...namely, from how few centers of command events in the world today are steered and directed.... [The average person] cannot attend [to these things], because they are smothered and buried under the—well, the same public life that is ruled over by the press." (The text quoted by Rudolf Steiner from Delaisi's book is italicized.)

2) What Rudolf Steiner addresses here is a vast theme: the exploitation of the population by an elite few. In order for this elite to achieve its goals, there is a continual creation of *maya* (illusion) from the press and media, consisting of a steady stream of cultural lies. These global cultural lies comprise the lens through which people's ethical and

moral conceptions are shaped, at least to a certain extent. Thereby the many honest and truthful accounts by recognized researchers and reporters are usually never mentioned by the media; they are simply ignored. It is vitally important in our time to cut through the illusion to be conscious of what is *really* taking place in the world, and almost the only way is via the Internet, in order to gain access to the accounts by independent researchers and reporters that are otherwise, by and large, unpublished. Although the Internet is an ahrimanic medium, it is still—at the present point in time (2009)—free and unrestricted, and allows for the publication of independent research. Having said this, it is clear that as there is no control whatsoever over what is published on the Internet, one has to be discerning. The responsibility for assessing the truth content of what appears on the Internet lies with oneself, with one's own sense for truth.

3) What is behind the global financial crisis? This vast theme could barely be touched on in this book. Yet, clearly, money (alongside military might) is the most important aspect of Satan/Ahriman's bid for world dominion. In 1933, Hitler came to power largely because of the appalling misery in Germany on account of the economic crisis there in the wake of the 1929 financial crash. And Hitler did not come empty-handed: he fueled an economic miracle which succeeded, from 1933 to 1937, in providing work for six million people. He also restored self-esteem to the German people—for example, through hosting the 1936 Olympic Games in Berlin—after the humiliation of defeat in World War I and the crushing conditions of the Treaty of Versailles, which required Germany to accept responsibility for causing the war, to disarm, to make substantial territorial concessions, and to pay exorbitant reparations to certain countries that had formed the Entente powers. What took place from 1933 to 1945 is history; nevertheless we can learn from it. Now, in relation to the present, the true story as to what underlies the current financial crisis has yet to be told, and hopefully there are some readers who might be encouraged to participate in further discussion regarding the present situation—in which case hopefully an Internet forum for reading the signs of the times can be started, intended as a means to enable active participation in an ongoing debate concerning these questions.

4) Related to number 3 is the theme of money and global finance. How many people have even a vague idea as to how the global financial system operates? Fortunately there are some researchers who have dedicated themselves to the task of unraveling the intricacies of the financial system. To have at least a rudimentary acquaintance with such research is a matter of great importance, if one wishes to be conscious of the grip that Satan/Ahriman/Mammon has on the modern world. (See, for example, www.whale.to/b/mullins5.html and www.monju.pwp.blueyonder.co.uk, the link to the website of Terry Boardman, a student of Rudolf Steiner who has published interesting articles related to themes addressed in this book.) In the words of Steiner, who devoted much research to exposing Ahriman's intention: "The endeavor is to found a [financial] ruling class in the West...with a terrible [financial] enslavement which [will]...in the course of time ensnare the entire civilized world and no one will be happy again" (lecture of December 1, 1918, CW 186, and lecture of December 31, 1918, CW 187).

5) In addition to financial enslavement through the power of money, the other main theme for gaining world control is military power. According to some researchers, the Global War on Terror is not simply about hunting down terrorists but is also about attaining strategic and economic objectives. Be that as it may, by redefining military doctrine to include the preemptive use of nuclear weapons, a dangerous threshold has been crossed. The attacks of September 11, 2001, are used to justify acts of war and conquest. Thereby a mammoth defense budget is justified at the expense not only of health and education, but of virtually every single category of public expenditure. "We've been warned there are evil people in this world. We've been warned so vividly...and we'll be alert. Your government is alert. The governors and mayors are alert that evil folks still lurk out there. As I said yesterday, people have declared war on America and they have made a terrible mistake.... My administration has a job to do and we're going to do it. We will rid the world of the evil-doers" (George W. Bush, CNN, September 16, 2001). To achieve this goal, *full-spectrum dominance* is the cornerstone of the new post-2001 military doctrine (en.wikipedia.org/wiki/Full-spectrum_dominance). In 2009,

hopes run high that the Barack Obama administration will reverse the recklessly destructive militarism of the Bush era. Initial indications (judging from Barack Obama's Cabinet appointments) do not reflect a fundamental change of heart in seizing a golden opportunity to initiate a new era of peace on Earth.

6) Apart from the striving to exercise military and financial power on a global scale, another area of growing concern to modern humanity, which has very much to do with our theme, is the genetic manipulation of organisms (GMO). Its relevance at this time is not surprising, since it is evident that it is actually part of the third temptation—the temptation of turning stones to bread—which is unfolding in the period 1988 to 2018. However, instead of the mineral realm ("stones") being manipulated to appear as if living ("bread"), it is a direct assault upon the "daily bread" itself. The words "Give us this day our daily bread" are directed to the Divine as the ultimate source of our daily bread. Food that is genetically manipulated is an attempted substitution of *inverted food* in place of the real food intended for us from our divine origin. By *inverted food* is meant the principle of taking that which is of divine origin and manipulating it so that it is changed while nevertheless still appearing to be like the original. It is again the principle of virtual reality, but now transposed to the organic realm. Moreover, GMO methods are promoted vigorously as an altruistic program: "To solve hunger in third world countries." In reality, there is a hidden agenda underlying the spread and proliferation of GMO, as exposed in F. William Engdahl's book *Seeds of Destruction: The Hidden Agenda of Genetic Manipulation* (Montreal/Canada: Global Research, 2007). The book outlines how a small elite is endeavoring to control the very basis of human survival, the provision of our daily bread. The inverted, anti-life nature of this endeavor is clear if one considers the use of "Terminator" seeds used to program a plant's DNA to kill its own embryos in order to force farmers and gardeners to repurchase seeds each year. Terminator genetically modified seeds "commit suicide" after one harvest season, thus compelling the purchase of new seeds each year: "No seeds, no food...unless you buy more seeds." If the proliferation of GMO organisms were to spread around the whole world, these seeds of destruction would replace

healthy seeds around the Earth—clearly a matter of concern for every thinking, caring human being on the planet. From the perspective of this book on Christ and the Maya calendar, since the Mystery of Golgotha—and in a new and more profound sense since the onset of the Second Coming—the Earth is the body of Christ, and thus not only human beings but also the animals, plants, and minerals of the Earth are sacred to Christ. This is the deeper meaning of the words, "Heaven is my throne, and Earth my footstool" (*Acts* 7:49). The endeavor of Satan/Ahriman is to take over the entire Earth and to populate the Earth with *his* creations—GMO—in place of the plant life sacred to Christ. The achievement of this goal would signify—at least, in the realm of food—the breaking of the link between humanity and nature. However, as the great Russian novelist Tolstoy said: "One of the first conditions of happiness is that the link between Man and Nature shall not be broken."

7) A contemporary of Tolstoy, the Russian philosopher Vladimir Solovyov (born 1853), passed away in the year 1900 at the threshold to the twentieth century. As well as being a philosopher, he was the founder of the spiritual stream of Sophiology (the theology of Divine Sophia), and he was also a mystic and a prophet. As early as 1882, in his "Second Discourse on Dostoevsky," Solovyov foresaw—and condemned—the sterility and cruelty of the collectivist tyranny which a few years later would oppress Russia. "The world must not be saved by recourse to force," Solovyov said. "One could imagine human beings toiling together toward some great end to which they would submit all of their own individual activity; but if this end is imposed on them, if it represents for them something fated and oppressive...then, even if this unity were to embrace all of humankind, universal brotherhood would not be the result, but only a giant anthill." This "anthill" was later constructed through the obtuse and cruel ideology of Lenin and Stalin. And in his final work, "A Short Story of the Antichrist" (finished Easter Sunday 1900), one is struck by how clearly Solovyov foresaw that "the epoch of great wars, civil strife, and revolutions" was coming. All this, he said, would prepare the way for the disappearance of "the old structure of separate nations" and "almost everywhere the remains of the ancient monarchical institutions would

disappear." He foresaw that this would pave the way for a "United States of Europe." The formation of the European Union in 1993 saw the fulfillment of this prophecy. Moreover, the accuracy of Solovyov's vision of the great crisis that would strike Christianity during the course of the twentieth century and culminating at the beginning of the twenty-first century is astonishing. He portrays the climax of this crisis as the coming of the Antichrist. In his portrayal, this fascinating personage succeeds in influencing and persuading almost everyone. The Antichrist, Solovyov says, will be an admirable philanthropist and he will not be hostile "in principle" to Christ. Indeed, he will appreciate Christ's teaching. But he will reject the teaching that Christ is unique, and he will deny that Christ is risen and alive today. Every reader is recommended to read Solovyov's prophetic work, "A Short Story of the Antichrist," which (alongside Steiner's prophecy of the incarnation of Ahriman and Jeane Dixon's visionary account of the birth and ascent to power of the Antichrist) offers insight into this monumental event of our time.

8) In the chapter on the redemption of Lucifer, something of the true significance of the New Age is indicated—however, only in outline. This is also another important and highly significant theme that we have only been able to touch on briefly in this book. What we have not been able to do, as it deserves a more complete treatment than is possible here, is to honor the achievements in the "New Age" movement in terms of awakening consciousness to spiritual reality, which is not to be underestimated in terms of the battle between Christ and Antichrist. Within the New Age movement there are many diverse streams, many of which, however, pay little or no attention to Christ. One stream which has been called into existence is that of *geomancy*— concerned with exploring the spirituality of the Earth and with healing the Earth. This stream, that is broadly represented within the New Age movement, has in Europe found a champion in Marko Pogacnik, who (like the authors of this book) is well aware of the whole dimension of *Earth changes* in connection with Christ's Second Coming. Marko's work is a significant contribution to awakening a connection with Christ in his Second Coming—an event that has to do with the spiritualization of the Earth. The work of geomancy, when aligned

with Christ in the etheric realm, opens up a new and vast dimension of spirituality as a counterpoint to the world of the Internet, in the sense that cyberspace is a shadowy lifeless realm (called by Terry Boardman "the belly of The Beast"), whereas the living experience of the spirituality of the Earth—together with Christ, the Spirit of the Earth—is a light-filled experience of life's great abundance. This theme itself is part of the vast one of Christ's Second Coming, his return in an ethereal raiment, which also deserves a much fuller treatment than we have been able to give it here.

9) In addition to the above eight themes, which are only a selection of important themes which, for reasons of space, have had to be omitted from this book, the theme of the Archangel Michael is of primary significance in relation to the titanic conflict with the Dragon/Satan/Ahriman, as is evident from the words: "Now war arose in heaven, Michael and his Angels fighting against the dragon; and the dragon and his Angels fought, but they were defeated and there was no longer any place for them in heaven. And the great dragon was thrown down, that ancient serpent, who is called the Devil and Satan, the deceiver of the whole world—he was thrown down to the Earth, and his Angels were thrown down with him" (Revelation 12:7–9). At the right-hand of Christ, the Archangel Michael is the "general of the celestial hosts." While not discussed in any detail in this book, the whole book is in service of the Archangel Michael, who is concerned that humanity awakens to the threat now posed by the coming of the Antichrist. As everyone who has studied Steiner's works knows, Steiner was a messenger/spokesman for the Archangel Michael in our time, and his works provide nourishment and spiritual support, and also offer a path of spiritual development leading to a living connection with the Archangel Michael.

One person, who later became a spiritual teacher in his own right, and who initially took the path outlined by Steiner, having already in his youth connected onto the spiritual stream of Sophiology, was the Russian esotericist Valentin Tomberg, who was born in St. Petersburg in 1900, the year of Solovyov's death. The following quote from Tomberg's *Christ and Sophia*, concerning the future destiny of Ahriman, offers a meditation that fits well to our theme:

The Defeat of Ahriman

Ahriman cannot be overcome either by *attacking* the ahrimanic element or by trying to convert it externally. The ahrimanic influence can neither be coerced by force nor inwardly transformed. The point is to *recognize* the ahrimanic element, not fear it. A courageous glance of recognition is the sword that limits Ahriman in the outer world, and the courage of self-knowledge is the force that renders the ahrimanic nature powerless in the human subconscious. As for Ahriman, the point is not to grant him power over the soul, and—with the weapon of recognition—to destroy all his attacks through uncompromising human courage. Stability and rocklike firmness are needed, not attacks or a desire to flee from ahrimanic onslaughts. The ahrimanic element is powerless if it cannot influence human beings with either fear or bribery. In such a condition of powerlessness, it receives no nourishment and disappears from the region, where it can no longer exercise power. Ahriman will be defeated, because he will not be nourished. His power in the universe looks enormous and overwhelming, but it is merely an illusion designed either to bribe or to frighten. Nonetheless, it is an *objective* illusion made up of *actual* external phenomena, but one that immediately shows itself as such when confronted by courageous recognition and incorruptibility—that is, a refusal to compromise, since all compromise is the result of bribery.

This has been shown as a fact of cosmic experience in the spiritual event of the Mystery of Golgotha traditionally called Christ's "descent into hell." ... Jesus Christ's "descent into hell" was the act that overcame Ahriman—not through superiority of power (that was not the issue), but by exposing the extent of Ahriman's true power over an alert and uncompromising consciousness. Since Jesus Christ walked that path, it has been proven that Ahriman's work in the world is hopeless, so long as people are willing to recognize and resist it. This attitude will continue into the future among those who do not succumb to Ahriman, and in this way Ahriman will be "shackled.".... Ahriman—who has always tried to lull human consciousness into a spiritual sleep and whose whole work was based on the hope that human beings would not be alert—will himself succumb to sleep, during which the things that happen to him will be the karmic counterpart of what he intended to do with the beings who became his prey.

In principle, therefore, the fate of the ahrimanic element is already sealed through Christ's descent into hell and his Resurrection; the prince of this world is defeated. [259]

The wisdom of the ancient calendars and their associated prophecies was in their anticipation of ever brighter dawns appearing after periods of darkness. The Maya Long Count's culmination at the thirty-six-year "window" marked by the alignment with the Galactic Center offers a promising image drawn from the cosmic pattern of the Earth and Sun's alignment with the Celestial Heart of our galaxy, to begin a new era of human alignment with the Divine. Similarly, the future according to the Apocalypse Code signifies a continuing unfolding and enactment of Christ's life—for the whole of humanity—over the next 36,000 years. There are many wondrous miracles ahead, once humankind makes it through the three temptations in the wilderness. We made it through the cosmic days of the first two temptations—1) 1929 to 1958 and 2) 1958 to 1988 (dates according to the Apocalypse Code)—and we will also make it through the cosmically appointed day of the third temptation: 3) 1988 to 2018. There is a precious and wondrous future ahead!

As Christ said, "You shall know the truth, and the truth shall make you free" (John 8:32). If one has ever had a feeling of uneasiness arising but does not know where it is coming from, it can actually be a great relief to come to know what is—or has been—amiss. And a real sense of freedom does arise when the truth becomes known, even if it is an uncomfortable truth. This book has been written to help lift a veil so that one can begin to become aware of what is truly amiss. Further, once one becomes aware of what is really going on in today's world, it is vitally important to behold the future calmly and with absolute trust in the ever-present help of Christ and his heavenly hosts, in the face of the unfolding of world destiny. Yet one has to *ask for* and *actively seek* this help.

Knowing clearly—at least to a certain extent—something of what the future holds in store, even if it is not exactly a rosy future, can bring an extraordinary sense of peace. Why? Because with *spirit beholding*, i.e., seeing into the future, it becomes a living experience that everything is watched over:

> Look at the birds of the air, that they do not sow, nor reap nor gather into barns, and yet your heavenly Father feeds them. Are you not worth much more than they? And who of you by being worried can add a single hour to his life?... Do not worry then, saying, "What will we eat?" or "What will we drink?" or "What will we wear for clothing?"... For your heavenly Father knows that you need all these things. But seek first his kingdom and his righteousness, and all these things shall be yours as well. (Matthew 6:26–33)

What emerges from these words is that it is the realm of spirit ("the kingdom") to which we have to turn first and foremost. This means that what takes place on the level of human consciousness is of great significance as a determining factor regarding the future. It is a matter of becoming active, first on an inner level in turning one's consciousness toward the realm of spirit, endeavoring to grasp what is right (in terms of divine righteousness), and then to act accordingly. Thus, each one of us is called upon to play our part, in whatever way we can, in the unfolding drama of humanity's destiny upon the Earth. And what is the essence of this destiny now? As already indicated in this book, the Second Coming of Christ—his return in the etheric aura of the Earth—is the primary event of our time, and the coming of the Antichrist is merely the shadow side of Christ's return.

This book has described the remarkable parallel between the "2012 window" (1980–2016) and the specification—by applying the Apocalypse Code—of the thirty-ninth day (1988–2018) of humanity "in the wilderness" on which the third temptation of humanity, the encounter with Satan/Ahriman takes place. As indicated in appendix 2, the period 2009 to 2014 is also the time, within this thirty-ninth day, when Pluto is at the same location (Sagittarius) in the zodiac as during the three and a half years of Christ's ministry. Given Rudolf Steiner's prophecy that the incarnation of Ahriman would take place *shortly after the year 2000* and that this incarnation is *inevitable*, the cosmic indicators point to the three and a half years of the incarnation of

Satan/Ahriman as occurring during the remaining time of the thirty-ninth day as an *inversion* of the three and a half years of Christ's ministry. Given the existence of freedom, however, the prophetic statements outlined in this book can only be *indications* and not certainties—and this needs to be borne in mind with regard to any discussion of the content of this book.

With this in mind, we offer a powerful meditation, given by the Russian esotericist Valentin Tomberg at Easter 1941, based on his clear beholding of Christ in his spiritual form—a meditation with which one can work actively and which can become an ever-growing source of strength and guidance, leading to a living experience of the presence of Christ in the life aura enveloping the Earth and interpenetrating the whole of nature.

MEDITATION ON THE RETURN OF CHRIST

Christ is already here.
From the south of the Earth, waves are proceeding from Him
    across the world.
Every human being is now able to create a connection with
    Him.
The human being has to do this out of free will.
He is opening the path to Shambhala,
And human beings are able to approach Him, to create a
    connection with Him.
For this, two things are necessary:
knowledge of Christ and Antichrist;
and aligning oneself with Christ.
If one chooses one of the two streams which are now streaming
    through the world:
Christ or Antichrist
—a radiant blue stream, and an ahrimanic stream—
when one chooses one is already taken into one of the two
    streams.
Through the Power of Christ one is immeasurably strengthened.
With Him one can pass through all trials and remain peaceful.
Through His Power one can endure to an extraordinary degree.
He bestows great Power.[260]

This meditation is a remarkable source of strength, as it directly addresses the spiritual situation in which humanity finds itself at the present time. Whether the three-and-one-half years of the Antichrist does or does not take place between July 2009 and the end of the Maya calendar in 2012, or during a later period associated with the "2012 Galactic Window," it is a fact that, since September 11, 2001, Ahriman has been preparing his incarnation with great intensity. This book was written to draw attention to his impending incarnation because only through meeting this apocalyptic event consciously can it be turned to good.

Appendix 1: The Central Sun

One important aspect indicated by Rudolf Steiner is that Sophia is a cosmic being, whose nature embraces the whole cosmos. Thus, when we contemplate the starry heavens, or even an image of the galaxy, we are able to gain insights into Sophia, who holds the blueprint for creation. Our Sun, and all the different Suns/stars in our galaxy, have ultimately all come into existence from the Galactic Center at the heart of the Milky Way Galaxy.[261] In the Platonic tradition reference is made to the *Transmundane* or *Supra-Celestial Sun*[262] and our Sun is conceived of as a miniature copy of this *Transmundane* or *Supra-Celestial Sun*—here we could also say *Central Sun*, if we identify Plato's *Supra-Celestial Sun* with the Galactic Center.[263] Could it be that Plato, in referring to the *Transmundane Sun*, had an inkling of the heart of our galaxy, conceived of as a *Central Sun* from which, ultimately, everything in our Milky Way Galaxy has proceeded?

Let us consider—along the lines of Platonic cosmology—that there is a *Central Sun* at the heart of our galaxy. However we designate what is at the Galactic Center, it is of immense power, as may be grasped by way of the following analogy. If one imagines the force exerted by our Sun in holding the nine planets[264] and countless asteroids and other cosmic objects in their orbits, one will get a sense of the power and majesty of our Sun. Now, think along the lines of Platonic cosmology of a *Central Sun* at the Galactic Center; the scope of its power is such as to hold more than one hundred billion Suns (not planets!), in their orbits around it, including our Sun!

To explain this immense power, modern astronomy postulates the existence of a "supermassive black hole" at the center of our galaxy. We have to bear in mind that this is a theoretical construction of modern astronomy. Moreover, from my perspective it is an inadequate theoretical explanation of what takes place at the transition point from the realm of material creation to the realm of pure spirit. The alternative perspective that is offered here is that at the Galactic Center there is a *Central Sun* (Plato's *Supra-Celestial Sun*) and that all the Suns/stars in the heavens, including our Sun, are—ultimately—offspring of the *Central Sun*.

By way of analogy and in support of this alternative perspective, let us consider Rudolf Steiner's description of our Sun, and then apply this on a galactic level to the *Central Sun* at the heart of our galaxy. This is actually how one can arrive at a true concept of what is really at the Galactic Center (rather than the current inadequate concept of a "supermassive black hole"). This true concept is offered by Steiner in at least three different lecture cycles.[265] In one of them, the *Astronomy Course*, he gives indications concerning the interior of the Sun: moving from the outside toward its center, it declines more and more in its physical-material composition to eventually become what he calls "negative, sucking matter." Hence, he says, our Sun exerts a tremendous sucking force and "then you do not need any other explanation of gravity than this, as this is already the explanation of gravity."[266] (He means, of course, the gravity exerted by our Sun to hold all the planets and other heavenly bodies in their orbits around the Sun). And elsewhere he says: "I have often said that the physicist would be greatly astonished if he could travel to the Sun and find there nothing of what he now imagines, but simply a hollow space; nay, even a hollow space of suction which annihilates everything within it. A space indeed that is less than hollow. A hollow space merely receives what is put into it; but the Sun is a hollow space of such a nature that anything brought to it is immediately absorbed and disappears."[267]

Here, in these words, Rudolf Steiner gives a true concept in place of that of a "black hole." This concept given by Rudolf Steiner to explain the gravitational pull exerted by our Sun can, by way of analogy, also be applied to describe on a much vaster scale the working of the *Central Sun* at the heart of our galaxy, which has been inadequately described as a "supermassive black hole." It is the "tremendous sucking force" of the *Central Sun* that holds all the billions of Suns/stars in their orbits in our Milky Way Galaxy. The *Central Sun* at rest at the Galactic Center, around which all the Suns/stars are moving in a clockwise direction, is evidently what Aristotle called the *Prime Mover*.[268] Everything in our galaxy is moving around this great center.

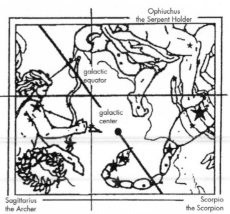

The Archer aims his arrow toward the Galactic Center (2° Sagittarius)
Image by Raymond Mardyks

Now we are in a better position to understand what the Galactic Center is. When we look up to the constellation of Sagittarius, we behold—traced out by the pattern of the stars— the figure of an Archer who is aiming his arrow. It is an extraordinary fact that his arrow is aimed directly at the Galactic Center (located at 2° Sagittarius), where an extraordinarily intensive point of infrared light has been discovered.[269] This energy source, approximately fifty light years in diameter—called Sagittarius A*—has been identified as the actual center of our Milky Way Galaxy. Located some 25,000 light years from our solar system, it is estimated that this energy source is about 500 million times more powerful than our Sun. From here emanates the power that holds our galaxy of more than 100 billion stars together. This is the *Central Sun*, if we adhere to the conception of Platonic cosmology, i.e., the *Transmundane* or *Supra-Celestial Sun* described by Plato as the source or origin of all the Suns/stars in the cosmos.

All the stars that we see in the heavens are Suns, like our Sun. All of them rotate slowly in a clockwise direction around the *Central Sun*, "*Like a wheel that is evenly moved by the love that moves the Sun and the other stars.*"[270] In light of Dante's words, could it be the fire of divine love emanating from the *Central Sun* that supports and sustains all the Suns/stars in the heavens such that it is literally "*Love that makes the world go round*"?

To gain an idea of the immensity of the *Central Sun* at the heart of our galaxy, let us imagine a second Sun alongside our Sun. And then in our imagination let us add a third Sun, and a fourth Sun, and a fifth

Illustration for Dante's Divine Comedy, Paradiso by Gustave Doré:
Dante and Beatrice beholding the Empyrean in the form of a
snow-white rose (Empyrean derives from the Ancient Greek
word Pyr meaning fire, which reminds us of Daniel Andreev's
term Astrofire for the Galactic Center)

Sun...and so on, until there are 500 million Suns there. This imaginative exercise can offer us a glimpse of the power, majesty, and glory of the *Central Sun* at the Galactic Center, which holds more than one hundred billion Suns/stars in their orbits around it.

Daniel Andreev once had a vision of the Galactic Center, which he called *Astrofire*, and which he describes in *The Rose of the World*: "I remember seeing a glowing mist of stunning majesty, as though the creative heart of our universe had revealed itself to me in visible form for the first time. It was *Astrofire*, the great center of our galaxy."[271]

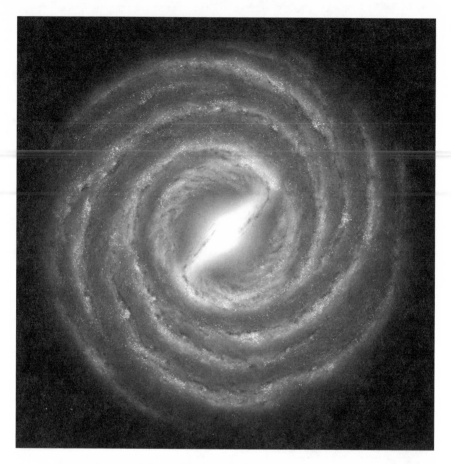

A rendering of the Milky Way Galaxy (NASA/JPL-Caltech)

Moreover, Divine Sophia has something to do with this great center, as we shall see.

Let us look back to someone who had a deep relationship with Sophia: the Italian poet Dante. In Dante's vision, which he had at Easter in the year 1300, and which he spent the rest of his life writing down as *The Divine Comedy*, he beheld the highest realm. In Dante's vision of the highest heaven he calls this highest realm the *Empyrean*, signifying a realm of fire—the fire of divine love. Let us now contemplate the depiction by the French graphic artist Gustav Doré of Dante's vision of the *Empyrean* (see above), and let us then compare this with an image of our Milky Way Galaxy (see above). One can immediately see the similarity. It appears that what Dante beheld in mystical (inner) vision has now been found outwardly by modern astronomy—in the shape of our galaxy—seven hundred years later. Dante describes in his vision the throne of God at the center and countless beings around the throne of God. According to Dante, the whole is fashioned in the form of "a snow-white rose."

Those who know the mystical tradition will recognize that this image invoked by Dante relates on a deeper level to Sophia. In the *Litany of Loreto*, for example, the Virgin Mary is referred to as the *Mystical Rose* and this appellation clearly applies also to Sophia, by way of her association with the Virgin Mary.[272] Further, often the Virgin Mary and the Christ child are found in the central rosette of the glorious rose windows in French Gothic cathedrals, thus associating the Virgin—and, again by way of association, Sophia—with the image of the rose. It is as if the creators of the rose windows were inspired by the same archetype spoken of by Dante as the "snow-white rose." Moreover, in the mystical tradition the creation itself is seen as a rose that is unfolding, or blossoming, over the six days of creation—this rose being Sophia, who is the plan of the creation and is thus called *Rosa Mundi*, the Rose of the World.

In contemplating an image of our galaxy, what are we actually beholding? Are we on some level beholding an image of Sophia in the form of a snow-white rose? Is Sophia, as the wisdom or plan of creation, one and the same with what we see revealed in the structure of our galaxy? Considering that Sophia—according to her own words from the book of Proverbs—has always had a relationship with our evolution "from the beginning of creation," is it reasonable to conclude that Sophia is a being connected with the heart of our galaxy, the Galactic Center being the source or origin of the entire creation of our Milky Way Galaxy?

One of the important things that Rudolf Steiner indicated was that the being whom we call Sophia is the same as the goddess whom the Egyptians called Isis.[273] We know of the great significance of Isis for the Egyptian culture and also of the significance of Osiris. Isis and Osiris were regarded as sister and brother and also as bride and groom. If we take this idea of Rudolf Steiner and work with it, that Sophia is the same as Isis, then whom were the Egyptians referring to as Osiris?

In various lectures Steiner describes that Osiris was how the Egyptian people saw Christ before his incarnation on the Earth. We could think of this as a pre-incarnatory revelation of Christ to the Egyptian people in the form of Osiris, before Christ incarnated on the Earth. Against this background we can understand the words of St. Augustine, who indicated that there was a "Christianity before Christ."[274] And this applies not only to the Egyptians, but to other cultures as well.

> Although Christ appeared only later, he was always present in the spiritual sphere of the Earth. Already in the ancient Oracles of Atlantis, the priests of those Oracles spoke of the "Spirit of the Sun," of Christ. In the old Indian epoch of civilization the Holy Rishis spoke of "Vishva Karman"; Zarathustra in ancient Persia spoke of "Ahura Mazda," Hermes [in Egypt spoke] of "Osiris"; and Moses spoke of the Power which, being eternal, brings about the harmonization of the temporal and natural, the Power living in the "Ehyeh asher Ehyeh" (I AM the I AM) as the harbinger of Christ. All spoke of the Christ.[275]

If we grasp this background concerning the ancient Egyptian mystery religion of Isis and Osiris, we can begin to understand that the Egyptians were indeed "Christians before Christ." Before Christ came into incarnation on the Earth, they worshipped him in his pre-incarnatory form as Osiris. The Egyptians recognized that Osiris and Isis have a deep relationship to each other; they are the same beings we know now, during the post-Christian era, as Christ and Sophia. This is addressed in the revelation to John, the last book in the Bible, which is the revelation of the Ascended Christ to John the beloved disciple on the island of Patmos. It is clear that the one who is called the "Lamb" in Revelation is Christ. That is also the name that John the Baptist gave to Christ, as indicated in John's words: "Behold the Lamb of God" (John 1:29). In chapter 21 of Revelation reference is made to the "Bride of the Lamb" who is Sophia. In conclusion, then, if Sophia is associated with the *Central Sun* at the heart of our galaxy, then so also is Christ, and thus the *Central Sun* is the provenance of both the Lamb and his Bride, who is called the Mystical Rose (*Rosa Mundi*), the Rose of the World.

The *Central Sun* is not only the provenance of the Lamb (the Son) and his Bride (Sophia), but is also the ultimate abode of the Holy Spirit—this being a discovery of spiritual research, a finding that is supported by the following astrosophical considerations. The archetypal historical manifestation of the Holy Spirit was at Pentecost, descending upon the disciples in the form of tongues of fire (*Acts* 2:3). At the event of Pentecost the Sun was located at 2½° Gemini.[276] The fact that at Pentecost at sunrise on May 24, C.E. 33 the Sun was located at 2½° Gemini signifies that the Earth—as seen from the Sun (thus diametrically *opposite* the Sun in the zodiac)—was at 2½° Sagittarius, in conjunction with the Galactic Center (2° Sagittarius). Divine love proceeded from the *Central Sun* in the shape of the Holy Spirit seen as tongues of fire above the heads of the disciples.[277] This emanation of divine love from the *Central Sun* was transmitted *directly* to the Earth at the cosmically effective moment in time of the Earth's conjunction with the Galactic Center on this day of the original, historical event of Pentecost.[278] This astronomical fact indicates that the ultimate abode of the Holy Spirit is indeed the *Central Sun*.[279]

The theme of fire symbolizing the divine love emanating from the *Central Sun* is a recurrent one. As indicated above, Dante refers to this highest world (the galactic plane at whose center is the *Central Sun*) as the *Empyrean*, and *Pyr* comes from the Greek, meaning fire. The *Empyrean* is thus a world of fire, the fire of divine love that pours forth from the *Central Sun* and sustains all existence. The source or heart ("hearth") of this fire is the *Central Sun*, which Daniel Andreev refers to by the name *Astrofire*, meaning *Star Fire*—the fire of divine love emanating from the *Central Sun* which is received, and then transmitted further, by every star in the heavens, including our "local star," the Sun. "The stars are the expression of love in the cosmic ether... To see a star means to feel a caress that has been prompted by love... To gaze at the stars is to become aware of the love proceeding from divine spiritual beings."[280]

Appendix 2: The Good News

"Good news," or good tidings, is the meaning of the word *Gospel*, which derives from the Old English *god-spell*. In turn, Gospel is the translation from the ecclesiastical Latin *evangelium*, itself deriving from the Greek word *euangelion*, which is also the source of the term Evangelist in English. The writers of the four Gospels—Matthew, Mark, Luke, and John—are known as the four Evangelists. St. Paul used the term in speaking of "the gospel (*euangelion*) I preached to you" in the passage where he speaks of the Mystery of Golgotha and the appearances of the Risen Christ (I Corinthians 15:1–8). Paul indicates here that the Gospel contains the power of redemption "by which you are saved, if you hold fast to it."

Nowadays the word Gospel generally carries the connotation of something belonging to the past, completed long ago with the four Gospels, so that in our time there is not the Pauline sense that the Gospel is a living force, a power of redemption.[281] An attempt was made in the early twentieth century by Rudolf Steiner to break through to a new level of "Gospel experience" when he held his 1913 / 1914 lectures entitled *The Fifth Gospel*.[282] These lectures were delivered shortly after Steiner began his proclamation of Christ's Second Coming in the etheric realm. This proclamation is generally believed to have begun on January 12, 1910, since this was the first time that he spoke about the dating of the onset of this event in the twentieth century: "Rudolf Steiner spoke in Stockholm for the first time about the reappearance of Christ in the etheric in the course of the twentieth century."[283] However, in 1917 Steiner indicated that the proclamation of Christ's Second Coming *began already in 1909.*

With the coming Christ, with the presence of Christ, will come the time when human beings will learn to enquire of him, not only concerning their souls, but also concerning the immortal part of their being on Earth. Christ is not a ruler of human beings, but their brother who, particularly in the near future, wishes to be consulted on all the details of life... Then human souls will see Christ standing by them as the beloved companion and they will not only obtain consolation and strength from the Christ being, but will also receive instruction from him as to what is to be done.... For Christ is with us always, even to the end of the Earth.... He will draw near to us and give us the strength and force in which we shall then live. The Christ will guide us, standing beside us as a brother, so that our hearts and souls may be strong enough to rise to the necessary level of the tasks awaiting humanity in its further development.... The esotericist is able to point out that since the year 1909 or thereabouts what is to come is being distinctly and perceptibly prepared for, that since the year 1909 we are inwardly living in a very special time. It is possible today, if we do but seek him, to be very near to Christ, to find him in a quite different way than has been hitherto possible.[284]

In occupying myself with this indication concerning the year 1909, I came across two lectures Steiner held at Easter 1909 called "Spiritual Bells of Easter." Before referring to the content of these lectures, it is important to bear in mind that 2009—the date highlighted in chapter 2 as possibly the beginning of the three and a half years of the Antichrist—also corresponds to the hundredth anniversary of the initial proclamation of Christ's enlivening presence in the etheric realm of the Earth. The positive significance of 2009 is then evident on taking into account the completion of three cycles of periods of 33 1/3 years, which is the rhythm of the Etheric Christ.[285] This is the *positive side*—the *good news*—in relation to the possible events which could fall within the shadow of the solar eclipse on July 22, 2009 (discussed in chapter 2).

The first proclamation of the reappearance of Christ in the etheric realm of the Earth was indicated in a veiled way in the two "Spiritual Bells of Easter" lectures referred to above, where the individual

Kashyapa is spoken of as a figure from the spiritual tradition of India. There are at least two Kashyapas, who have to be distinguished. The first—particularly revered in the Hindu tradition—was one of the seven Holy Rishis who revealed the primal wisdom early in the ancient Indian culture. The second—especially honored in the Buddhist tradition—was one of Kashyapa's later incarnations in India as a disciple of the Buddha in the fifth/sixth centuries B.C.E., when he again bore this name. He was Gautama Buddha's chosen disciple to whom the Buddha gave his gold brocade mantle, thus indicating Kashyapa to be the Buddha's successor—the one who will become the next Buddha, the Maitreya Buddha. In Steiner's 1909 lectures he speaks of a legend "that when Kashyapa came to the point of death and on account of his mature wisdom was ready to pass into *nirvana*, he made his way to a steep mountain and hid himself in a cave. After his death his body did not decay but remained intact. Only initiates know of this secret and of the hidden place where the incorruptible body of the great initiate rests. But the Buddha foretold that one day in the future his great successor, the Maitreya Buddha, the new great teacher and leader of humankind, would come, and reaching the supreme height of existence to be attained during earthly life, would seek out the cave of Kashyapa and touch with his right hand the incorruptible body of the enlightened one. Whereupon a miraculous fire would stream down from heaven and in this fire the incorruptible body of Kashyapa, the enlightened one, would be lifted from earthly into spiritual existence."[286] Having described this legend concerning Kashyapa in relation to the spiritual fire brought down by the Maitreya Buddha, Rudolf Steiner then goes on to proclaim *the return of Christ* with these words: "He will be revealed to us in a spiritualized fire of the future. He is with us always, until the end of the world, and he will appear in the spiritual fire to those who have allowed their eyes to be enlightened through the Event of Golgotha. *Human beings will behold him in the spiritual fire.* They beheld him, to begin with, in a different form; they will behold him for the first time in his true form, in a spiritual fire."[287] In contrast to his subsequent 1910 lectures on the reappearance of Christ in the etheric, here Steiner does not give specific dates, but he nevertheless proclaims this event, through which human beings "will behold him [Christ] for the first time in his true form," i.e., in an etheric body, *in spiritual fire.*

These two lectures, held at Easter 1909, were inspired by Kashyapa, the bodhisattva who will become the Maitreya Buddha. Who is this bodhisattva? "He is a great individuality who, since the time of Buddha, since about 600 B.C.E....has been incarnated nearly every century since that time, is now [1911] also already incarnated, and will be *the real* herald of the Christ in etheric raiment."[288] With the expression *the real* (German, *der eigentliche*), Rudolf Steiner brought to expression that he saw this bodhisattva as the *actual* proclaimer of the Etheric Christ, and that he (Rudolf Steiner) was proclaiming the event of Christ's return by way of the inspiration that he was receiving from this bodhisattva. "We must allow ourselves to be inspired by the bodhisattva who will become the Maitreya Buddha. The inspiration makes us aware of a future when those who develop new forces through renewed Essene wisdom will be blessed and enlivened by the appearance of the Christ in a new etheric guise."[289] It is clear from the context of the two lectures "Spiritual Bells of Easter" that they are dedicated to Kashyapa, and that through the inspiration of this bodhisattva, Rudolf Steiner was able to proclaim the reappearance of Christ in the etheric.[290]

The hundredth anniversary of this proclamation on Easter Saturday/Sunday, April 10 and 11, 1909, is at Easter 2009 (Good Friday falls on April 10 in 2009). Beginning with the proclamation at Easter 1909, there follows the possibility one century later[291]—this is the *good news*—of a widespread manifestation of Christ's reappearance in the etheric realm beginning at Easter 2009. This event, prepared in advance by the powers of Good, is on the positive side of the scales of world destiny.

Confirmation of the possibility of an enhanced three-and-a-half-year period through which the manifestation of the Etheric Christ will bring "life and blessing" was communicated by the Russian esotericist Valentin Tomberg in his 1939 lectures on the reappearance of Christ in the etheric realm. These lectures, recently republished in the book *Christ and Sophia*, indicate that these will be three extraordinary years. Like Steiner, Valentin Tomberg always referred to the "three years" of Christ's life, which may be understood as a shorthand abbreviation for the actual three and a half years.

> Three years will come during which nature will radiate goodness. For example, when people are in despair they will find remarkable consolation in trees. Goodness will flow from plants into human souls. People will have the experience that trees bend before them in goodness and generosity. Goodness will be felt in nature to such a degree that people will not forget it...A breath of goodness will flow from the world of nature, and human nature will feel it as regeneration and healing...It will really be the breath of Christ moving in a certain direction over the face of the Earth. For a short period of three years, there will be reconciliation between humankind and the world of nature. This is the second event that will take place for nature in relation to the coming of the Etheric Christ.[292]

Could it be that the three and a half years of this special manifestation of the Etheric Christ in the world of nature will be the *cosmic balance on the positive scales of world destiny* for the three and a half years of the Antichrist? And that these three and a half years of the Etheric Christ will begin at Easter 2009, three and a half months before the solar eclipse of July 22, 2009?

Given its importance in dating the coming of the Antichrist, I would like to conclude with a brief review of my research on the Apocalypse Code.[293] The Apocalypse Code came to light during my research on the chronology of Christ's life, the results of which were published in *Chronicle of the Living Christ*.294 Although the *Chronicle* was only published in 1996, I knew about the Apocalypse Code already in 1990, and first wrote about it in *Christian Hermetic Astrology: The Star of the Magi and the Life of Christ*[295] and then in more detail in *The Christ Mystery: Reflections on the Second Coming*.[296] At that time (1990) my attention was not focused on the three and a half years of the Antichrist in relation to the end date of the Maya calendar—which is new to this book on the year 2012— nor was I aware in 1990 of the significance of the July 22, 2009, solar eclipse as the longest eclipse of the twenty-first century. What my attention was focused upon at that time was the recurrence of *the same planetary configuration in 2010* as at the third temptation of Christ in the wilderness, and that this event falls in the period of humanity's undergoing the third temptation between 1988 and 2018. This I found to be so striking that I wrote about it in the aforementioned books. For the benefit of the reader of this book, what I mean by this recurrence of *the same planetary configuration in 2010* is the following:

On the historical date—November 29, C.E. 29—of the third temptation in the wilderness (on the thirty-ninth day of the forty days), there was a conjunction of the Sun and Pluto at 9° Sagittarius.[297] What was the significance of that conjunction? On this day Christ (symbolized by the Sun) had an encounter with the Prince of Darkness (symbolized by Pluto), who tried to tempt him to "turn stones into bread." The way this temptation manifests now, for humanity as a whole, is through materialism and, in particular, through the temptation presented by the technological production of a "virtual reality" in place of the reality of Divine Creation.[298] The creation of the appearance of something real and living, but which in fact is only something mechanical and lifeless ("stones"), in place of the reality of the creation ("bread"), is the third temptation. It is this third temptation—summarized by the expression *virtual reality*—which has swept the world since 1988 (although it was in preparation long before). It was in 1989 that Al Gore introduced the National High-Performance Computer Technology Act, a five-year $1.7 billion program to expand the capacity of the information highway to connect government, industry, and academic institutions. Signed by President George Bush Senior in 1991, the bill supported research and development for an improved national computer system, and assisted colleges and libraries in connecting to the new network. Around that time the World Wide Web was founded by Sir Tim Berners-Lee, the Briton who is credited with the creation of this instrument that has transformed the world—with more than one billion people now connected to the Internet. It is interesting to consider Christ's response to the third temptation: "Man shall not live by bread alone, but by every word that proceeds from the mouth of God" (Matthew 4:4). With these words he implicitly acknowledges the necessity of that which the material world provides, but at the same time draws attention to Divine Creation as the source of everything.[299] As indicated in appendix 1, the ultimate source manifests itself in our galaxy through the Galactic Center as the *creative heart* of our existence.

Against the background of the archetype of the life of Christ, the conjunction of the Sun and Pluto on the thirty-ninth day of the forty days in the wilderness was the cosmic sign of the third temptation, the temptation now manifesting by way of materialism, supported by technology, which is assaulting humanity at the present time in an unprecedented way.[300] There is another archetypal significance of the conjunction of the Sun and Pluto that revealed itself one year later in Christ's life, on December 1, C.E. 30, when he raised the daughter of Jairus from the dead (Mark 5:35–43)—again the Sun and Pluto were in exact conjunction.[301] Here Christ clearly reveals the higher side of the conjunction of the Sun and Pluto—the pouring out of divine love (Christ's nature, represented by the Sun) uniting with the primal life of existence that still lives in the outermost realm of the solar system (represented by Pluto) to the extent of overcoming death. Thus, in these two archetypes from the life of Christ, the meeting of the Sun with Pluto-Hades (the encounter with the Prince of Darkness) and then the meeting of the Sun with Pluto–Phanes (calling forth, through love, the primal life) are revealed.[302]

During the course of the year 2010 Pluto crosses the exact position (9° Sagittarius) where it was at the third temptation in the wilderness three times: January 15, July 7, and November 17.[303] Moreover, shortly after having crossed this position for the third time, just over one month later there is a conjunction of the Sun and Pluto very close to this position. Since Pluto moves so slowly through the zodiac, at the conjunction of the Sun and Pluto on December 26 and 27, 2010, the zodiacal location of this conjunction is 10° Sagittarius, which was the location of the Sun on the day of the Tsunami (December 26, 2004) in which some 283,000 people lost their lives. Pluto's return in 2010 to its position at the third temptation in the wilderness is the eighth since the historical occurrence of the temptations in the wilderness. Since Pluto takes 247 ½ years to orbit the zodiac, it makes eight orbits

in 8 x 247½ = 1,980 years (the exact amount is 1,981 years) added to
C.E. 29, leads to the year 2010. What makes this eighth return special
is that it is taking place *within* the historical period 1988 to 2018 of
the third temptation for humanity which, as indicated in chapter 2,
coincides closely with the "2012 Window" from 1980 to 2016 during
which the Sun at the winter solstice crosses the galactic equator—the
cosmic event that, according to many people, is the distinguishing
feature predicted by the Maya calendar as a *galactic alignment.*

The conjunction of the Sun and Pluto on December 26/27 in 2010
is evidently a most significant cosmic event. In light of the conjunction
of the Sun and Pluto not only at the third temptation in the wilderness
(at 9° Sagittarius), but also in relation to the raising of the daughter
of Jairus from the dead (at 11° Sagittarius), there is a twofold aspect
to this conjunction. There is the foretelling of a possibility for great
good, or toward something highly negative; much depends upon
human beings finding a positive relationship to the cosmic impulse of
the Sun-Pluto conjunction.

The Sun-Pluto conjunction at 9° Sagittarius at the time of the third
temptation of Christ in the wilderness is repeated not only in 2010.
Summarizing:

1. In 2009 Pluto crosses the exact position (6°54' Sagittarius) where
   it was located at the baptism of Jesus in the River Jordan. It
   crosses this position three times: on January 15, July 1, and
   November 17/18.
2. On December 24, 2009, the Sun-Pluto conjunction occurs at 8°
   Sagittarius.
3. On December 26/27, 2010, it takes place at 10° Sagittarius.
4. On December 29, 2011, it is at 12° Sagittarius.
5. On December 30, 2012, it is at 14° Sagittarius. This is just nine
   days after the end of the Maya calendar on December 21, 2012.
6. On January 1, 2014, it is at 16° Sagittarius, which is the location
   of the Sun at the birth of Jesus of Nazareth.
7. In the year 2014—on January 30, on July 5, and on December
   5—Pluto crosses 17°19' Sagittarius, where it stood at the completion of the three and a half years of Christ's ministry *on the day
   of the Resurrection* (April 5, C.E. 33).

8. *Throughout this time (2009–2014), Pluto is in the same region of the zodiac (Sagittarius) as during the ministry of Christ* (C.E. 29–33).

With regard to the prophecies brought to light through the research presented in this book concerning the approaching trial for humanity, there are two important considerations. First: "Through evil one can come to know what is most sublime. For initiates everything evil is also a revelation of God."[304] Second: "Our future is possible only by way of miracles—and we may hope for miracles, because the past consists *only* of miracles."[305] Whereas it is understandable as an initial response to the cognition that we are living in the time of the coming of the Apocalyptic beast (the incarnation of Ahriman) and the prophet of The Beast (the human being who is the focus of inspiration from Sorath) to feel fear, it is important to grasp that this experience of fear is an indication of the direct influence of these beings (Ahriman and Sorath) *within oneself*.[306] It is therefore here—within oneself—that initially the work of overcoming evil is to be carried out. This is the meaning of the words from the Lord's Prayer, "Deliver us from evil." Ultimately, deliverance from evil is attained by way of initiation by the Master, who is Christ.[307] Then, for the initiate, "Everything evil is also a revelation of God."

Further, initiation itself is a miracle—and the fact that humanity and the world exist at all is a miracle, an ongoing miracle or series of miracles. "Life is only a series of miracles...*Faith* is the source of magic power and all the miracles spoken of in the Gospels are attributable to it."[308] These miracles are taking place all the time. Although we are normally not aware of the constancy of the interventions of Christ, Sophia, the Archangel Michael, and the spiritual hierarchies on our behalf, they are all the more active during times of crisis. The goal on the spiritual path is to begin to participate in these miracles, the requirement being faith, which brings us back to the *good news* of the Gospels. We are called upon to *live the Good*—this is the new or *fifth Gospel*, connected with the Etheric Christ—"That Good may become, what from our hearts we found, and from our heads direct with single purpose."[309]

A singular miracle is manifesting to the world in our time in the person of Judith von Halle, decribed here by Peter Tradowsky:

> Today we want to report on a specific event which has occurred right in our midst. It is a cosmic event manifesting in Judith von Halle. In Passiontide 2004, the stigmata, the wounds of Jesus Christ, appeared on Judith von Halle.... The stigmatization was accompanied by a radical change.... The altered body of Judith von Halle, who previously loved cooking and eating, now vehemently refuses any physical food.... The Christ being provides humans with the power to develop their individual self, and also at the same time the possibility to transform, to spiritualize and individualize the sheaths of their being... [including] the individual form of the Resurrection body newly created by Christ.... Humans will be reconnected by means of the Resurrection body with the karmic stream of nutrition which builds the substances in the human being.... The astonishing fact of someone living without eating or drinking... [is] an expression of a new form of health... a gradual stage-by-stage process of fusion with the Resurrection body.[310]

Through a personal meeting with Judith von Halle on November 24, 2008, I was able to experience the miracle that she is representing to the world: the overcoming of the third temptation, as expressed in Christ's words, "Man does not live by bread alone, but by every word that proceeds from the mouth of God" (Matthew 4:4). Since Easter 2004 she is bearing witness to the reality of these words of Christ. "The life force emanating from the Resurrection strengthens me inwardly so much that I can be outwardly nourished by it."[311] At the time of my meeting with her, she had not eaten for four and a half years, yet she appeared radiantly healthy. My experience of her is that she is representing a new kind of human being, a new way of being in the world, living from the sustenance that she receives directly through a "process of fusion with the Resurrection body" of Christ.

What is referred to in the above quote is one aspect to this miracle, the physical aspect.[312] Another is the consciousness aspect relating to her ongoing experience of the Etheric Christ, which she is in the process of bringing to expression through her descriptions in her various books.[313] This consciousness aspect is also part of the miracle that she is representing to the modern world, and which could be described as a continuation of the four Gospels, along the same (or similar) lines as Rudolf Steiner's *Fifth Gospel*. In this capacity, she is a messenger on behalf of the third teacher—of the three spiritual teachers referred to in *The Most Holy Trinosophia*.[314]

> It has been predicted (see chapter 3, "The Holy Soul") that the third spiritual teacher of the twentieth century, who represents Sophia, would incarnate in female form.... The coming of the third spiritual teacher signifies the last stage in the unfolding of the triune impulse that is guiding the community of the Second Coming. [315]

What is referred to here is the existence of three spiritual teachers, whose mission is to serve as teachers and guides of the community of those seeking Christ in his Second Coming, appearing one after the other in the course of time. "The work of the three teachers may be seen as bearing a direct relation to the stages of incarnation of the Etheric Christ, with the teachers acting as 'ambassadors of Christ' in the New Age."[316] After the first two Christ teachers of the twentieth century,[317] whose spiritual work centered around proclaiming (or even facilitating) Christ's return in the etheric realm, Judith von Halle—although not identical with the third spiritual teacher in person—is nevertheless acting as a public representative of the third teacher who remains hidden behind the scenes. In this respect, Judith von Halle's work is a fulfillment of that of the two teachers before her, bringing the work of the Etheric Christ a stage further at this crucial time in the twenty-first century. It has to be borne in mind that my book prophesying the coming of the third teacher in female form was published in the year 2000, four years before Judith von Halle became known on account of receiving the stigmata on Good Friday in the year 2004. In writing this, I am fully aware that she has no pretension of being a spiritual teacher— she is far too modest to accept such a title—and yet it is clear that in the essence of her being she is representing to the world the triumph of the Etheric Christ, and in this sense she is a teacher. This is the *good news*—and, moreover, in her books she is bringing forth the *good news* for our time, new knowledge of Christ—what might be called the *Gospel of the Etheric Christ.*

Notes

1   *The Book of Chilam Balam of Chumayel,* Ralph L. Roys, trans., p. 79.

2   Rudolf Steiner (1861–1925) was a twentieth-century clairvoyant and spiritual teacher of enormous probity, depth of perception, and scope. He was clairvoyant from childhood. As a young man he studied philosophy and various sciences in order to acquire a thorough grasp of the modern scientific world-view and method, and to discipline his natural clairvoyance with a trained scientific consciousness. He went on to develop a "scientific clairvoyance"—or spiritual science, which he also called Anthroposophy—in place of the natural clairvoyance of his youth. The list of his innovations in the fields of science, social development, and the arts, all of which result from the application of spiritual science as he developed it, is breathtaking. Most of his works are available in English from www.steinerbooks.org.

3   See "About the Authors" at the end of this book.

4   For a full explanation of this chronology, see chapter 3 in Robert Powell, *Hermetic Astrology,* vol. I.

5   As will emerge in our study of the year 2012 in relation to the Christ mystery, Christ is a majestic cosmic being. It is important to emphasize this in order to clearly distinguish between Cosmic Christianity, as represented in this book, and the purely human conception of Jesus Christ prevalent nowadays, particularly in fundamentalist circles.

6   Robert Powell, *Chronicle of the Living Christ: Foundations of Cosmic Christianity,* pp. 424–432. As the title indicates, it is a matter of *Cosmic Christianity.* In other words, in contrast to the conception of Jesus Christ simply as a good man from Nazareth (which on the purely human level he was), the research presented in *Chronicle of the Living Christ* shows that Christ was a being of cosmic dimensions.

7   Robert Powell, "The Apocalypse Code," *Christian Star Calendar 2009,* pp. 10–18.

8   See Robert Powell, *Chronicle of the Living Christ* (SteinerBooks, 1996) concerning the Saturn rhythm in history. His inspiration was the provocative statement made by Rudolf Steiner in 1911, that every step taken by Christ during his ministry was in harmony with—and an expression of—the entire cosmos, Powell set out to exactly identify the chronology of Christ's ministry, from the baptism in the Jordan until the Crucifixion. Despite the fact that Christianity rests squarely on historical events—the life, death, and Resurrection of Jesus Christ—the actual birth and death dates were never transmitted. The four Gospels—the historical record of Jesus' life—do not mention any

explicit dates. To this day, scholars disagree about the timing of all the important dates in Jesus Christ's life.

Powell worked both from his knowledge of astronomy and from the indications of Rudolf Steiner and Anne Catherine Emmerich, a German woman who, between 1820 and 1824, communicated visions of the day-to-day life of Jesus, including the period of Christ's ministry. Anne Catherine's eyewitness account gave Powell important details for corroborating his chronology, allowing him to precisely determine Jesus' date of birth (around midnight on December 6/7, 2 B.C.E.), the date of the baptism (September 23, C.E. 29) and Resurrection (April 5, C.E. 33). Since the time interval from the birth to the Resurrection is exactly thirty-three and one-third years, Powell's research corroborates Rudolf Steiner's indication that the life of Jesus Christ was thirty-three and one-third years long.

9   All references made to the zodiac in this book are to the original zodiac of the Babylonians, Egyptians, Greeks, and Romans—now called the *sidereal zodiac*. See Robert Powell, *History of the Zodiac*.

10   See "Appendix 2: The Good News."

11   In the Gospel of St. Matthew and the Gospel of St. Luke the three temptations are described in the reverse order to that in which they actually occurred, as Rudolf Steiner points out in his lectures *The Fifth Gospel: From the Akashic Record* (see especially pp. 93–97 and pp. 154–158). According to this account, the third temptation in the wilderness was that presented by Ahriman (Satan) to Christ. It was the temptation of changing stones into bread. In his description of this, Rudolf Steiner also points out that the turning of stones into bread has to do with money: "Ahriman communicated to Christ something that could indeed be known on Earth...that here on Earth it was necessary to turn mineral substance—metal—into money, into bread. Ahriman had said that human beings on Earth had to nourish themselves by means of gold" (p. 96). Given that humanity is currently living through this ahrimanic temptation, it is not surprising that humankind is in the grip of a global financial crisis. This has to be seen as one aspect of the great spiritual battle now taking place on the Earth, in which humanity as a whole is living through what Christ lived through on his thirty-ninth day in the wilderness—the encounter with Ahriman and the corresponding temptation of turning stones into bread.

12   Judith von Halle was born in Berlin in 1972. She attended school in Germany and the U.S. and studied architecture, graduating in 1998. She encountered Anthroposophy in 1997 and began working as a staff member at Rudolf Steiner House in Berlin, where she also lectured from 2001, while maintaining an architectural practice. In 2004, her life was transformed when she received the stigmata. Her first book was published in German in 2005, and she now works principally as a lecturer and author. She lives part of the time in Berlin and for the

remaining time in Dornach, Switzerland. Among her books in English translation are the following: *And If He Had Not Been Raised: The Stations of Christ's Path to Spirit Man* (2007); *Illness and Healing: The Mystery Language of the Gospels* (2008); *The Lord's Prayer: The Living Word of God* (2007); and *Secrets of the Stations of the Cross and the Grail Blood: The Mystery of Transformation* (2008).

13   Judith von Halle, *And If He Had Not Been Raised: The Stations of Christ's Path to Spirit Man*, p. 23.

14   Rudolf Steiner, *Egyptian Myths and Mysteries*, pp. 23–25.

15   "Before only a part of the third millennium of the post-Christian era has elapsed, there will be in the West an actual incarnation of Ahriman—Ahriman in the flesh." This prophetic statement relating to now was made in a lecture held on November 1, 1919; Rudolf Steiner, *The Incarnation of Ahriman: The Embodiment of Evil on Earth*, p. 37.

16   See also the lectures on the subject in *The Incarnation of Ahriman: The Embodiment of Evil on Earth*.

17   Ibid., pp. 26–27.

18   Robert Powell, *The Christ Mystery: Reflections on the Second Coming*, chapter 5 discusses the Second Coming and the approaching trial of humanity posed by the coming of the Antichrist.

19   *The Bundahisn, Sacred Books of the East*, vol. 5, translated by E. W. West, Part I, pp. 6–8.

20   Rudolf Steiner, *Human Questions and Cosmic Answers*, lecture of June 25, 1922.

21   In terms of the astronomical way of writing B.C.E. dates, the starting date of the Maya calendar—3114 B.C.E.—is written -3113. Adding 2,012 to -3,113, equals 5,125 years. Historians skip the year zero, since they go straight from 1 B.C.E. to C.E. 1, but in order to count correctly, one needs the year 0, and thus for astronomers: 1 B.C.E. = 0, 2 B.C.E. = -1, 3 B.C.E. = -2, etc.

22   Rudolf Steiner, *The Bhagavad Gita and the Epistles of Paul*, p. 98 (now contained in *The Bhagavad Gita and the West: The Esoteric Meaning of the Bhagavad Gita and Its Relation to the Letters of St. Paul*).

23   In the words of one of the great interpreters of the *Bhagavad Gita*, Yogananda: "The Spirit (Krishna) became the devotee's charioteer, or guiding power" (Paramahansa Yogananda, *God Talks with Arjuna: Royal Science of God-Realization* (2 vols.), vol. 1, p. 129.

24   Robert Powell, *Chronicle of the Living Christ*, pp. 108–109, dates and describes the baptism in the River Jordan. Concerning the gradual incarnation of Christ over millennia, descending from celestial heights, see chapter 9; see also Robert Powell, *Sophia and the Rose of the World* (www.sophiafoundation.org/articles).

25   The Krishnamurti affair is what led Rudolf Steiner to separate himself from the Theosophical Society and found the Anthroposophical Society. On January 11, 1911, the Order of the Star of the East was founded

and supported by leading theosophists such as C. W. Leadbeater and Annie Besant to herald the young Krishnamurti (at that time only fifteen years old!) as the World Teacher. On account of this absurd claim, Rudolf Steiner withdrew and founded the Anthroposophical Society on February 3, 1913. In the course of time, Krishnamurti came to see that he had been misused by his "benefactors"—C. W. Leadbeater and Annie Besant—and on August 3, 1929, the thirty-four-year-old Krishnamurti disbanded the Order of the Star of the East.

26   In Adolf Hitler, who came to power on January 30, 1933, we find a fulfillment of the prophecy that "before the Etheric Christ can be comprehended by human beings in the right way, humanity must first cope with encountering The Beast who will rise up in 1933" Rudolf Steiner, *The Book of Revelation and the Work of the Priest* (London: Rudolf Steiner Press, 1998), p. 231. Against this background, Hitler was a true forerunner of the Antichrist. The conflict with Hitler's Nazi party lasted from 1933 to 1945, a twelve-year period. We find this twelve-year period is very significant, for it has to do with Christ's descent into the underworld. Many twentieth-century events can only be understood against this background—for example, in 1945: the July 16 explosion of the first atomic bomb at Los Alamos, then the attack upon Hiroshima, Japan, on August 6, then upon Nagasaki on August 9. These atomic explosions represented a physical opening of the interior of the Earth in 1945. See Robert Powell, "Subnature and the Second Coming," in *The Inner Life of the Earth: Exploring the Mysteries of Nature, Subnature, and Supranature*, Paul V. O'Leary, ed., pp. 69–141.

27   These are just a few examples of the systematic inversion implemented by Hitler.

28   Judith von Halle, *Secrets of the Stations of the Cross and the Grail Blood: The Mystery of Transformation*, pp. 58–152.

29   Fray Diego de Landa, *Yucatán Before and After the Conquest, Relacion de las cosas de Yucatán*, translated by William Gates.

30   Bernal Diaz, *The True History of the Conquest of New Spain*.

31   Tlacaellel (circa 1397–1487) was the son of Huitzihuitl, nephew of Itzcoatl, and half-brother of Montezuma I. Tlacaellel was the advisor to no less than four kings, and he was a promoter of human sacrifice with a vehemence and on a scale that bears comparison with the holocaust of the Jewish people in Nazi Germany.

32   The "Coatepec" hill of the Huitzilopochtli myth may refer to Tepeyac, the hill which bore a temple to Tonantzin, and in 1531 was the site of the apparition of the Virgin of Guadalupe. See Wayne Elzey, "A Hill on a Land Surrounded by Water: An Aztec Story of Origin and Destiny," *History of Religions* 31 (2) (1991): 105–149.

33   Fundamental to understanding this tendency is a knowledge of the polarity between the luciferic (light) and ahrimanic (dark) forces of

opposition, with Christ in between, who holds the balance between Lucifer and Ahriman (see chapter 8). Lucifer seeks to lead human beings away from earthly reality through flights of fantasy, etc. Thereby Lucifer tries to entice human souls into his kingdom, a false paradise removed from the Earth, never to reincarnate upon the Earth again, and the cult practice described here played straight into Lucifer's hands by causing human souls to flee from the Earth. On the other hand, Ahriman endeavors to bind human beings to the Earth, to enslave humanity under his sole direction as vassals in his dark kingdom in opposition to the rest of the universe. Hence Ahriman's striving—through incarnating upon the Earth—to become world ruler.

34 Further elucidation regarding the Mexican mysteries is offered in chapter 10.

35 Huitzilopochtli's name, "Hummingbird of the South," seems suggestive of the image of Resurrection, since in colonial times, it was commonly believed that the hummingbird hibernated over the winter and then "resurrected" in the spring.

36 See chapter 7.

37 Concerning Sorath, see chapters 7 and 8.

38 One student of Maya culture, José Diaz-Bolio (*Why the Rattlesnake in Mayan Civilization*), suggests that the worship of Kukulkan led to the Maya practice of the *pulkan* (*pul* = head; *kan* = serpent), a technique to deform the heads of newborn children, in the shape of the snake. The child's head was placed in a tight frame, to create a slanting forehead and slant eyes, to look like the *Ahau Kan—Crotalus durissus*, a small rattlesnake of the Yucatán rainforest region.

39 See chapter 8.

40 This is the first of six apparitions of the Virgin of Guadalupe in the time frame indicated below. With gratitude to John Hipsley for providing this time frame and for his helpful editorial comments regarding the apparitions of the Virgin of Guadalupe:

December 9: Message for the bishop and Juan Diego tells it to the bishop

December 9: Juan Diego tells Guadalupe that the bishop does not believe him

December 10: Juan Diego sees the bishop again, who asks for a sign

December 11: Juan Diego cares for his uncle, who is ill

December 12: The Virgin of Guadalupe intercepts Juan Diego, then the roses miracle and subsequently the image miracle occur

December 12: The Virgin of Guadalupe appears to Juan Diego's uncle, who is cured

41 The similarity between the Nahuatl word *Coatlaxopeuh* ("who crushes the stone serpent") and the name of the town of Guadalupe is a topic of debate. The conclusion for *Coatlaxopeuh* is generally supported by comparing the image of the Virgin of Guadalupe to the

(Revelation 12:1) image of "the woman clothed with the Sun, with the Moon under her feet, and on her head a crown of twelve stars." In 1666, church authorities concluded that the Virgin used the word *Tequantlaxopeuh*, translating it as "who saves us from the devourer." Recent scholarly examination of the early texts almost unanimously dismisses these church accounts; see, for example, D. A. Brading, *Mexican Phoenix: Our Lady of Guadalupe: Image and Tradition across Five Centuries*. The true significance of an image of this magnitude is an enduring mystery to be contemplated and is timeless in its unfolding.

42 Anonymous, *Meditations on the Tarot* (trans. Robert Powell), p. 405: "The Canaan Moloch who demanded the bloody sacrifice of the first-born, mentioned so often in the Bible, is not a hierarchical entity— either of good or of evil—but rather an evil *egregore*, i.e., a demon created artificially and collectively by human communities infatuated with the thrill of fear. The Mexican Quetzalcoatl is a similar instance of this. There, also, it was a matter of a demon created and worshiped collectively." As discussed in chapter 3, the (later) bloodthirsty Aztec culture worshiped the Quetzalcoatl *egregore* under the name "Huitzilopochtli."

43 The return of Quetzalcoatl, the "plumed" or "feathered" serpent god, had been long awaited in Mexico. However, some interpreters of the sacred Nahuatl prophecy refer to the return of Huitzilopochtli.

44 The *tilma* is an over-garment that drapes downward. The arrangement of the roses and the tying of the two bottom corners of the garment are touching reminders of the physical placement of the Virgin's hands and the care with which she dealt with Juan Diego.

45 There is some confusion regarding which flowers are "crosses" and which are other types of Mexican flowers with their corresponding symbolism. The flowers are regional to the area and, both in their variety and in their placement and number, each symbolizes something significant.

46 These three examples of the miraculous *tilma* are among the most important and actually defy the explanations of present-day science.

47 This is right and left from the perspective of the Virgin of Guadalupe. As viewers, we look at the *tilma* and see the northern constellations on the left and the southern constellations on the right of the image.

48 This is indicated by the Angel's right hand (left side from the perspective of the viewer).

49 Research indicates that the myth did center on Quetzalcoatl. However, Rudolf Steiner's indication could lead one to conclude that it is a matter of the return of Huitzilopochtli in the sense of the reincarnation of this great initiate who lived in Mexico at the time of Christ.

50 In 1525, Princess Papantzin was baptized into the new faith, in the same year in which Cuauhtlatoatzin, the Indian peasant who took the name Juan Diego, was baptized.

51 In 1946, Pope Pius XII declared the Virgin of Guadalupe to be the *Patroness of the Americas* and in 1961 Pope John XXIII invoked her as the *Mother of the Americas*.

52 The manifestation from celestial heights of Sophia through the Virgin of Guadalupe is evident in the imprint of the heavenly star constellations of that day, the winter solstice in 1531, upon the *tilma* image. A veritable Astro-Sophia ("star wisdom") is evident here, as indicated by the above description of the astronomical constellations in relation to the various parts of the Virgin's mantle.

53 David Freidel, Linda Schele, and Joy Parker, *Maya Cosmos: Three Thousand Years on the Shaman's Path*, p. 51.

54 On Aztec concepts of the subtle body, see Jill McKeever Furst, *The Natural History of the Soul in Ancient Mexico*, pp, 138–183.

55 Lacquanna Paul and Robert Powell, *Cosmic Dances of the Planets*, and Lacquanna Paul and Robert Powell, *Cosmic Dances of the Zodiac;* see also Lacquanna Paul, *The Prayer Sequence in the Sacred Dance of Eurythmy*, and Robert Powell, *The Morning Meditation in Eurythmy*.

56 Jeane Dixon, *My Life and Prophecies*, pp. 178–179.

57 Ibid., pp. 167–168.

58 Ibid., pp. 189–190.

59 Ibid., pp. 168–169.

60 Ibid., p. 170.

61 Ruth Montgomery, *A Gift of Prophecy: The Phenomenal Jeane Dixon;* and Jeane Dixon, *My Life and Prophecies*, pp. 142–154.

62 Robert Powell, *Hermetic Astrology, vol. II: Astrological Biography*, p. 11.

63 Rudolf Steiner, *Karmic Relationships*, vol. I, pp. 143–158, describes Nietzsche's previous incarnation as an ascetic Franciscan monk. The identity of this monk as St. Peter of Alcantara was established by Robert Powell, *Hermetic Astrology, vol. I: Astrology and Reincarnation*, appendix iii, where also brief biographies of Peter of Alcantara and Friedrich Nietzsche are to be found.

64 Paul Marshall Allen's excellent biography, *Vladimir Soloviev: Russian Mystic*, pp. 366–410, contains the *Short Story of the Anti-Christ*.

65 In the November 1998 issue of the *Journal of Forensic Science* (43: 6), forensic psychiatrist Dr. David Post theorized that Adolf Hitler's belief he was meant to rule the world may have stemmed in part from a hypnotic suggestion given during treatment for hysterical blindness after a mustard gas attack in 1918. Lacking any knowledge of the spiritual world, contemporary behavioral science fails to grasp that Hitler's radical change in personality is a clear case of demonic possession. In the words of Sri Aurobindo's coworker, the Mother: "Hitler was in contact with a being whom he considered to be the Supreme. This being came and gave him advice, told him all he had to do. Hitler

used to retire into solitude and remain there as long as it was necessary to come into contact with his 'guide' and receive from him inspiration which he carried out later very faithfully. This being whom
Hitler took for the Supreme was plainly an Asura, one who is called
'the Lord of Falsehood' in occultism, but who proclaimed himself 'the
Lord of Nations.'... He had decided clearly to make Hitler commit all
possible extravagances till the day he would break his neck." Wilfried
Huchzermeyer, *The Mother: A Short Biography*, pp. 59–60—concerning Asuras, see below in the chapter entitled "The Redemption of
Lucifer."

66 "Before only a part of the third millennium of the post-Christian era
has elapsed, there will be in the West an actual incarnation of Ahriman—Ahriman in the flesh." This prophetic statement relating to now
was made in a lecture held on November 1, 1919: Rudolf Steiner, *The
Incarnation of Ahriman: The Embodiment of Evil on Earth*, p. 37.

67 See, for example, this translation of the *Ahunvar* prayer by Piloo
Nanayutty: www.zarathushtra.com/z/article/ahunavar.htm: "O living
God, even as you work your will so may the prophet act by following your Truth, your Divine Law, for the love of Righteousness. The
riches of Vohu Mana, the Good Mind, come to him who dedicates
every act of his earthly life to Mazda, and who strives to establish the
Sovereignty of Ahura in the world by loving and serving the homeless,
the dispossessed, the afflicted of the Earth."

68 Rudolf Steiner, *The Reappearance of Christ in the Etheric*, see also the
lecture of January 25, 1910.

69 The Greek poet Hesiod (seventh century B.C.E.) used the terms Golden,
Silver, Bronze, and Iron Ages, instead of the traditional Hindu names
for these periods.

70 www.hinduism.about.com/od/basics/a/goldenage.htm.

71 Helene Petrovna Blavatsky, *Collected Writings*, vol xii, pp. 491–492;
quoting from *The Book of Rules*. E.S.T. published in 1888, three years
before Blavatsky's death in 1891.

72 Ibid.

73 Robert Powell, *The Sign of the Son of Man in the Heavens: Sophia
and the New Star Wisdom*, pp. 120–121. See also Robert Powell, *Hermetic Astrology, volume I: Astrology and Reincarnation*, chapter 3,
for an overview of the dating of the zodiacal ages.

74 Robert Powell, *The Christ Mystery: Reflections on the Second Coming*, the foreword and pp. 84–91.

75 Rudolf Steiner, *Foundations of Esotericism*, footnote 72.

76 Carlos Barrios, "The Mayan Calendar: The World Will Not End":
www.mayamysteryschool.com/pdf%20files/Carlos_Barrios.pdf.

77 This quote from Carlos Barrios is in the article "2012: The Start of a
New Era" by Janosh in *The Mystery of 2012: Predictions, Prophecies
& Possibilities*, p. 266.

78 Any reader who is interested in following up on the various currently prevalent perspectives concerning the Maya calendar should refer to *The Mystery of 2012: Predictions, Prophecies & Possibilities.*

79 Gene D. Matlock, "Will the Mayan Prophecy Really Happen?": www. viewzone.com/chatur.html.

80 See note 76.

81 Robert Powell, "The Apocalypse Code," *Christian Star Calendar 2009,* pp. 11–18.

82 Rudolf Steiner, *The Apocalypse of St. John: Lectures on the Book of Revelation,* pp. 197–200. See also Rudolf Steiner, *The Book of Revelation and the Work of the Priest,* p. 113.

83 Rudolf Steiner, *Three Streams in the Evolution of Humanity,* pp.76–77; in this quotation and in some other quotes in part II of this book, words in brackets [ ] have been added by R.P.

84 "The Elohim created human beings in their own image...male and female they created them" (Genesis 1:27). The Elohim of the Hebrew Bible, and other beings connected with them, are what Rudolf Steiner had in mind when he refers to the "primal gods." In English translation, the plural word *Elohim* from the Hebrew Bible is usually translated simply as *God* or *the Lord.*

85 Gondishapur was a city located in southwest Iran, in Shah-Abad near Susa in Khuzestan Province. The city was founded—or, rather, rebuilt—by Shapur I (224–241). The prophet Mani, the founder of Manichaism, was executed there in 276 or 277. Shapur II (309–379) made the city his capital, which soon became famous as a center of science and culture. The exact date of the founding of the Academy of Gondishapur, now often referred to as the Gondishapur School of Medicine, or simply the Gondishapur School, is unknown, but it is generally believed that it was established during the reign of Shapur II. It attracted scholars and physicians not only from Persia but also from such diverse countries as Greece, India, Egypt, and Syria. Engraved on its portal stood the words: "Knowledge and virtue are superior to sword and strength." By the seventh century, the Gondishapur School was regarded as the leading medical school of the world. It had a library with books in Greek, Syriac, and Pahlavi, as well as a hospital, which after the Muslim conquest became the model for hospitals throughout the Islamic world.

86 Rudolf Steiner, *Three Streams in the Evolution of Humanity,* pp. 78–89.

87 Mohammed-Hossein Azizi, "Gondishapur School of Medicine: The Most Important Medical Center in Antiquity," *Archives of Iranian Medicine* (2008), Volume 11, Number 1, pp. 116–119.

88 H. Momtahen, *The Story of Jundishapur,* pp. 37–44.

89 Rudolf Steiner, *Three Streams in the Evolution of Humanity,* p. 89.

90 Majid Fakhry, *Averroes: His Life, Works and Influence,* p. 31.

91 Rudolf Steiner, *Three Streams in the Evolution of Humanity*, pp. 91–92.

92 Rudolf Steiner, *The Book of Revelation and the Work of the Priest*, p. 112.

93 Ibid., pp. 113–114.

94 The Templars were forced, under torture, to make false and out-rageous statements about themselves and their spiritual practices, thereby opening themselves to the influence of Sorath. See the excel-lent study by Malcolm Barber, *The Trial of the Templars*, "Appen-dix A: The Articles of Accusation," which lists the things that the Templars were forced to confess to, things that could be described as demonic.

95 Ibid., pp. 117–119. Regarding "the entry of [the Archangel] Michael into the spiritual evolution of humanity," Rudolf Steiner indicated the year 1879 as the point in time in the nineteenth century of the begin-ning of the regency of the Archangel Michael, which he considered would last until about the year 2233—Rudolf Steiner, *The Archangel Michael: His Mission and Ours*.

96 Jeane Dixon, *My Life and Prophecies*, pp. 178–179. It is clear from the context that the pharaoh of this vision is Akhenaton (note that Jeane Dixon used the transliteration *Ikhnaton* instead of *Akhenaton* or *Akhenaten*).

97 Robert Powell, *Christian Hermetic Astrology: The Star of the Magi and the life of Christ*, p. 259.

98 Rudolf Steiner, *Isis Mary Sophia: Her Mission and Ours*, p. 102.

99 Jeane Dixon, *My Life and Prophecies*, p. 187.

100 In consideration of the ongoing conflict described in various reli-gions: in the Zoroastrian religion as the battle between Ahura Mazda and his evil twin Ahriman, in the Egyptian religion as the struggle between Osiris and his evil brother Seth, and in the Chris-tian religion between Christ and Satan, it is important for our theme to understand that, in the light of Rudolf Steiner's research, Ahura Mazda and Osiris are pre-incarnatory manifestations of Christ to two different peoples (ancient Persians and ancient Egyptians) and that, likewise, Ahriman, Seth, and Satan are one and the same being—with different names in different cultures.

101 *The Ancient Egyptian Pyramid Texts* translated into English by R. O. Faulkner.

102 See chapter 9; see also, Robert Powell, *Sophia and the Rose of the World*—sophiafoundation.org/articles.

103 Jeane Dixon, *My Life and Prophecies*, pp. 180–182.

104 Sources vary regarding Akhenaton's date of death: the most commonly cited dates are 1336, 1334, and 1332 B.C.E. For our considerations it is of interest that his date of death lies 5 x 666 years ago (5 x 666 = 3,330 = 1,332 + 1,998), that is, five cycles of 666 prior to the date 1998.

105 John Anthony West, *The Traveler's Key to Ancient Egypt*, p. 19.

106   Rudolf Steiner, *Three Streams in the Evolution of Humanity* (London: Rudolf Steiner Press, 1965), p. 78.

107   Judith von Halle, *Der Abstieg in die Erdenschichten* (*The Descent into the Layers of the Earth*), pp. 92–129.

108   Paul V. O'Leary (ed.), Christopher Bamford, Dennis Klocek, David S. Mitchell, Marko Pogacnik, Robert Powell, Rachel C. Ross, *The Inner Life of the Earth*; see Robert Powell, "Subnature and the Second Coming," pp. 69–141, for an account of the subearthly layers and their significance in our time.

109   *The Gospel of Judas.*

110   Jeane Dixon, *My Life and Prophecies*, pp. 190–192.

111   There are also all the hosts of spiritual beings aligned with Christ in his work—first and foremost Divine Sophia, who is discussed at the end of this chapter and in the next chapter, and also the Archangel Michael, who is the leader of the celestial hosts in the conflict with Ahriman/Satan, as is clear from the quotation from Revelation 12.

112   Rudolf Steiner, *The Deed of Christ and the Opposing Spiritual Powers: Lucifer, Ahriman, and the Asuras*; lecture in Berlin, March 22, 1909 (out-of-print editions are usually available from Rudolf Steiner Library, 65 Fern Hill Road, Ghent, NY 12075; 518-672-7690; rsteinerlibrary@taconic.net).

113   Since the date (February 5, 1962) of the birth of a human vessel for the Antichrist has become widely known, it goes without saying that this human being will endeavor to conceal his true date of birth. Otherwise, it would be too easy to identify the Antichrist, if one could simply say, "Look, you see, he was born on February 5, 1962, so he must be the Antichrist."

114   Rudolf Steiner, *The Deed of Christ and the Opposing Spiritual Powers—Lucifer, Ahriman, and the Asuras*. Lecture held in Berlin on March 22, 1909.

115   Rudolf Steiner, *Esoteric Lessons 1904–1909*, p. 135.

116   Valentin Tomberg, *Christ and Sophia*, pp. 42–43. The word *karma*, from the Sanskrit, refers to the law of cause and effect in the sense that performing good deeds will result in good effects and performing bad deeds will result in bad effects. In this context, the actions of Lucifer opened the door for the "bad effects" associated with Ahriman. Likewise, the Asuras are the karma of Ahriman, i.e., the actions of Ahriman lead inevitably to the destructive consequences connected with the Asuras.

117   Jeane Dixon, *My Life and Prophecies*, p. 131.

118   See, for example, James DiEugenio, Lisa Pease, Judge Joe Brown, and Zachary Sklar, *The Assassinations: Probe Magazine on JFK, MLK, RFK, and Malcolm X*.

119   Judith von Halle, *Der Abstieg in die Erdenschichten* ("The Descent into the Layers of the Earth"), pp. 57–58.

120   Anonymous, *Meditations on the Tarot*, p. 188.

121   Valentin Tomberg, *Christ and Sophia*, p. 349.

122   Rudolf Steiner, *The Deed of Christ and the Opposing Spiritual Powers—Lucifer, Ahriman, and the Asuras*; lecture in Berlin, March 22, 1909.

123   I am well aware of the difficulties besetting any kind of prophecy, since there is always the factor of human freedom. While everything points to this three-and-a-half-year period ending at the winter solstice 2012 as that of the Antichrist—or "The Beast," to use the language of Revelation 13—it is possible that this three-and-a-half-year period could be the time of the "prophet of The Beast" and that December 21, 2012, could denote the *start* (rather than the end) of the three and a half years of The Beast. In terms of the Apocalypse Code discussed in chapter 2, since 2018 denotes the end of the thirty-ninth day in the wilderness (1988–2018 being the period for humanity as a whole of the ahrimanic temptation of turning stones to bread), the years 2015 to 2018 signify the *terminus ante quem* for the three and a half years of The Beast (Antichrist).

124   "Before only a part of the third millennium of the post-Christian era has elapsed, there will be in the West an actual incarnation of Ahriman—Ahriman in the flesh." This prophetic statement relating to now was made in a lecture on November 1, 1919; see Rudolf Steiner, *The Incarnation of Ahriman: The Embodiment of Evil on Earth*, p. 37.

125   Rudolf Steiner, *The Book of Revelation and the Work of the Priest*, p. 118.

126   Rudolf Steiner, *Three Streams in the Evolution of Humanity*, p. 78: "The aim of the being who hoped to intervene in 666 was to make himself God."

127   Rudolf Steiner, *The Fifth Gospel: From the Akashic Record*, pp. 93-98,154–158. Steiner describes the actual sequence of the three temptations as: 1) the will to power (Lucifer); 2) plunging from the pinnacle of the temple (Lucifer and Ahriman together); and 3) turning stones into bread (Ahriman).

128   Rudolf Steiner, *Der Baugedanke des Goetheanums* (*The Architectural Conception of the Goetheanum*), p. 51.

129   Valentin Tomberg, *Christ and Sophia*, pp. 162–189 offers a profound elucidation of the three temptations in the wilderness. See, for example, concerning the second temptation, on p. 178: "The temptation to cast himself down from the pinnacle of the temple into the abyss of the instinctive also assailed Jesus Christ, but he overcame it by allowing only the clear light of consciousness to be the arena for the covenant between the human and the suprahuman."

130   In the first place, however, it is necessary to *know* that the three temptations are at work upon all human beings—throughout history and also at the present time. Robert Powell, *Chronicle of the Living Christ*,

pp. 424–432, describes the three temptations as presented to humanity at the present time, as found through the Apocalypse Code—1) the will to power in the period 1929–1958; 2) plunging from the pinnacle of the temple in the period 1958–1988; and 3) turning stones to bread in the period 1988–2018. See also Robert Powell, *The Christ Mystery*, p. 92.

131   The case of the stigmatist, Judith von Halle, who received the stigmata at Easter 2004 and has not eaten since then, defies the ahrimanic temptation altogether, since she does not need bread (food) to live, and instead receives her nourishment through her direct and immediate contact with the living Christ.

132   Valentin Tomberg, *Christ and Sophia*, pp. 296–297. The "other" referred to here is, of course, Christ.

133   Rudolf Steiner & Edouard Schuré, *The East in the Light of the West: The Children of Lucifer and the Brothers of Christ*, lecture of August 31, 1909.

134   Ibid., lecture of August 27, 1909.

135   Rudolf Steiner, *The Spiritual Hierarchies and the Physical World: Zodiac, Planets, and Cosmos*, evening lecture, April 18, 1909, pp. 121–122.

136   Ibid., p. 136.

137   Rudolf Steiner, *The Deed of Christ and the Opposing Spiritual Powers: Lucifer, Ahriman, and the Asuras;* lecture in Berlin, March 22, 1909.

138   Valentin Tomberg, *Christ and Sophia*, p. 307.

139   The following biblical reference is generally interpreted to mean that Lucifer was created as one of the cherubim, a spirit of wisdom and harmony: "You were the signet of perfection, full of wisdom and perfect in beauty. You were in Eden, the garden of God…On the day that you were created…with an anointed guardian cherubim I placed you…on the holy mountain of God…and you sinned, so I cast you as a profane thing from the mountain of God, and the guardian cherubim drove you out" (Ezekiel 28:12–16).

140   Thomas Schipflinger, *Sophia-Maria*, afterword by Robert Powell, pp. 397–403, discusses the two perspectives: Sophia as a created being and Sophia as a "God-born" being, i.e., an eternal being.

141   Valentin Tomberg, *Christ and Sophia*, pp. 303–307.

142   Rudolf Steiner, *Man in the Light of Occultism, Theosophy, and Philosophy*, p. 191.

143   José Díaz-Bolio, *La Serpiente Emplumada: Eje de Culturas* [*The Plumed Serpent: Axis of Cultures*] was first published in 1942 and appeared in its fifth edition in 1998, the year of the author's death (available only in Spanish).

144   Robert Powell, *Hermetic Astrology*, vol. I, pp. 58–63, describes the Venus pentagram.

145   Valentin Tomberg, *Lazarus, Come Forth!*, p. 281.

146 Anonymous, *Meditations on the Tarot*, p. 405: "The Canaan Moloch who demanded the bloody sacrifice of the firstborn, mentioned so often in the Bible, is not a hierarchical entity—either of good or of evil—but rather an evil *egregore*, i.e., a demon created artificially and collectively by human communities infatuated with the thrill of fear. The Mexican Quetzalcoatl is a similar instance of this. There, also, it was a matter of a demon created and worshiped collectively." As discussed in chapter 3, the (later) bloodthirsty Aztec culture worshiped the Quetzalcoatl *egregore* under the name "Huitzilopochtli."

147 Daniel Pinchbeck, *2012: The Return of Quetzalcoatl*.

148 Anonymous, *Meditations on the Tarot*, pp. 629–647, offers a profound analysis of the working of the "belt of lies," also known as the "sphere of mirages" or the "sphere of the false Holy Spirit."

149 See appendix 1. See also, Robert Powell, "Saturn in Gemini," *Christian Star Calendar 2003*, pp. 7–14.

150 See "Appendix 1: The Central Sun," page 221, the figure of the Archer pointing his arrow at the Galactic Center.

151 Viewed heliocentrically, i.e., from the Sun, the Earth was opposite in the zodiac at 2½° Sagittarius, in conjunction with the Galactic Center at 2° Sagittarius.

152 The Venus transit of 2012 will be visible from the west coast of the United Stares and also in the Pacific region. There was a Venus transit, visible in Europe, on June 8, 2004—see Wain Farrants, "Transit of Venus," *Christian Star Calendar 2004*, pp. 15–22. The previous Venus transit, however, was in 1882, and the next Venus transit will not be until the year 2117, from which it can be seen that the Venus transits are rare astronomical events.

153 Robert Powell, *Hermetic Astrology, vol. II: Astrological Biography*, pp. 292–295.

154 Daniel Andreev, *The Rose of the World*.

155 Daniel Andreev, *The Rose of the World*, p. 358.

156 Ibid., p. 356.

157 Robert Powell, *The Most Holy Trinosophia and the New Revelation of the Divine Feminine*.

158 Daniel Andreev, *The Rose of the World*, p. 357.

159 Robert Powell, *Hermetic Astrology*, vol. I, chapter 3 describes the sequence of zodiacal ages and corresponding cultural epochs, each 2160 years in length. The unfolding of ages/cultures in connection with the Apocalypse Code is referred to in chapter 2: *The Gospel in the Stars*.

160 Daniel Andreev, *The Rose of the World*.

161 Ibid., pp. 8–9.

162 Rudolf Steiner, *The Incarnation of Ahriman*, p. 37; see note 15.

163 Jeane Dixon, *My Life and Prophecies*, p. 190.

164 Paul M. Allen, *Vladimir Soloviev: Russian Mystic*, pp. 385–409.

165   Daniel Andreev, *The Rose of the World*, p. 73.

166   Ibid., p. 23.

167   Rudolf Steiner, *The Fall of the Spirits of Darkness*, pp. 19–20.

168   Although officially China is still communist, the world's most popu-
       lous country began its open-door policy in 1981, and under *laissez
       faire* capitalism the economy has boomed. This process began just five
       years after Mao's death in 1976.

169   This is not to diminish the significance of the very real threat of ter-
       rorism. It is simply to cognize that *fear* is the atmosphere that Ahri-
       man feeds on, and thus seeks to create, whereas *love* is the substance
       that Christ creates and which nurtures and sustains us in our true
       humanity.

170   Daniel Andreev, *The Rose of the World*, p. 357.

171   Thomas Schipflinger, *Sophia-Maria*.

172   Paul M. Allen, *Vladimir Soloviev: Russian Mystic*, p. 117.

173   It is interesting that Chairman Mao called his version of the *Commu-
       nist Manifesto* for China *The Little Red Book*, although a more appro-
       priate title would have been *The Quotes of Chairman Mao*. During
       the Chinese Cultural Revolution this red book had enormous power
       and was popularly used by the young people who called themselves
       the *Little Red Guard* to implement Mao's brand of Communism.

174   Daniel Andreev, *The Rose of the World*, pp. 20–21, 68.

175   Jeane Dixon, *My Life and Prophecies*, pp. 189–190.

176   Ibid., 172–173.

177   It is of interest that the first public announcement of the New World
       Order, which was by President George H. W. Bush on September 11,
       1990, was at the time when the demise of Soviet Communism was
       shaping up—a clear indication that Revelation 12 was drawing to a
       close and the new scenario of chapter 13 was announcing itself. Presi-
       dent Bush spoke before a joint session of Congress, regarding the need
       to go to war, which led over four months later to the Gulf War to end
       the Iraqi invasion of Kuwait. Among other topics, he stated that the
       war presented an opportunity for a "New World Order" to emerge.
       The address was broadcast live nationwide on television and radio.
       Eleven years later to the day, the event of September 11, 2001, then
       became a new galvanizing impulse toward the implementation of the
       New World Order.

178   Satan, Ahriman, and Mammon are three names for the same being,
       each name expressing a discrete aspect of this being.

179   According to a message transmitted by the Virgin Mary at an appear-
       ance in the little village of Medjugorje in Bosnia-Herzegovina on Sep-
       tember 25, 2001, just two weeks after the event of September 11, and
       twelve days prior to the commencement of the war in Afghanistan, she
       said: "Satan wants war and hatred.... Pray and fast that God may give
       you peace. Witness peace to every heart and be carriers of peace in this

world without peace. I am with you and intercede before God for each of you. And do not be afraid": www.medjugorjeweb.org/msg01.htm.

180 Unfortunately, there are also definite errors in this book. Perhaps these have arisen in translation. Nevertheless, the general message of the book about the coming Sophia culture, the Rose of the World, is very inspiring.

181 Daniel Andreev, *The Rose of the World*, pp. 338–342. See www.gutenberg.org/dirs/etext05/inqus10.txt for the text of an English translation (by H. P. Blavatsky) of Dostoevsky's *The Grand Inquisitor*.

182 Ibid., p. 342.

183 See "Appendix 1: The Central Sun."

184 There are four spiral arms—two major and two minor—proceeding from the center of the galaxy and some side arms, one of these being the Orion Arm, located between the Sagittarius and Perseus Arms—see figure. Our Sun is located on the inside of the Orion Arm, looking toward the Galactic Center in the direction of Sagittarius.

185 See "Appendix 1: The Central Sun" for a graphic depiction of the *Empyrean*.

186 All references to the zodiac are in terms of the original zodiac—also known as the sidereal zodiac (*sidereal*, "of the stars")—as defined by the Babylonians; see Robert Powell, *History of the Zodiac*.

187 Rudolf Steiner, *The Reappearance of Christ in the Etheric*.

188 Rudolf Steiner, *Esoteric Christianity and the Mission of Christian Rosenkreutz*, p. 101.

189 Rudolf Steiner, *The Archangel Michael: His Mission and Ours*. Rudolf Steiner, *Becoming the Archangel Michael's Companions: Rudolf Steiner's Challenge to the Younger Generation*.

190 Johannes Kiersch, *A History of the School of Spiritual Science: The First Class*.

191 *Cosmos* is a Greek word that conveys the sense of the *visible* starry heavens, and since the stars belonging to other spiral arms of our galaxy are, with a handful of exceptions, not visible (at least, not to the naked eye), our cosmos, in the Greek sense of the word, comprises by and large stars belonging to our local part of the galaxy, the Orion Arm, making up the starry heavens which we see when gazing up at the night sky.

192 This six-hundred-year rhythm is connected with the planet Venus. See Robert Powell, *Hermetic Astrology*, vol. I, chapter 3. See also Robert Powell, "Sophia and Venus," *Christian Star Calendar 2004*, pp. 7–14. This rhythm is also referred to by Rudolf Steiner, who speaks of the six-hundred-year rhythm as an important rhythm of cultural history. See Rudolf Steiner, *Background to the Gospel of St. Mark*, p. 153. We may recall, also, as mentioned earlier, that Venus and her rhythms played a central role for the Maya.

193 Robert Powell, *History of the Zodiac*, appendix i.

194　Neil Michelsen, *The American Sidereal Ephemeris*, the introduction. There, the date for the beginning of the Age of Aquarius is given as 2376, a slight difference of only one year.

195　Daniel Andreev, *The Rose of the World*, pp. 356–357.

196　Rudolf Steiner, *The Incarnation of Ahriman*, p. 18.

197　Ibid., p. 36.

198　Ibid., pp. 66–67.

199　Richard Dickens & Lisu Chen Dickens, *Divine Sophia and the Goddess of Mercy (Kwan-Yin)* (self-published manuscript, 1997), p. 24.

200　According to Steiner, the one who served as the physical vessel for Lucifer's incarnation lived around 3000 B.C.E., also the date indicated by some historians for the birth of Huang-Ti. Most modern sources give his dates as 2600–2500 B.C.E. (he is said to have lived for 100 years). We have indicated a median date of 2800 B.C.E. for the birth of the Yellow Emperor.

201　Ling Lun is the legendary founder of music in ancient China. In Chinese mythology, he created bamboo flutes that made the sounds of many birds, including the mythical phoenix. The Yellow Emperor is said to have ordered the casting of bells in tune with those flutes.

202　Translated by Nelson Liansheng Wu and Andrew Qi Wu.

203　Paul Golden, *Culture of Sex in Ancient China*.

204　Sima Qian, *Ssuma Ch'ien: Including History of the Hsia Dynasty and Yin Dynasty*.

205　I have chosen to write Tao and Taoism rather than Dao and Daoism. "T" and "D" are phonetically equivalent, and Tao and Dao are simply two ways of transcribing the Chinese characters for this word into the English language.

206　The lightning in the heavens could have been a meteor shower. One thing that is not clear is whether this lightning phenomenon associated with Huang-Ti's birth is a legendary account that has been confounded with the story that his mother conceived him after being struck by lightning, or whether these are two stories, one having to do with his conception and one having to do with his birth.

207　The cosmic lightning, or meteor shower, in the region of the Big Dipper seen by Huang-Ti's mother, precipitating his birth, has been mentioned already. See also, Paul Stonehill, *Mysteries of the Yellow Emperor*—www.mystae.com/streams/ufos/emperor.html.

208　"It [Regulus] is known in Chinese as...the Yellow Emperor": en.wikipedia.org/wiki/Regulus.

209　Regulus (5° Leo in the sidereal zodiac) is 77 light years away and has a luminosity 150 times that of our Sun. It is one of the four royal stars— the other three being Aldebaran (15° Taurus), Antares (15° Scorpio), and Fomalhaut (9° Aquarius). These royal stars—in particular Aldebaran and Antares—define the central axis of the sidereal zodiac—Robert Powell, *History of the Zodiac*.

210 Robert Powell, *Hermetic Astrology*, vol. I, chapter 3. According to *Astrogeographia*, the science of correspondence between the starry heavens and the Earth, China comes under the constellation of Leo—www.astrogeographia.org.

211 Rudolf Steiner, *Inner Impulses of Evolution: The Mexican Mysteries*, pp. 48–49.

212 Rudolf Steiner, *Die Welträtsel und die Anthroposophie* ("Anthroposophy and the Riddles of the World"), lecture of November 16, 1905 (CW 54).

213 Quoted from *The Biography of Huang-ti*: "When the Emperor met the West Empress at the Mountains of Wangwu, twelve large mirrors were wrought for use month by month": "Mysteries of the Yellow Emperor": www.dankalia.com/paranoia/emperor.htm.

214 The endeavor of the Yellow Emperor to mirror the light of the Moon has been recreated in our time with the help of modern technology by the Interstellar Light Collector, which cost more than $2 million to construct. It consists of a large frame sunk into a forty-five-foot-deep crater, on private land in sparse desert, in an area known for its dark skies, a few miles from the Kitt Peak National Observatory (56 miles southwest of Tucson). The device is five stories tall and weighs twenty-five tons, and is covered with eighty-four mirrored panels set on a hydraulic mount that can focus the light of the Moon with the precision of a Swiss watch. There is no charge to use the facility. So far it has been visited by more than one thousand visitors, with interest from as far afield as Australia, Japan, India, and Saudi Arabia from people seeking either a new experience or in the hope of some kind of medical benefit. Some dress in robes, others strip to their underwear to bask in the glow of the Moon's light reflected from the glittering bank of mirrors, spending anywhere from three minutes to fifteen minutes at a time: www.reuters.com/article/inDepthNews/idUSN046 3343020071205?feedType=RSS&feedName=inDepthNews&rpc=22&sp=true.

215 Paul Stonehill, *Mysteries of the Yellow Emperor*: www.mystae.com/streams/ufos/emperor.html. Regulus is the "fourteenth star" in Syuan Yuan, which is an asterism in the constellation of Leo, but as the brightest star in this asterism, the name Syuan Yuan for the whole asterism is used here in the sense of applying to the star Regulus alone.

216 Rudolf Steiner, *The Incarnation of Ahriman*, p. 68.

217 Ibid., pp. 15–16.

218 Ibid., pp. 94, 108–109.

219 Robert Powell, *Chronicle of the Living Christ* presents the fruits of the research, and Robert Powell, *Christian Hermetic Astrology: The Star of the Magi and the Life of Christ* offers a meditation on the correspondences between the Christ events and the stellar configurations at the time of those events.

220 Robert Powell, *Christian Star Calendar*. The 2009 calendar is the final issue in which the monthly commentaries appear.

221 Rudolf Steiner, *Intuitive Thinking as a Spiritual Path: A Philosophy of Freedom*, pp. 19, 20, 25, 84, 236.

222 Rudolf Steiner, *The Occult Significance of the Bhagavad Gita*, pp. 25–26 (now included in *The Bhagavad Gita and the West*).

223 Love in its highest sense, exemplified through the deeds of the saints and benefactors of humanity, who have acted selflessly for the benefit of their fellow human beings.

224 Rudolf Steiner, *Inner Impulses of Evolution*, p. 49.

225 Rudolf Steiner, *The Incarnation of Ahriman*, p. 23.

226 Some modern "Taoist thoughts" are quoted by Thomas Meyer (*Clairvoyance and Consciousness: The Tao Impulse in Evolution*, p. 58) from Rudolf Steiner's book *The Philosophy of Freedom* (*Intuitive Thinking as a Spiritual Path*); see page 180 of this volume.

227 See "Appendix 1: The Central Sun."

228 Rudolf Steiner, *The Mission of the Individual Folk Souls*, p. 109.

229 Rudolf Steiner, *An Outline of Esoteric Science* offers a comprehensive description of the entire process of creation through the cooperation of the various ranks of the spiritual hierarchies working in the service of the divine source of existence.

230 *Yahweh Elohim* is first used in Genesis 2:4, whereas beforehand, in chapter 1, *Elohim* is the divine name that is used. *Yahweh Elohim* is then usually abbreviated to *Yahweh*, as in: " I am Yahweh; that is my name" (Isaiah 42:8). The following passage indicates that it was Moses who introduced the name *Yahweh* and that previously the name *El Shaddai* was used: "I appeared to Abraham, to Isaac, and to Jacob as *El Shaddai*, but by my name *Yahweh* I did not make myself known to them" (Exodus 6:3). The different names of God used in the Bible indicate different hierarchical beings in the service of the Creator. The Creator, the one whom Christ calls the Father, was first revealed to humanity by Christ, just as Yahweh was first revealed by Moses.

231 From Chief Seattle's famous speech made in 1854: www.halcyon.com/arborhts/chiefsea.html.

232 Big Thunder (Bedagi) Wabanaki Algonquin: www.greatdreams.com/wisdom.htm.

233 Rudolf Steiner, *Inner Impulses of Evolution: The After Effects of the Atlantean Mysteries in America and Asia*. Lecture of September 18, 1916.

234 Ibid.

235 Ibid.

236 Ibid.

237 Anonymous, *Meditations on the Tarot*, p. 405: "The Canaan Moloch who demanded the bloody sacrifice of the firstborn, mentioned so often in the Bible, is not a hierarchical entity—either of good or of

evil—but rather an evil *egregore*, i.e., a demon created artificially and collectively by human communities infatuated with the thrill of fear. The Mexican Quetzalcoatl is a similar instance of this. There, also, it was a matter of a demon created and worshiped collectively." As discussed in chapter 3, the (later) bloodthirsty Aztec culture worshiped the Quetzalcoatl *egregore* under the name "Huitzilopochtli."

238 The original mantric word is AUM, but the way this is pronounced in the Hindu tradition has led it to be written OM.

239 A—Father (*Atma*); U—Son (*Buddhi*); M—Holy Spirit (*Manas*). AUM relates to the Holy Trinity, and thus to the *Central Sun*, and Christ is the Divine I AM from the *Central Sun*, who through his incarnation and sacrifice upon the Earth became the bestower of the Divine I AM upon human beings.

240 Because the sculpture was not quite complete by the end of 1922, it was not in located in the Goetheanum at the time of the fire on New Year's Eve 1922/1923; it was still in Steiner's workshop, which was not destroyed by fire that night.

241 This was called the small cupola to distinguish it from the large cupola above the auditorium.

242 Rudolf Steiner's description of Lucifer is along the lines of what his listeners were used to hearing. His words at that time served as a veil to a mystery that only becomes apparent through closer contemplation of the image of Lucifer in this painting—the mystery (discussed here) of Lucifer's redemption.

243 Rudolf Steiner, *Der Baugedanke des Goetheanum* (*"The Architectural Conception of the Goetheanum"*), pp. 50–51.

244 Judith von Halle, *And If He Has Not Been Raised...*, pp. 154–155.

245 Ibid., pp. 76, 87.

246 Hans-Joachim Aderhold, "Die Erdwandlung durch die Eröffnung geistiger Quellen" ("The Transformation of the Earth through the Opening of Spiritual Sources"), *Erlebnis Erdwandlung*, pp. 400–402 (italics by R.P.).

247 Anonymous, *Meditations on the Tarot*.

248 Robert Powell, *Hermetic Astrology*, vol. I, chapter 3.

249 Valentin Tomberg, *Christ and Sophia*, pp. 176–189.

250 David Black, *The Computer and the Incarnation of Ahriman*; David Black, "Further to *The Computer and the Incarnation of Ahriman*," *Shoreline*, vol. 1 (1988), pp. 26–30. See also: www.anthroposophie. net/Ahriman/ahriman.htm.

251 There are some eye-opening short videos on the latest developments in microchipping people: www.wethepeoplewillnotbechipped.com.

252 Valentin Tomberg, *Christ and Sophia*, p. 225.

253 Rudolf Steiner, *The Book of Revelation and the Work of the Priest*, p. 149.

254 Robert Powell, "Subnature & the Second Coming," *The Inner Life of the Earth*, p. 118.

255 On this day there was a solar eclipse and an extraordinarily powerful alignment of the seven classical planets in Capricorn.

256 Robert Powell, "Subnature & the Second Coming," *The Inner Life of the Earth*, pp. 116–118. The emergence of the true Kalki Avatar in 2014 is being preempted from various quarters—one example being Sri Kalki Bhagavan, the self-styled "Living Avatar."

257 Anonymous, *Meditations on the Tarot*, p. 614

258 *Vishnuyasha* is the Hindu name for the human being who will be the bearer of the Kalki Avatar, and for the Kalki Avatar to emerge in the year 2014, it follows that *Vishnuyasha* must already be in incarnation.

259 Valentin Tomberg, *Christ and Sophia*, pp. 297–300.

260 From an esoteric lecture held at Easter 1941 for a small group of people in Amsterdam during World War II. Translated by Robert Powell.

261 New stars are born in different parts of the galaxy, yet they are offspring of stellar regions which originally were born from the Galactic Center, and in this sense the center of our galaxy is the ultimate source for all existence in the Milky Way Galaxy.

262 Reference to the *Intelligible Sun*, i.e., not the visible Sun but the Sun belonging to the intelligible world, as the source of divine goodness is found in Book VI of Plato's *Republic* (509b). Immediately after, at the start of Book VII, in the famous allegory of the cave, the *Supra-Celestial Sun* is indicated to be the source of truth and intelligence, and the visible Sun, together with its light, is said to be an offspring thereof: "In the visible realm it gave birth to light and its sovereign; in the intelligible realm, itself sovereign, it provided truth and intelligence" (517 b–c). Subsequently this reference recurs often in the Platonic tradition. For example, the Neoplatonist Proclus refers to the *Supermundane Sun* in his Commentary on Plato's *Timaeus*: "There is the true Solar World and the Totality of Light [where] the Sun, also being *Supermundane*, sends forth the Fountains of Light"—Proclus, *Commentary on Timaeus*, in: *The Chaldean Oracles*, p. 45.

263 The term *Central Sun* is a simplification of Plato's *Transmundane Sun,* or *Supra-Celestial Sun*. The term *Central Sun*—conceptually identical with Plato's *Supra-Celestial Sun*—brings to expression its central location, i.e., its location at the center of the Milky Way Galaxy. Note that Plato himself did not explicitly use the expressions *Intelligible Sun, Transmundane Sun, Supermundane Sun,* or *Supra-Celestial Sun*, but these expressions, which were used in the Platonic tradition, are implicit in Plato's work and are employed by later commentators on Plato's works when referring to the *Sun* in the intelligible world spoken of by Plato.

264 Nine planets, including Pluto, or eight planets, if Pluto is no longer considered to be a planet; see Robert Powell *Pluto and the Galactic Center*: https://sophiafoundation.org/articles/.

265 See, for example, Rudolf Steiner's lecture of January 18, 1921, as part of the *Astronomy Course* (CW 323—unpublished in English [2009]).

266 Ibid.

267 Rudolf Steiner, *Man: Hieroglyph of the Universe* (current ed. *Mystery of the Universe: The Human Being, Model of Creation*), p. 47.

268 In his work *Metaphysics*, Book Lambda, Aristotle calls the source of all movement the *Prime Mover*, which is at rest at the center of all movement around it.

269 The two-dimensional image of the Archer aiming his arrow at the Galactic Center has to be thought of in three dimensions in order to grasp that the two-dimensional perspective is really an optical illusion, since the visible stars making up the constellation of Sagittarius are relatively close to our solar system (the most distant stars—with some exceptions—being not more than a few thousand light years away), whereas the Galactic Center is located at an enormous distance of about 25,000 light years.

270 Dante, *The Divine Comedy: Paradise* 33:144–145.

271 Daniel Andreev, *The Rose of the World*, p. 198.

272 Thomas Schipflinger, *Sophia-Maria*.

273 Rudolf Steiner, *Isis Mary Sophia: Her Mission and Ours*.

274 St. Augustine: "That which is known as the Christian religion existed among the ancients" (*Retractiones* I, xiii).

275 Rudolf Steiner, *The Deed of Christ and the Opposing Spiritual Powers. Lucifer, Ahriman, Asuras*, lecture of March 22, 1909 (CW 107).

276 Robert Powell, *Chronicle of the Living Christ*, p. 178.

277 At the same time an emanation from Sophia, who at that time was still united with the Central Sun, passed into the Virgin Mary; see chapter 9.

278 Normally that which streams out from the *Central Sun* is received by our Sun and is "stepped down" in the process of being transmitted to the Earth. Christ, having descended from the *Central Sun*, prepared the disciples to receive *directly* from the *Central Sun* at Pentecost.

279 This localization of the ultimate abode of the Holy Spirit to the *Central Sun* in no ways limits the omnipresence of the Holy Spirit but simply points to the ultimate source from which the Holy Spirit proceeds.

280 Rudolf Steiner, *Karmic Relationships*, vol. 7, lecture of June 8, 1924.

281 Rudolf Steiner, *Cosmic and Human Metamorphoses*, lecture of February 6, 1917; "What pulsated in the Gospels is no earthly language but cosmic words, heavenly words, possessing an immeasurably greater force than anything else on Earth. It is also true that humankind in the present age has become estranged from the form in which these words were laid down in the Gospels at the time of the Mystery of

Golgotha.…The Gospels, in the form accessible to us today, are really not the original Gospels, [as] they do not possess their original force."

282 Rudolf Steiner, *The Fifth Gospel.*

283 Christoph Lindenberg, *Rudolf Steiner: Eine Chronik* ("Rudolf Steiner: A Chronicle"), p. 289—here Lindenberg is referring to the lecture of January 12, 1910, which was held in Stockholm.

284 Rudolf Steiner, *Cosmic and Human Metamorphoses,* lecture, February 6, 1917, "Materialism and Spirituality, Life and Death."

285 Concerning the Christ rhythm of 33 1/3 years, see the Postscript (pp. 125–141) of my article "Subnature and the Second Coming," *The Interior Life of the Earth*, pp. 69–141.

286 Rudolf Steiner, *The Festivals and Their Meaning,* "Spiritual Bells of Easter," lecture, Easter Saturday, April 10, 1909.

287 Rudolf Steiner, "Spiritual Bells of Easter," lecture, Easter Sunday, April 11, 1909.

288 Rudolf Steiner, *Esoteric Christianity and the Mission of Christian Rosenkreutz*, lecture of November 4, 1911.

289 Rudolf Steiner, *According to Matthew*, p. 178.

290 Robert Powell, *Rudolf Steiner, Valentin Tomberg, and the Return of Christ in the Etheric*: sophiafoundation.org/articles/.

291 Rudolf Steiner, *Mysterienwahrheiten und Weihnachtsimpulse* ("Mystery Truths and the Impulses of Christmas"), lecture of December 26, 1917 (CW 180): "One can recognize the intensity of an impulse that is implanted into the historical process by virtue of its effect through three generations, through a whole century."

292 Valentin Tomberg, *Christ and Sophia*, p. 400.

293 The Apocalypse Code brings to expression that the three and a half years of Christ's ministry are a seed for the living out of the Christ Impulse "unto the end of the Earth," i.e., that humankind collectively lives through the events lived through by Christ during these three and a half years. The cosmic equation underlying the Apocalypse Code is that *one day* in the ministry of Christ, which lasted for 1,290 days between the baptism in the Jordan and the Resurrection, *corresponds to 29½ years* (Saturn rhythm) in human history. Applying the Apocalypse Code, the thirty-ninth day in the wilderness, when Christ encountered Satan/Ahriman, who presented the third temptation, corresponds to the present historical period from 1988 to 2018.

294 Robert Powell, *Chronicle of the Living Christ.*

295 Robert Powell, *Christian Hermetic Astrology*, pp. 71–81 (2nd edition).

296 Robert Powell, *The Christ Mystery*, pp. 57–67 (chapter 4: The Second Coming and the Approaching Trial of Humanity)—this chapter is a reprint of my article with the same name that appeared in *Shoreline*, vol. 5 (1992), pp. 27–34.

297 Robert Powell, *Chronicle of the Living Christ*, p. 207. On page 163 is the horoscope of the fortieth day (November 30, C.E. 29), the day

on which "Angels came and ministered unto him" (Matthew 4:11), and in this horoscope the Sun is one degree advanced from its position on the previous day (November 29, C.E. 29) in conjunction with Pluto at 9° Sagittarius (since the Sun travels approximately one degree every day).

298 As referred to in chapter 2, according to the Apocalypse Code the period 1988–2018 is the time when humanity as a whole is undergoing the third temptation.

299 As the words of Christ indicate, it is not a matter of rejecting the material realm—the realm of "bread"—but of seeing and acknowledging the priority of the spiritual realm, that which "proceeds from the mouth of God." By the same token, it is not a matter of rejecting the Internet or the other extraordinary creations of modern technology, but of placing the use of technology in the right context *as a tool* and not as a dominating "life principle."

300 A recent statistical survey made in 2006 of young people in England (and no doubt similar results would be found in other countries of the modern world) estimated that by the age of 13 some 40% already have not only their own mobile phone but also their own computer and TV in their bedroom. These kids tend to withdraw from family life into their bedrooms and lead a "technologically savvy" life there, sometimes resulting in addiction to computer games, one of the most pernicious and destructive forms of modern addiction. Contrast this with the life of young people in earlier times, where the experience of nature—for example, through hiking in the mountains—was normal and natural. What kind of human race is being bred through this over–exposure to cyberspace and images of the media? What is the effect on young people in the United States of the estimate that the average American teenager has already—via TV, cinema, or videos—seen on screen more than 500,000 murders by the age of sixteen?

301 Robert Powell, *Chronicle of the Living Christ*, p. 167, gives the horoscope of this event, showing the conjunction of the Sun and Pluto at 11° Sagittarius.

302 See my articles, *Pluto and the Galactic Center* and *Pluto-Phanes and Pluto-Hades* (the latter written together with Krista Koesters)—sophiafoundation.org/articles/.

303 On January 15, 2009, coinciding closely with the date (January 20) of the inauguration of Barack Obama as president of the United States, Pluto was at exactly the same position in the zodiac where it was located at the baptism of Jesus in the Jordan, which signified the start of Christ's three-and-a-half-year ministry.

304 Valentin Tomberg, *The Lord's Prayer Course/Our Mother Course* (study material distributed by the Sophia Foundation of North America, 3143 Avalon Court, Palo Alto, CA 94306), p. 341.

305 Ibid., p. 352.

306 Judith von Halle, *Das Christliche aus dem Holze herausschlagen*, p. 66: "Again and again Rudolf Steiner spoke of the spiritual path that has to be taken by the beholder in order to grasp *The Group* as a living image of one's own inner being"—meaning that the spiritual forces represented by the various spiritual beings portrayed in *The Group* have to be experienced as a reality living in the depths of one's own inner being.

307 Ibid., p. 62: "The sole hierophant is now 'the Christ in us.'"

308 Anonymous, *Meditations on the Tarot*, pp. 67, 72.

309 Rudolf Steiner, *The Foundation Stone Meditation*, closing words; see, for example, Lacquanna Paul & Robert Powell, *The Foundation Stone Meditation in the Sacred Dance of Eurythmy*.

310 Report by Peter Tradowsky, in: Judith von Halle, *And If He Had Not Been Raised...*, pp. 10–20.

311 Ibid., p. 23.

312 Although physical, it is at the same time profoundly spiritual.

313 The basis for Judith von Halle's experience of the Etheric Christ is communicated in the words of Rudolf Steiner quoted earlier in this appendix: "He [Christ] will appear in the spiritual fire to those who have allowed their eyes to be enlightened through the Event of Golgotha." Judith von Halle's focus is upon the Mystery of Golgotha, and it is this that has opened up for her the experience of Christ in the etheric realm.

314 Robert Powell, *The Most Holy Trinosophia and the New Revelation of the Divine Feminine*.

315 Ibid., p. 141. The significance of the third teacher—in contrast to the first two Christ teachers—appearing in female form can be seen as a metamorphosis from two thousand years ago, when Christ incarnated physically into a male body and had twelve male disciples. Now his incarnation is in an etheric body, and on account of the polarity between the physical and etheric bodies, it is understandable that Christ's manifestation in an etheric body is being proclaimed by a woman. (The polarity referred to here is that the etheric body of a male person is female, and the etheric body of a female person is male.)

316 Ibid., p. 147.

317 Ibid., p. 153: "The three teachers referred to here are, so to speak, the three 'elders' of the metamorphosed community in the twentieth century. *However, there are more teachers than these three we are considering.*"

BIBLIOGRAPHY

The Ancient Egyptian Pyramid Texts, trans. R. O. Faulkner (Oxford: Clarendon Press, 1910).

The Book of Chilam Balam of Chumayel, trans. Ralph L. Roys (Norman, OK: University of Oklahoma Press, 1967 [1933]).

The Bundahisn, Sacred Books of the East, vol. 5, trans. E. W. West (Oxford: Oxford University Press, 1880).

The Chaldean Oracles (Fintry, UK: Shrine of Wisdom, 1979).

Codex Chimalpahin, vol. 1: society and politics in Mexico Tenochtitlan, Tlatelolco, Texcoco, Culhuacan, and other Nahua altepetl in central Mexico; the Nahuatl and Spanish annals and accounts collected and recorded by don Domingo de San Antón Muñón Chimalpahin Quauhtlehuanitzin, Civilization of the American Indian Series, no. 225. Arthur J.O. Anderson and Susan Schroeder, eds. and trans. (Norman, OK: University of Oklahoma Press, 1997 [1621]).

The Gospel of Judas, trans. and eds. Rodolphe Kasser, Marvin Meyer & Gregor Wurst (Washington, DC: National Geographic Society, 2006).

Yellow Emperor's Canon of Internal Medicine, trans. Nelson Liansheng Wu and Andrew Qi Wu (Beijing: China Science & Technology Press, 1999).

Aderhold, Hans-Joachim. "Die Erdwandlung durch die Eröffnung geistiger Quellen," ("The Transformation of the Earth through the Opening of Spiritual Sources"), *Erlebnis Erdwandlung* ("Earth-Transformation Experiences"; Borchen, Germany: Verlag Ch. Möllmann, 2008).

Allen, Paul Marshall. *Vladimir Soloviev: Russian Mystic* (Great Barrington, MA: SteinerBooks, 2008).

Andreev, Daniel. *The Rose of the World* (Great Barrington, MA: Lindisfarne Books, 1997).

Anonymous. *Meditations on the Tarot: A Journey into Christian Hermeticism* (trans. Robert Powell; New York: Putman, 2002).

Azizi, Mohammed-Hossein. "Gondishapur School of Medicine: The Most Important Medical Center in Antiquity," *Archives of Iranian Medicine* 11(1) (2008): 116–119.

Barber, Malcolm. *The Trial of the Templars*, 2nd ed. (New York: Cambridge University Press, 2006).

Barrios, Carlos. "The Mayan Calendar: The World Will Not End": www.mayamysteryschool.com/pdf%20files/Carlos_Barrios.pdf.

Black, David. *The Computer and the Incarnation of Ahriman* (Spring Valley, NY: St. George Publications, 1981).

———. "Further to The Computer and the Incarnation of Ahriman," *Shoreline*, vol. 1 (1988).

Blavatsky, Helene Petrovna. *Collected Writings*, vol xii (Wheaton, IL: Theosophical Society Publishing Company, 1890).

Boone, Elizabeth H. "Incarnations of the Aztec Supernatural: The Image of Huitzilopochtli in Mexico and Europe," *Transactions of the American Philosophical Society, New Series*, 79(2) (1989): i–107.

Braden, Gregg, et al. *The Mystery of 2012: Predictions, Prophecies & Possibilities* (Boulder, CO: Sounds True, 2007).

Brading, D. A. *Mexican Phoenix: Our Lady of Guadalupe: Image and Tradition Across Five Centuries* (New York: Cambridge University Press: 2002).

Brinton, Daniel Garrison. *Rig Veda Americanus: Sacred Songs of the Ancient Mexicans, With a Gloss in Nahuatl* (New York: AMS Press, 1969 [1890]).

de Landa, Diego. *Yucatán Before and After the Conquest*, trans. William Gates (Maya Society: Baltimore, 1937 [1566]).

Díaz del Castillo, Bernal. *The True History of the Conquest of New Spain* (Harmondsworth, UK: Penguin, 1973).

Díaz-Bolio, José. *Why the Rattlesnake in Mayan Civilization* (Area Maya: Merida, 1988).

Dickens, Richard and Lisu Chen Dickens. *Divine Sophia and the Goddess of Mercy (Kwan-Yin)* (Phoenix: self-published manuscript, 1997).

DiEugenio, James, Lisa Pease, Judge Joe Brown, and Zachary Sklar. *The Assassinations: Probe Magazine on JFK, MLK, RFK, and Malcolm X* (Los Angeles: Feral House, 2003).

Dixon, Jeane & Rene Noorbergen. *Jeane Dixon: My Life and Prophecies* (New York: William Morrow, 1969).

Durán, Diego. *The History of the Indies of New Spain* (Norman, OK: University of Oklahoma Press, 1994).

Elzey, Wayne. "A Hill on a Land Surrounded by Water: An Aztec Story of Origin and Destiny," *History of Religions* 31 (2) (1991): 105–149.

———. "The Nahua Myth of the Suns: History and Cosmology in Pre-Hispanic Mexican Religions," *Numen* 23(2) (1976): 114–135.

Fakhry, Majid. *Averroes: His Life, Works, and Influence* (Oxford, UK: Oneworld Publications, 2001).

Farrants, Wain. "Transit of Venus," *Christian Star Calendar 2004*, ed. Robert Powell (Palo Alto, CA: Sophia Foundation of North America, 2003).

Freidel, David, Linda Schele, and Joy Parker. *Maya Cosmos: Three Thousand Years on the Shaman's Path* (New York: William Morrow, 1993).

Furst, Jill McKeever. *The Natural History of the Soul in Ancient Mexico* (New Haven, CT: Yale University Press: 1997).

Golden, Paul. *Culture of Sex in Ancient China* (Honolulu: University of Hawaii Press, 2002).

Huchzermeyer, Wilfried. *The Mother: A Short Biography* (Pondicherry, India: Sri Aurobindo Society, 2007).

Jenkins, John Major. *Galactic Alignment: The Transformation of Consciousness According to Mayan, Egyptian, and Vedic Traditions* (Rochester, VT: Inner Traditions, 2002).

Kiersch, Johannes. *A History of the School of Spiritual Science: The First Class* (London: Temple Lodge Publishing, 2007).

León-Portilla, Miguel. *Aztec Thought and Culture: A Study of the Ancient Nahuatl Mind* (Norman, OK: University of Oklahoma Press, 1963).

Lindenberg, Christoph. *Rudolf Steiner: Eine Chronik* ("Rudolf Steiner: A Chronicle"; Stuttgart: Verlag Freies Geistesleben, 1988).

Lothrop, Samuel K. 1924 *Tulum, An Archæological Study of the East Coast of Yucatán* (Washington, DC: Carnegie Inst., pub. no. 335).

Meeus, Jean. *Mathematical Astronomy Morsels* (Richmond, VA.: Willmann-Bell, 1997).

Michelsen, Neil. *The American Sidereal Ephemeris* (San Diego: Astro Communications Services, 1981).

Moctezuma, Eduardo Matos. "Archaeology & Symbolism in Aztec Mexico: The Templo Mayor of Tenochtitlan," *Journal of the American Academy of Religion,* 53(4) (1985): 797–813.

Momtahen, H. *The Story of Jundishapur* (Ahwaz, Iran: Jundishapur University Press, 1977).

Montgomery, Ruth. *A Gift of Prophecy: The Phenomenal Jeane Dixon* (New York: William Morrow, 1965).

Meyer, Thomas H. *Clairvoyance and Consciousness: The Tao Impulse in Evolution* (London: Temple Lodge Press, 1991).

Padden, R. C. *The Hummingbird and the Hawk: Conquest and Sovereignty in the Valley of Mexico, 1503–1541* (Columbus: Ohio State University Press: 1967).

Paul, Lacquanna. *The Prayer Sequence in the Sacred Dance of Eurythmy* (Palo Alto, CA: Sophia Foundation of North America, 2003).

Paul, Lacquanna, and Robert Powell. *Cosmic Dances of the Planets* (San Rafael, CA: Sophia Foundation Press, 2007).

———. *Cosmic Dances of the Zodiac* (San Rafael, CA: Sophia Foundation Press, 2007).

———. *The Foundation Stone Meditation in the Sacred Dance of Eurythmy* (Palo Alto, CA: Sophia Foundation of North America, 2005).

Pinchbeck, Daniel. *2012: The Return of Quetzalcoatl* (New York: Penguin, 2006).

Post, David. "The Hypnosis of Adolf Hitler," *Journal of Forensic Science,* 43(6) (1998).

Powell, Robert. "The Apocalypse Code," *Christian Star Calendar 2009* (San Rafael, CA: Sophia Foundation Press, 2008).

————. *The Christ Mystery: Reflections on the Second Coming* (Fair Oaks, CA: Rudolf Steiner College Press, 1999).

————. *Christian Hermetic Astrology: The Star of the Magi and the life of Christ* (Great Barrington, MA: SteinerBooks, 1998).

————. *Chronicle of the Living Christ: Foundations of Cosmic Christianity* (Great Barrington, MA: SteinerBooks, 1996).

————. *Hermetic Astrology, Vol. I, Astrology and Reincarnation (*San Rafael, CA: Sophia Foundation Press, 2007).

————. *Hermetic Astrology, Vol. II: Astrological Biography* (San Rafael, CA: Sophia Foundation Press, 2007).

————. *History of the Zodiac* (San Rafael, CA: Sophia Academic Press, 2007).

————. *The Morning Meditation in Eurythmy* (Palo Alto, CA: Sophia Foundation of North America, 2005).

————. *The Most Holy Trinosophia and the New Revelation of the Divine Feminine* (Great Barrington, MA: SteinerBooks, 2000).

————. "Pluto and the Galactic Center": www.sophiafoundation.org/articles/.

————. "Rudolf Steiner, Valentin Tomberg, and the Return of Christ in the Etheric": www.sophiafoundation.org/articles/.

————. "The Second Coming and the Approaching Trial of Humanity," *Shoreline*, 5 (1992): 27–34.

————. *The Sign of the Son of Man in the Heavens: Sophia and the New Star Wisdom* (San Rafael, CA: Sophia Foundation Press, 2008).

————. "Saturn in Gemini," *Christian Star Calendar 2003* (Palo Alto, CA: Sophia Foundation of North America, 2002).

————. "Sophia and Venus," *Christian Star Calendar 2004* (Palo Alto, CA: Sophia Foundation of North America, 2003).

————. "Sophia and the Rose of the World": www.sophiafoundation.org/articles.

————. "Subnature and the Second Coming," in *The Inner Life of the Earth: Exploring the Mysteries of Nature, Subnature, and Supranature*, Paul V. O'Leary, ed. (Great Barrington, Ma.: SteinerBooks, 2008).

Powell, Robert, and Krista Koesters. "Pluto-Hades": www.sophiafoundation.org/articles/.

Qian, Sima. *Ssuma Ch'ien: Including History of the Hsia Dynasty and Yin Dynasty* (Charleston, SC: Forgotten Books, 2007).

Schele, Linda and Mary Ellen Miller. *The Blood of Kings: Dynasty and Ritual in Maya Art* (New York: George Braziller, 1986).

————. Peter Matthews and Justin Kerr. *The Code of Kings: The Language of Seven Sacred Maya Temples and Tombs* (New York: Scribner, 1998).

Schipflinger, Thomas. *Sophia-Maria* (York Beach, ME: Samuel Weiser, 1997).

Solovyov, Vladimir. *War, Progress, and the End of History: Three Conversations Including a Short Story of the Anti-Christ* (Great Barrington, MA: Lindisfarne, 1990).

Steiner, Rudolf. *According to Matthew: The Gospel of Christ's Humanity* (Hudson NY: Anthroposophic Press, 2003).

———. *The Apocalypse of St. John: Lectures on the Book of Revelation* (Hudson, NY: Anthroposophic Press, 1993).

———. *The Archangel Michael: His Mission and Ours* (Hudson NY: Anthroposophic Press, 1994).

———. *Background to the Gospel of St. Mark* (London: Rudolf Steiner Press, 1968).

———. *Der Baugedanke des Goetheanums* [*The Architectural Conception of the Goetheanum*] (Dornach/Switzerland: Verlag am Goetheanum, 1986).

———. *Becoming the Archangel Michael's Companions: Rudolf Steiner's Challenge to the Younger Generation* (Great Barrington, MA: SteinerBooks, 2007).

———. *The Bhagavad Gita and the West: The Esoteric Meaning of the Bhagavad Gita and Its Relation to the Letters of St. Paul* (Great Barrington, MA: SteinerBooks, 2009).

———. *The Book of Revelation and the Work of the Priest* (London: Rudolf Steiner Press, 1998).

———. *Cosmic and Human Metamorphoses* (Blauvelt, NY: Garber Communications, 1989).

———. *The Deed of Christ and the Opposing Spiritual Powers: Lucifer, Ahriman, Mephistopheles, Asuras* (Vancouver, BC: Steiner Book Centre, 1954).

———. *Egyptian Myths and Mysteries* (Hudson NY: Anthroposophic Press, 1971).

———. *Esoteric Christianity and the Mission of Christian Rosenkreutz* (London: Rudolf Steiner Press, 2005).

———. *Esoteric Lessons 1904–1909* (Great Barrington, MA: SteinerBooks, 2007).

———. *The Fall of the Spirits of Darkness* (London: Rudolf Steiner Press, 2008).

———. *The Festivals and Their Meaning: Christmas, Easter, Ascension and Pentecost, Michaelmas* (London: Rudolf Steiner Press, 1996).

———. *The Fifth Gospel: From the Akashic Record* (London: Rudolf Steiner Press, 1998).

———. *Foundations of Esotericism* (London: Rudolf Steiner Press, 1982).

———. *Human Questions and Cosmic Answers* (London: The Anthroposophical Publishing Company, [1922] 1960).

———. *The Incarnation of Ahriman: The Embodiment of Evil on Earth* (London: Rudolf Steiner Press, 2006).

————. *The Influences of Lucifer & Ahriman: Human Responsibility for the Earth* (Hudson, NY: Anthroposophic Press, 1993).

————. *Inner Impulses of Evolution: The Mexican Mysteries and the Knights Templar* (Spring Valley, NY: Anthroposophic Press, 1984).

————. *Intuitive Thinking as Spiritual Activity: A Philosophy of Freedom* (Hudson, NY: Anthroposophic Press, 1995).

————. *Isis Mary Sophia: Her Mission and Ours* (Great Barrington, MA: SteinerBooks, 2003).

————. *Karmic Relationships*, vol. 7 (London: Rudolf Steiner Press, 2002).

————. *Man in the Light of Occultism, Theosophy, and Philosophy* (Blauvelt, NY: Garber Communications, 1989).

————. *The Mission of the Folk-Souls in Relation to Teutonic Mythology* (London: Rudolf Steiner Press, 2005).

————. *Mystery of the Universe: The Human Being, Model of Creation* (London: Rudolf Steiner Press, 2001); previously *Man: Hieroglyph of the Universe*.

————. *Mysterienwahrheiten und Weihnachtsimpulse* ("Mystery Truths and the Impulses of Christmas"), lecture of December 26, 1917 (CW 180).

————. *An Outline of Esoteric Science* (Hudson NY: Anthroposophic Press, 1997).

————. *The Reappearance of Christ in the Etheric* (Great Barrington, MA: SteinerBooks, 2003).

————. *The Spiritual Hierarchies and the Physical World: Zodiac, Planets & Cosmos* (Great Barrington, MA: SteinerBooks, 2008).

————. *Three Streams in the Evolution of Humanity* (London: Rudolf Steiner Press, 1965).

————. *Die Welträtsel und die Anthroposophie* ("Anthroposophy and the Riddles of the World"), Lecture of November 16, 1905 (CW 54).

Steiner, Rudolf & Edouard Schuré, *The East in the Light of the West / The Children of Lucifer and the Brothers of Christ* (Blauvelt, NY: Garber Communications, 1986).

Stonehill, Paul. *Mysteries of the Yellow Emperor*: www.mystae.com/streams/ufos/emperor.html.

Thomas, Cyrus. *Day Symbols of the Maya Year*, sixteenth Annual Report of the Bureau of American Ethnology to the Secretary of the Smithsonian Institution, 1894–1895, Government Printing Office, Washington, DC, 1897.

Tomberg, Valentin. *Christ and Sophia: Anthroposophic Meditations on the Old Testament, New Testament, and Apocalypse* (Great Barrington, MA: SteinerBooks, 2006).

————. *Lazarus, Come Forth! Meditations of a Christian Esotericist on the Mysteries of the Raising of Lazarus, the Ten Commandments, the Three Kingdoms & the Breath of Life* (Great Barrington, MA: Lindisfarne Books, 2006).

————. *The Lord's Prayer Course/Our Mother Course* (Study material distributed by the Sophia Foundation of North America, Palo Alto, CA).

von Halle, Judith. *Der Abstieg in die Erdenschichten* (*The Descent into the Layers of the Earth*; Dornach, Switzerland: Verlag am Goetheanum, 2008).

————. *And If He Had Not Been Raised: The Stations of Christ's Path to Spirit Man* (London: Temple Lodge Press, 2007).

————. *Das Christliche aus dem Holze herausschlagen* (Dornach, Switzerland: Verlag am Goetheanum, 2007).

————. *Illness and Healing: And the Mystery Language of the Gospels* (London: Temple Lodge Press, 2008).

————. *The Lord's Prayer: The Living Word of God* (London: Temple Lodge Press, 2007).

————. *Secrets of the Stations of the Cross and the Grail Blood: The Mystery of Transformation* (London: Temple Lodge Press, 2008).

West, John Anthony. *The Traveler's Key to Ancient Egypt: A Guide to the Sacred Places of Ancient Egypt* (Wheaton, Ill.: Quest Books, 1995).

Yogananda, Paramahansa. *God Talks with Arjuna: Royal Science of God-Realization,* 2 vols. (Los Angeles: Self-Realization Fellowship, 1995).

Zarebska, Carla. *Guadalupe* (Albuquerque: University of New Mexico Press, 2004).

About the Authors:

 **Robert Powell, PhD** is an internationally known lecturer, author, eurythmist, and movement therapist. He is founder of the Choreocosmos School of Cosmic and Sacred Dance, and cofounder of the Sophia Foundation of North America. He received his doctorate for his thesis on the History of the Zodiac, now available as a book from Sophia Academic Press, and he is on the adjunct faculty of Wisdom University. His published works include: *The Sophia Teachings*, a six-tape series (Sounds True Recordings), as well as the following books: *Divine Sophia-Holy Wisdom; The Most Holy Trinosophia and the New Revelation of the Divine Feminine; The Sophia Teachings; The Mystery, Biography, and Destiny of Mary Magdalene; Chronicle of the Living Christ; Christian Hermetic Astrology; The Christ Mystery; The Sign of the Son of Man in the Heavens; The Morning Meditation in Eurythmy;* and the yearly *Christian Star Calendar*, as well as other works published by Sophia Foundation Press. He translated the spiritual classic *Meditations on the Tarot* and co-translated Valentin Tomberg's *Lazarus, Come Forth!* He is coauthor, with Lacquanna Paul, of *Cosmic Dances of the Zodiac* and *Cosmic Dances of the Planets*. He teaches a gentle form of healing movement: the sacred dance of eurythmy (from the Greek, meaning "harmonious movement") as well as the cosmic dances of the planets and signs of the zodiac. Through the Sophia Grail Circle he facilitates sacred celebrations dedicated to the Divine Feminine. Robert offers workshops in Europe and North America and, with Karen Rivers, cofounder of the Sophia Foundation, leads pilgrimages to the world's sacred sites (1996, Turkey; 1997, Holy Land; 1998, France; 2000, Britain; 2002, Italy; 2004, Greece; 2006, Egypt; 2008, India). Websites: www.sophiafoundation.org and www. astrogeographia.org.

 **Kevin Dann** teaches history at the State University of New York, Plattsburgh. His books include: *Lewis Creek Lost and Found* (University Press of New England: 2001); *Across the Great Border Fault: The Naturalist Myth in America* (Rutgers University Press: 2000); and *Bright Colors Falsely Seen: Synaesthesia and the Search for Transcendental Knowledge* (Yale University Press: 1998). In conjunction with his latest book, *A Short Story of American Destiny: 1909–2009* (LogoSophia: 2008)—inspired both by the quadricentennial commemoration of the voyages of Samuel de Champlain and Henry Hudson and by the Apocalyptic significance of 2009—Kevin is planning a "Corridor of Amity" pilgrimage from Montreal to Manhattan in May/June of 2009. For more information, see: www.corridorofamity.org.